MOTHERS AND AMAZONS
The First Feminine History of Culture

Helen Diner is the pseudonym of Bertha Eckstein-Diener, who published widely in German between 1929 and 1940. She used another pseudonym as well, especially during the early years of her literary career: Sir Galahad. Under this suggestive disguise some of her most controversial books were written and duly received wide notoriety. One of these, *Imperial Byzantium,* was published in the United States in 1938.

MOTHERS AND AMAZONS

The First Feminine History of Culture

HELEN DINER

Edited and Translated by John Philip Lundin
Introduction by Brigitte Berger

Anchor Books
Anchor Press/Doubleday
Garden City, New York

MOTHERS AND AMAZONS: The First Feminine History of Culture was originally published in the United States by The Julian Press, Inc. in 1965. The Anchor Press edition is published by arrangement with The Julian Press.

ANCHOR BOOKS EDITION: 1973

INTRODUCTION

In *Mothers and Amazons* Helen Diner tries to present a first feminine history of culture. She states boldly at the very outset of her venture that she is going to be as one-sided as possible since "the other side is fairly well known" anyway. The reason for her partisanship is brilliantly and succinctly formulated: "The history of cultures, time and again, thoroughly describes those phases in which man coined his image of the world, while the feminine element could not achieve its realization at all or, at best, could do so only indirectly through him. Consciously or unconsciously, the male stage remains the darling object of historical contemplation."

Quite clearly, then, this book is a reaction from a masculine era that passionately engaged in the glorification of the male element in life, love, art, and thought. Helen Diner is determined, at long last, to give the female principle its proper place in history and culture. Implicitly she hopes to open up new avenues of thought for the destiny of humanity thwarted in the past by the conquest of the male. For that reason, *Mothers and Amazons* is a very timely book.

The book was originally published in German more than forty years ago. The perspective, however, is still surprisingly new, the insights are still provocative, and the highly individualistic opinions of the author are still apt to produce the same startled reaction, even outrage, as they did when first presented. Moreover, if pure pleasure is to be a criterion of a book, one can only acknowledge that this challenging and brilliantly executed endeavor to provide woman with her own history has been successful. This is an arresting and enchanting and, at times, even a strikingly exotic book. However, since the book was first presented four decades ago, it will be necessary to put it into contemporary perspective.

There are a number of notable reasons why we feel that *Mothers and Amazons* deserves to be brought once more to the attention of a wider audience. For one, there does not exist any recent general historical or ethnological work on this topic. If we wish to obtain information on the role of women in prehistorical and early societies, we are forced to engage in lengthy and tedious historical research. By the same token, if we wish to know more about the position of women in primitive societies, it is necessary to go to the sources, the many ethnographic monographs—a truly laborious task. The second reason is connected to the first and deserves some thought. It cannot be purely accidental that no attempt has been made in the past decades to bring together the results of modern historical and anthropological research into one single study. It surely cannot be due to a lack of interest since—as one prominent (male) anthropologist not very long ago suggested—the status of the woman in our own society "ceased to be an acute public issue." The reasons, I suspect, are more complex and difficult to unravel. They will become clear, I hope, when we turn to take a closer look at Helen Diner's important attempt.

Any evaluation of the book before us must be done in two stages: first, by determining the viability of the large-scale ideas that dominate the entire enterprise, and second, by rendering a critique of the minutiae, the tremendous number of details that are woven together so skillfully in this book, which have to be affirmed or corrected by the scholarly evidence presented since the time of its original publication. In proceeding in this manner, I am intentionally reversing the scientific method. The purpose for adopting this course is quite simple. For if we were to start out in the accepted way with the collection and assessment of the details, this book could not have been written—nor could any other book that attempts what Diner has done. Only a daring mind can aim at a synthesis as ambitious as the one we find in *Mothers and Amazons*. The book, then, cannot claim "scientific" accuracy, nor should it be understood primarily as a scholarly presentation. Helen Diner knowingly threw to the winds the caution with which more careful researchers present ideas. Each chapter, therefore, demonstrates the author's strength and weakness at the same time. Her summaries are sources of insight and strength, for they make it possible to see an entire complex of questions in one magnificent sweep. Yet, in all candor, I must add here that this peculiar disregard of the rules of the game of scholarship (I personally find the omission of proper references most annoying) may have done more harm to the basic ideas developed in the book than it has helped to further the acceptance of the important novel arguments on the role of the woman in social life. Because the ideas as well as the data—and there are ample data—are presented in a manner that inspires little confidence, they can easily be misunderstood and misinterpreted. Human beings have unhappily learned to distrust poetic and sweeping generalizations. Only unorthodox thinkers have recognized some of the implications contained in this revolutionary way of looking at history. For what could be more revolutionary than to present a female vision of history and life in an age that has been shaped by millennia of male thought?

Mothers and Amazons stands in the tradition that seriously discredits the belief in the natural basis of the monogamous and patriarchal family. It was the genius of the Swiss scholar Johann Jakob Bachofen that drew the attention of intellectuals and the wider public to this perspective in the middle of the nineteenth century with a series of publications that finally appeared together in the much disputed *Das Mutterrecht (Motherright)* in 1861. Helen Diner pays enthusiastic respect to Bachofen's heritage as well as to the extensive research that emerged at his original instigation toward the turn of the twentieth century—after a period of stunned silence—and continued to come to the fore sporadically until the middle of the 1930s. In comparing *Mothers and Amazons* with Bachofen's monumental opus—which, unfortunately, was never translated into English—we discover that Diner leans heavily upon Bachofen's findings and makes the same use of mythological interpretation in order to arrive at prehistorical processes.

The extensive use of mythology presents a set of problems more complicated and obscure than would appear at first sight. Already Diodorus Siculus, a Greek historian who lived during the first century B.C., stated perceptively, "As a rule the ancient myths are not found to yield a simple and consistent story, so that nobody need wonder if details of my recension cannot be reconciled with those given by every poet and historian." This is not the place to engage in a somewhat specialized discussion of the problems centering around the validity of the use of mythology. Diner herself takes passionate issue with some interpretations, especially the psychoanalytic one. Neither is this the place to challenge Diner—and through her Bachofen—on their scanty use of etymology. Let me point here to merely the astounding discovery Bachofen was able to arrive at through the use of myth interpretation which is of direct concern to our theme, a theme that is so ably and passionately transmitted to us by Diner.

The claim is made, and it is made very eloquently, that there existed once in the dim past of the Mediterranean, Babylonian, Indian, and possibly other cultures as well an age where woman was the master of man's destiny. It is she who was the initial creator of social life, it is she who was the mother of all things; she had absolute power, she was the impartial creator and destroyer. There were no fathers, only group marriages of all female members of a particular totem society with all members of another totem society. Every child's maternity was certain, its paternity irrelevant. The emergence of the idea of fatherhood is understood to have been a revolutionizing element which brought with it the institution of individual marriage. Once this revolution occurred, the social status of the woman changed fundamentally. Now men took over many of the sacred practices from which they had been barred by virtue of their sex. Finally, man declared himself head of the household and gradually his ascendancy in all other spheres of social life and thought was established firmly as well. So firmly, indeed, that the traces of the original stages have disappeared over the ages.

Bachofen proposed a three-stage theory for this whole process. Originally there was a stage of sexual promiscuity for which he used the term "chthonic hetaerism." Out of this emerged a second stage, which he called the stage of genuine matriarchy, characterized by such features as the reckoning of descent in the female line and property inheritance in the female line; in this stage women held a position of such high respect that it became the foundation for a rule of women (gynocracy). In the third stage, matriarchy was finally supplanted by patriarchy.

The ancient myths reflect this transition as a quasi-religious conflict between the supporters of the matriarchal Moon Goddess of the Pelasgians (the original inhabitants of the Greek peninsula) and those of the patriarchal gods of the Greeks. Traces of this transition can be found in considerable numbers, as for instance in the poems of Homer. If read under this perspective, the Homeric poems clearly reflect this conflict between two irreconcilable social systems, for the bickerings between Zeus and Hera are far more than a satire on the domestic differences in Greek families.

Robert Graves, the English writer and poet, tried to follow some of these ancient traces in his book *The White Goddess* (1948) (regrettably never mentioning his indebtedness to Bachofen), and observed the subsequent change in mythology: "But even after male dominance was established, the male intellect became self-sufficient, the ancient language survived purely enough in the secret mystery-cults of Eleusis, Corinth, Samothrace and elsewhere; and when these, along with the male mystery cults, were suppressed by early Christian emperors, the secret language was still taught in the poetic colleges of Ireland and Wales and in the witch covens of Western Europe."

Clearly then, there exist a number of versions, mainly mythical and poetic, that reflect the theory that woman was originally the master of all social life, that this stage, for whatever reasons, was transplanted by the one we know so well that it seems to be the natural one. When Diner once more reweaves the haunting tragedy of Aeschylos' *Oresteia*, it is difficult for even the most cautious scholar to close himself off from the power of the argument. Her recasting of the tragedy is truly masterful.

However, what about some "hard" data, that is, data of an empirical-scientific nature? If we reexamine our theme in light of the archaeological and documentary material now available, especially in the Middle East and eastern Mediterranean, the unique position occupied by the Mother Goddess cult is prominently prevalent. In the words of one expert (E. O. James, *The Cult of the Mother Goddess: An Archaeological and Documentary Study,* Thames and Hudson, London, 1959), "Clearly it was an essential element very deeply laid in the long and complex history of the body of beliefs and practices which centered in and around the mysterious processes of fecundity, birth and generation, alike in nature, the human species and in the animal kingdom." In fact, we are permitted to observe today that while there has been a strange silence in the field of anthropology on the significance of the early Bachofen findings, their widespread importance is becoming increasingly recognized in archaeological circles. Obviously, no conclusions can be drawn from these archaeological findings on whether or not the Mother Goddess was the earliest manifestation of the concept of deity, nor can any pronouncements be made on this basis with respect to general cultural evolutionary processes. To quote once more our previously cited archaeological source:

> Her [the Mother-Goddess'] symbolism unquestionably has been the most persistent feature in the archaeological record of the ancient world, from the sculptured Venuses of the Gravettian culture in the Upper Paleolithic and the stylized images of the decorated caves, to the emblems and inscriptions of the cult when it became established in the Fertile Crescent, Western Asia, the Indus Valley, the Aegean and Crete between the 5th and 3rd millennia B.C. Moreover it is now becoming increasingly evident that in its dispersal from its cradleland in the Southern Russian steppe and Eastern Asia, it was destined to have a widespread influence and to play a very significant role in the subsequent development of the Ancient Near Eastern religions from India to the Mediterranean from Neolithic times to the Christian era.

Helen Diner, however, is swept by a veritable crusader's spirit far beyond such relatively safe grounds. In her first chapter, "Parthenogenesis" (i.e. the asexual creation of life by the female), she proposes an audacious theory on the creation of all physical life that will have a hard time standing up against the flood of criticism that is likely to be advanced

by modern physical anthropology and biology. Yet, we encounter in Elaine Morgan's recent *The Descent of Woman*
(Stein & Day, New York, 1972) a contemporary proponent
of a rather similar theory. I, for one, wish our author had not
championed this theory, for I am convinced that it does a
disservice to the very important general theme of the book.
But then . . . in her own words, "we all find it necessary to
set ourselves goals farther than our strength can take us, in
order not to achieve less in the end than we might." We will
have to understand the first chapters of the book as Diner's
great strike to establish independence of the female from the
male. For her this also means that the mother is the life-
producing eternal womb, the root, the source, which in no
way corresponds to masculinity. The mother, in other words,
is the nucleus. In the context of the primacy of the female
principle the author seeks as well to reinterpret the phenomena of circumcision, totemism, exogamy, and couvade. And
once more she mixes great learnedness with audacious and
independent interpretations that deserve serious consideration
by contemporary analysts.

Let us now return to the central quest of *Mothers and
Amazons* and grant—at least for the moment—that there once
existed, in the dim past of human life, a general social stage
of matriarchy. The question then arises whether we can find
any remnants of this stage in historical records, written by
eyewitnesses. Here our author, firmly placed on the shoulders
of Bachofen, is in a safe position, for such records abound.
She literally overwhelms us with this documentation, citing
especially those societies of the past where, in spite of the
apparent rule of the men, clear traces of preceding matriarchies can be established. A good part of *Mothers and
Amazons* is concerned with precisely this task. Unfortunately,
the execution of this task is unnecessarily marred by Diner's
debatable use of etymology for this purpose. Without want-
ing to sound tiresome, I must regretfully observe that Helen
Diner does not possess the scientific equipment for tracing the
origin of the meaning of words. But then, neither have many
others (as for instance the founding fathers of psychoanalysis) who try the same under the cloak of scholarship claiming
universal validity.

Once one is set on such a course, the argument has to be carried further still. Having uncovered historical records testifying to the preexistence of a matriarchal stage—in at least fourteen societies according to Bachofen—it is reasonable to assume by the same token that matriarchal social systems can be encountered if we take inventory of those societies, still found in the far reaches of this shrinking globe, as yet untouched by civilization (which, by definition, is patriarchal).

As expected, a great many so-called primitive societies can be singled out where some form of a matriarchal system or remnants thereof—and the qualification "some form" is the crux of the matter, as we shall presently see—can, indeed, be found. An enumeration of them as well as a very general characterization of the phenomenon is presented in another great part of the book. Here, however, we meet with some serious shortcomings of *Mothers and Amazons*. At the time when Diner researched her material, historical ethnologists, especially the dedicated scholars of the *Kulturkreis* tradition, such as Graebner, Koeppers, Schwab, Bastian, Frobenius, and Pater Schmidt, had already presented numerous ethnographic studies pertaining to the motherright complex. Indeed, some of their attempts at theorizing their findings had by then already caused heated controversies, opening up glimpses of the complexity of the subject. But Diner chose to base much of the anthropological data of her monumental task upon a more shaky source: Robert Briffault's *The Mothers: A Study of the Origins of Sentiments and Institutions* (London, 1927), in which a colossal amount of material is tendered, alas indiscriminately and without method or knowledge of scientific presuppositions. Briffault himself tells us in the introduction to his work that he began his task (singlehanded!) "with still youthful buoyancy" and ended with "broken wings." This, however, is not the place to render a critique of Briffault's writings. Others, such as Edward Westermarck, have done this most competently.

Within the theme of *Mothers and Amazons* we must emphasize once more that it is the author's unequivocal aim to draw our attention to a much neglected aspect of social life without claiming final validity for her material. In fact, when she sets out in her last chapter to present some of the theories on matriarchy, she clearly demonstrates her awareness of the complexity of the problems involved, and I personally find her statement "In recent years, a great deal of research has been done on human nature, which is why once more so little is known about it" not only very witty but also singularly timely. She herself provides a brief, amusingly formulated critique of her hero Bachofen's three-stage theory of matriarchy revealing her knowledge of the anthropological controversies.

It may perhaps be useful for the reader if I try to summarize briefly some of the chief general objections to Bachofen's —and thereby Helen Diner's—propositions:

1) Even though it is clear that matriarchal societies once existed, indeed, in great numbers, especially in the Mediterranean area, the claim of universality for the existence of the social institution of matriarchy cannot be maintained. Indo-European peoples, for instance, as well as many others, probably never had a matriarchal stage. What is more, the notion of a law of development or social evolution, whereby all societies have to go through similar stages, cannot be generalized.

2) Even though there may once have existed "promiscuity" somewhere in the primate past of man (see especially S. L. Washburn and Irven DeVore, "Social Behavior of Baboons and Early Man," in S. L. Washburn [ed.], *Social Life of Early Man*, Aldine, Chicago, 1961), an original cultural stage of general sexual promiscuity—for which Bachofen and Diner use the awkward term "chthonic hetaerism"—cannot be verified and it is quite likely that it never existed in this pure form. The existence of practices and customs in contemporary primitive societies (based upon nineteenth-century material within the context of the book) associated with the matriarchal complex—for instance, unrestricted sexual intercourse before marriage, cultic initiation rites, certain marriage rites, etc.—can all also be explained in different terms and may, in all probability, be of a different function. Even though Lewis Henry Morgan's discovery of the classificatory sys-

tems of relationships (in *Ancient Society: Researches in the Lines of Human Progress from Savagery Through Barbarism to Civilization*, 1878, reprinted by Harvard University Press in 1964 with an excellent introduction by Leslie White) seemed to lend support to the assumption that there originally existed a stage of sexual promiscuity, the theory will have to be discarded in light of modern research. An exposition of these data and arguments, unfortunately, is beyond the framework of this introduction. Let me just mention, however, that historical ethnology can demonstrate convincingly that those societies that are culturally perhaps the most ancient never knew a general stage of sexual promiscuity—that, in fact, the matriarchal stage may very well be of a more recent cultural origin.

3) Moreover, there exist a number of common confusions in connection with the terms matriarchal, matrilineal, and matrilocal. It is important to keep in mind that societies may be matrilocal and matrilineal and even property may be passed on in the female line, and yet the status of the woman may very well be inferior to that of the man. What difference does it make to the status of the woman whether her husband or her brother control her and her property—after all, both are men!

In short, then, human societies exhibit a never-ending variety of social institutions in which many elements are found in a multitude of combinations; there exists no one law of social development or evolution. Alternatives have always and will always be possible, just as there have been, there are, and there will be different modes of social existence and consciousness.

As the reader can readily see now, the matriarchal complex has been a touchy subject ever since it made its first appearance—and it is most likely to continue to be a controversial one in the future as well. As I have tried to show, this is partly due to the intricacy of the questions and theories surrounding this cultural complex. Partly, however, it is also due to the peculiar emphasis the field of cultural anthropology received by its founders Malinowski and Radcliffe-Brown in England and the Boas school of anthropology in the United States. This influential structural-functional school supplanted successfully the ethno-historical approach at just about the time when Helen Diner wrote *Mothers and Amazons*. However, recently Leslie White, in the aforementioned excellent introduction to the republication of Morgan's *Ancient Society*, pointed out perceptively that there are signs today that the tide of the anti-evolutionism of the Boas school is turning again in the wake of the 1959 Darwin centennial. Yet much remains to be done to restore to respectability the theory of cultural evolution and the questions raised by the ethno-historians among American anthropologists. Whereas students of society in the past four decades could get along very well without a consideration of the perspectives opened up in *Mothers and Amazons*, students of society today—to use the words of the anthropologist Paul Bohannan in his introduction to the republication of Lewis Henry Morgan's *Houses and House-Life of the American Aborigines* (University of Chicago Press, 1965)—"will find it necessary to turn back to these questions that arise from this perspective." I personally hope that Helen Diner's *Mothers and Amazons* will aid in reopening this important and often unjustly maligned approach.

There exist still other complications. One is that the prominent treatment given the matriarchal question complex by Karl Marx and Friedrich Engels (see especially Friedrich Engels, *The Origin of the Family, Private Property and the State*, republished by International Publishers, New York, 1942) has moved it still more into the center of controversy. Because Marx and Engels both based their views of the early forms of social life upon Morgan's reaffirmation of the Bachofen perspective and findings and incorporated the universal existence of an original "natural" stage of matriarchy and preceding sexual promiscuity into their redesign of social life, Communist theoreticians today still abide more or less by these presuppositions. The peculiar twist that Morgan gave to the role of the matriarchal complex in linking it to the stages of human progress was uniquely suited to Marx's intention for finally "making man into man." Within the context of our theme let me mention here that no other theory connected with the matriarchal complex has been more heatedly discussed than that on the original stage of sexual promiscuity. Helen Diner, in her bold and daring style, stated her own notions most vociferously and independently of any dogma.

Nowhere in the literature I know of do I find mention of the most obvious reason why a book like *Mothers and Amazons,* for all its realism, for all its insights and significance, has remained without the final sanction of the wider learned public. And that is beyond any doubt the fact that until now a primarily masculine intellect and spirit have dominated in the interpretation of society and culture—whether this interpretation is carried out by males or females. I find disregard of this factor, especially in more recent literature, truly amazing. For instance, when I read the highly regarded anthropologist Evans-Pritchard's rather delightful little lecture on the "Position of Women in Primitive Societies and in Our Own" (published under the same title by the Free Press of New York in 1965), I cannot help but be convinced by Diner's assertion that fundamentally masculine assumptions have shaped our whole moral and intellectual history. In light of this one-sidedness, Diner's own overstatements and judgments appear minor indeed. However, it is up to us now not to continue the tradition in one-sided interpretations. The interests of women and the cause of knowledge both would be badly served by presenting yet another distorting view. Because of the existing inadequacy, in fact almost complete lack, of serious research into the questions opened up by Diner, I would suggest that we will have to be partial to developing the much neglected female perspective in studying the primitive field as well as our own society so that a more balanced picture of social reality may finally emerge. Moreover, in order to arrive at an adequate "feminine history of culture" many aspects not considered by Diner need to be pursued. What has struck me most in my readings has not been this or that individual study or observation, but the failure to understand that woman has always had an important role and vital function in patriarchal societies as well—

certainly more important than has hitherto been recognized. On the whole, I would venture, the status of woman and the significance of her role among primitive peoples as well as in the history of Western and non-Western societies up to our own days has been misunderstood and misinterpreted. The history of the entire Middle Ages as well as the period since the Renaissance will have to be rewritten from the feminine perspective Helen Diner has drawn to our attention. To give just one example, I have yet to see a competent analysis of the role of the daughters of the rising bourgeoisie of the seventeenth and eighteenth centuries upon the formation of our modern times.

Even though this book intends to be the first feminine history of culture the reader will encounter many an issue that is alive and relevant to the points under debate today. So for instance, we most certainly can profit from Diner's insights into the connection between the type of social system and the knowledge of the functions of the body. According to her findings, patriarchal societies have a tendency to keep women not only sexually under the yoke of male supremacy but also generally ignorant of the functions of the body, whereas matriarchal societies give rise to the free disposition of woman over her body leading to a "good knowledge of its laws." Or, her reiterated statements on the "natural" rule of mothers as opposed to the more "intellectual" rule of fathers—although in need of clarification and precision—are pertinent to contemporary reflections. Furthermore, in the final chapter of the book where Diner enters into the old arguments on the effects of the ownership of and the control over the means of production, she makes a contribution to the questions pertaining to "sexual politics" that cannot easily be ignored even though her insights may not at all be in line with the arguments over "sexual politics" today.

In sum, this book not only takes up old unsolved questions and opens up new ones, but what is more it provides us with a much needed vital perspective upon social life. In developing this perspective, Helen Diner dug deeper, but built less securely than others; she constructed grandiose visions which may be attacked bitterly; she was passionate and may have created confusion; she either would not or could not assimilate the rules of the various games of scholarship. And yet, she achieved something others could not, for she knew something others did not—something about the nature of life.

BRIGITTE BERGER
New York, 1972

AUTHOR'S PREFACE

This is the first feminine history of culture. It endeavors to remain as one-sided as possible, one-sided in that direction which has never so far enjoyed a graphic representation. The other side is fairly well known to anyone who takes an interest in intellectual things. The histories of cultures, time and again, thoroughly describe those phases in which man coined his image of the world, while the feminine element could not achieve its realization at all or, at best, could do so only indirectly through him. Consciously or unconsciously, the male stage remains the darling object of historical contemplation.

What, on the other hand, is the world like in those areas where it is arranged by the woman, according to her nature, to the exclusion of the male as a personality? Once more, it is one-sided. Certainly. But it may be that these deliberate halves, viewed from a superior perspective, make up the whole, for "Truth lies in contemporaneous opposites." A misrepresentation of the world image through paternalistic prejudices can be freely compensated in the consciousness of mankind if its soul experiences the renewed image of sufficiently pure female-oriented societies with their matriarchal precepts. It is intended that the woman shall thus receive a tradition, so that she should not seem without tradition in her own eyes in relation to those things that she can do.

Cultural histories are cross sections through developments. The results are determined by where the cross cut sets in, the direction in which it runs, what is to be touched, and what is to be exposed. In this representation, the incision is aimed across our globe and through races and cultures in such a manner that it cuts through as many layers of the soul as possible, for the roots of female realms are really found only in the magic foundations of blood and soil, even if their pinnacles often have survived civil activity in the top stratum. They are never states but realms, irrational, profoundly vital, welded together—because of their solid substance—by no more than a kind of magic incubation heat of mysticism and feeling, veneration of the created for its creatress and of moral subjects for the authoress of their morality. This relationship is not without its frictions; the frictions, however, are structured differently. That is what makes them so interesting. Even in the polarity of the sexes, the partners and counterplayers here are not lover and beloved, husband and wife, as in the patriarchal state. In the matriarchy, world events correlate with the polarity mother-son, brother-sister. This, in turn, leads us to substructural areas and becomes understandable only through the primal origins of female existence, leading us back to an aboriginal phenomenon.

After a demonstration of the norm in biology, mythology, the psychology of magic, and the fountainheads of social institutions, there follows a matriarchal pilgrimage across the globe. It is an excursion into ethnographic and historical miniatures of everything that shows an attractive peculiarity in color or dynamics while based on matriarchy, gynocracy, or other forms of female predominance, until the picture of the whole arises from the alignment of individual facets. It is the revelation of a solemn and joyous spectacle rich in forms that finally arrives on our horizon and points the way beyond.

The reader's notoriously easy spiritual exhaustion, since it is an organic defect, has been taken into consideration, but not his equally notorious laziness and superficiality, since these are mere bad habits. Therefore, plentiful tidbits have been incorporated into the body of the work in such a devilish fashion that it should be far easier to swallow the whole than to find the juicier passages. "Thing, eat the crumbs, too."[1]

Unfortunately, it was not possible to include exhaustive notes or a bibliography. The book and its price would have

---

[1] The author herself derives this saying from "The Fairytale of the Toad," a reference that is not entirely clear to the editor translator.

been expanded intolerably by an enumeration of all source materials, magazine articles, papyruses, and pamphlets from the diverse disciplines necessary to bring about this feminine history of culture. Nor did it prove possible to make room for the bibliography through an abbreviation of the text, for the contents are already condensed. But in the most important passages, quotations and sources have been included.

Two personalities are responsible for the best portion of this work: for its depth, it was J. J. Bachofen, the great discoverer of matriarchal society; its ethnographic breadth was added by Robert Briffault.[2] The latter's life work provided in-

---

[2] Johann Jakob Bachofen (1815–1887) was a famous Swiss anthropologist and cultural historian. He studied law and legal history at the universities of Basel, Berlin, Oxford, Cambridge, and Paris. He was appointed to the chair of Roman law upon completion of his studies and return to Basel, but he resigned from the Basel faculty in 1844 to study the history of art. After some years of satisfying his curiosity, he accepted an appointment as a judge in the criminal court in 1877. His publications on legal topics include *Ausgewählte Lehren des römischen Civilrechts* (Selected Lessons from Roman Civil Law), published in 1848. His anthropological publications were recognized as very significant at the time and included the following:

> *Versuch über die Gräbersymbolik der Alten* ("Essay on the Grave Symbolism of the Ancients"), 1859
> *Das lykische Volk und seine Bedeutung für die Entwicklung des Altertums* (The Lycian People and Its Significance for the Development of Antiquity), 1862
> *Das Mutterrecht; eine Untersuchung über die Gynaikokratie der alten Welt nach ihrer religiösen und rechtlichen Natur* (Matriarchy; an Investigation of the Gynocracy of Antiquity according to its Religious and Legal Nature), 1861
> *Antiquarische Briefe, vornehmlich zur Kenntnis der ältesten Verwandtschaftsbegriffe* (Antiquarian Letters, Especially Regarding the Knowledge of the Oldest Concepts of Family Relationships), 2 vols., 1880–1886

Bachofen's major contribution, developed in *Matriarchy*, is his theory of a social evolution experienced by all peoples, starting with a universal stage of promiscuity, developing into a family group organized strictly by the mother and consisting of her children without regard to paternity, graduating into a matriarchally controlled family with acknowledged fathers, and replaced finally by the patriarchally controlled family so familiar to the Europe of Bachofen's day. In his works, he accumulated voluminous evidence

valuable assistance through its references to an otherwise overwhelming mass of ethnological sources. These two men are responsible for the "mothers" part.

As for the "Amazons" part, I am indebted to Ephoros, Pherecydes, Isocrates, Hellanicus, Cleidemus, Eusebius, Dionysius Scythobrachion, Herodotus, Diodorus, Plutarch, Pliny, Strabo, Pompeius Trogus, and many nameless gentlemen still older, who preserved their ancestral heritage with the tact of the great gentlemen of the world that they were. They transmitted all the material about the rise of mankind unedited, in true wordings and religious subordination to tra-

---

to the effect that, indeed, all tribes and nations had undergone this evolution in varying degrees, depending upon their relative state of civilization. His theories have been challenged in the century that has passed since the publication of his works, and important exceptions to his rules have been discovered, but his evidence was too massive ever to be totally discarded.

Robert Briffault was born in London, the son of an exiled French diplomat, received most of his education in Florence, studied medicine in London, and became a practicing physician in New Zealand. He volunteered in the British Army when World War I broke out, was decorated twice for conspicuous bravery, and received a severe wound at Nieuport. Settling down in Paris, he published his first book at the age of 43 (He was born in 1876). He sympathized with Communism but broke with the Reds because he could not stomach Stalinism. In addition to his anthropological works, he published several less successful novels. He is best known for his psychoanthropological books, which include:

> The Making of Humanity, 1919
> Psyche's Lamp: A Revaluation of Psychological Principles, 1921
> The Mothers: A Study of the Origins of Sentiments and Institutions, 1927
> Rational Evolution, 1930
> Sin and Sex, 1931

Briffault's work was contemporary to, and somewhat related to, the work of Freud. It was at least as revolutionary in its implications. The author proved, better than anyone had that far, that "morality is a matter of geography." He brought the scientific mind of the medical practitioner to a field still very much influenced by religiously dictated taboos. In part, his observations bore out Bachofen's theory that the primitive nations of his day were merely repeating the experience of Europe's ancestors thousands of years before.

dition, even at the risk of being called "unimaginative copyists" in a bourgeois anachronism. Therefore, new sources are unnecessary, if one will only read the old ones in a spirit receptive to the contents, even though the results of new research are proliferating. "The sources," as J. Burckhardt says in his observations regarding the history of the world, "are inexhaustible, because they show a different face to each reader and to each century, and even to every stage of the individual's development. But this is not a misfortune; rather, it is a consequence of continuously vital communication."

I especially attempted to include the historical and ethnographical material only where it was specifically needed for the structure of the whole edifice, so that none of it should be abandoned somewhere in the text like unused building material, for "We all find it necessary to set ourselves goals farther than our strength can take us, in order not to achieve less in the end than we might."

HELEN DINER

CONTENTS

I

PARTHENOGENESIS[1]

In the beginning, there was woman. The man only appears as the son, as a biologically younger and later phenomenon. The female is the older, the more powerful, and the more aboriginal of the two mysterious, fundamental forms in which everything vital unfolds in its race through time, now locked in an inimical embrace, now yearningly separated. Virgin conception reaches far into our animal ancestry as parthenogenesis, through epochs incomparably longer than those that have passed since its termination. And more: the original female in the animal species not only reproduces herself but also is the sole creatress of the male; the male never is anything without the female. Thread worms, wheel animalcules, plant lice, and many branchiopodia, as well as diverse types of wasps and butterflies are all virginal mothers. Parthenogenesis reaches up to the crustaceans. "Daphnia produce eleven or

[1] The author, as becomes evident later in the text, lays especial stress upon the difference between parthenogenesis, which is an asexual reproduction on the part of the female, and immaculate conception, which is sexual reproduction without the usual means of fertilization. There is an implied carry-over, or transfer, of ideas, but there still is a difference between the two. For the purpose of this book, the primary difference lies in the fact that the female element precedes the male in parthenogenesis, but the male, divine or magical, element is essential for immaculate conception.

One cannot deny the astounding similarity that she points out between the myths of early or primitive peoples regarding the origin of the gods and the world. The role played by the Great Mother in this world-wide myth, however, is probably to be attributed to the creative role of the woman in the creation of human society, as proved at such great length and depth by Bachofen, rather than to any consciousness among mankind, no matter how remote, of our Darwinian ancestors. (Editor–translator)

twelve females every two weeks from March to August; only then do they produce the males with which they mate."

Woman, then, created man, not the other way round. She is the postulate, he is the creature; she is the cause, he is the effect. In the guise of the mother, she anticipates him, rises up from primeval world spaces up into the personal stratum of individual existence. The deepest sensitivity does not bear the imprint of a father, because fathers at the beginning of consciousness were only brothers.

Aboriginal phenomena ought to be realized rather than explained, realized and effectively recognized, not only in fully unfolded matter but also in that which has been coolly shed and is drifting without a visible source. Human destiny always has been decided anew from its magical wells by the aboriginal phenomenon of female primacy, while the male principle, separated from the female, appears later and matures later into independence and creativity. Mythology has always known this: above the gate of the Egyptian goddess Neith, it says: "I am what is, what will be, and what has been. No one uncovered me. The fruit to which I gave birth was the sun." On other tombstones, she is called, "Nut, the old one, who gave birth to the sun and laid the seeds of gods and men." Or again, "The mother of the morning sun, the creatress of the evening sun, who existed when there was nothing and who created what was after her." Her symbol, the immortal scarab, rolls his original egg, the globe, before him, the ball of dung, only to crawl out of it anew after every rotation of the moon, winged and rejuvenated.

In the earliest versions of the myth of creation, female substance is considered the only creative force. In Babylonia, this original being was called Thalat, who only in the second generation gave birth to a divine couple called Apsu and Thiamat. They are the "world parents" of so many cosmogonies, who, resting upon one another incessantly, are torn apart to make Heaven and earth when their children crowd outward. According to the earliest Greeks, too, Gaea, the female earth, first emerges from the primal vagina, "the abyss sensing everything." Gaea, while remaining a virgin, creates Uranos, the sky, who is her son, but who procreates with her to found the race of Titans. According to old Norse legends,

Ymir, the wind god, comes out of the abyss of Ginnungagab
—declivity, cavern, crevice are always female symbols; he
comes out of the silvery world egg, the "uterus expositus,"
like Eros, the oldest and most venerable of the gods, according to the worshipers of Orpheus.

Brahma also dwells hidden in the original egg for a long
time and divides it into heaven and earth after he emerges.
The Hittite Agdistis is androgynous, like almost all god-
mothers of the Near East, and carries a male member within
herself. Later, that member is separated from her and grows
up to be Attis, the handsome youth and son-lover. In the
much later fairytales of the steppe tribes, the woman appears
contemporaneously in the role of both parents: she is called
Our Mother, the Hero Caracus.

> Only the woman is extant from the beginning and im-
> mutable; the man has evolved and is therefore condemned
> to perish. In the realm of physical existence, therefore,
> the male principle is secondary. Gynocracy takes its ex-
> ample and has its reason from this fact, which also con-
> tains the roots of that prehistoric concept of a union be-
> tween an *immortal* mother and a *mortal* father. Plutarch
> relates in a Venus myth how Theseus sacrificed a goat to
> the goddess at the seashore and the she-goat suddenly
> changed into a he-goat. Since that time, Plutarch claimed,
> the goddess had been portrayed riding a billy goat. Here
> also the mother animal appears as original, whereas the
> male arises from the female by a wondrous metamorphosis.
> The billy goat is no more than an attribute of Venus, sub-
> ject to her and destined for her service. But her eye rests
> delightedly upon her creation. The man becomes her be-
> loved, the billy goat her bearer, the phallus her constant
> companion. . . . She is happy with the spirit she has cre-
> ated. But Cybele the God Mother is greater than Attis,
> Diana greater than Virbius, Aphrodite greater than Phaë-
> ton. The female, material principle of Nature always pre-
> cedes. Like Demeter with Cista, she raises the male to her
> lap, the secondary principle existing only in mortal and
> continuously changing form. That is the highest expression
> of gynocracy. (Bachofen)

Statisticians—as far removed from mythology as one can
be—proved a long time ago that the male lines die out more

quickly. The male element is essentially mortal; the female essentially indestructible.

Early myths reflect biological primal conditions in a parthenogenetic image consisting of scenes so revolutionary and fantastic that they transpire in life nowadays only in the deep sea. There is a general and primordial belief in parthenogenesis and in the excellence of such an origin. It is greatly valued by all those who would excel: saviors, heroes, gods, demigods, ancestors, kings, and magi. Buddha and Quetzalcoatl, Huizipochli and Plato, Montezuma and Genghis Khan claimed to have been born of virgins. The Ainus of Japan, the tribes of central Asia, Chinese philosophers, Siamese demigods, Indian (American) heroes, and Tibetan prophets—they all want to be considered the products solely of their mothers and disclaim any bodily fathers.

This idea also may be made, aided by a certain amount of symbolism, to include some semipure concepts. Thus a Mongol princess is impregnated by the northern lights, a Japanese goddess conceives after partaking of a cherry, Chinese princesses are made gravid by lotos flowers. The Shang dynasty traces its origins to the Princess Kien-ti, into whose mouth a swallow's egg fell, and the Manchu claim descent from a girl and a red fruit. There are countless examples. But at this point, pure parthenogenesis is obscured and suffers a transition into immaculate conception, which is something entirely different. The two concepts share only the peculiarity that they do not necessarily connect the rise of life with the physical sex act. Whereas, however, the female in parthenogenesis accomplishes everything by herself, she remains passive in immaculate conception, only "conceives," even though the conceiving does not occur with a mundane man but with a god, with something amaterial, in a mythical or otherwise supernatural manner. This does not necessarily imply an emphatic respect before the female, only a deprecation of the sex act. Thus the Virgin, in the extreme spiritual religion called Christianity, means only the vessel waiting in purity for the bearing of the Saviour.

The Australian aborigines—they are the most primitive races on earth, now dissolving completely—do not know anything but immaculate conception. Such primitive peoples believe that women may be impregnated by almost any means other than men. Spencer and Gillen had to contend with a general disbelief, when they reported in their famous book that the Australian bushmen, though close to nature, in the midst of an uninhibited animal kingdom whose mating and birth seasons they constantly witnessed in their regular sequence, would not recognize any relationship between sex act and reproduction but rejected all of the causalities explained to them. B. Spencer's and F. J. Gillen's statements were verified again and again.

These aboriginal races, at least in their present state, are primitive animists. Formerly they underwent a highly mythological phase, surrounded by the spirits of their ancestors. The invisible swarms abound on the ground and around woods and stones and, with the aid of a sunbeam or a breath of wind, penetrate into the woman as ancestral dust in dozens of ways. Dead children, for this reason, are best buried at crossroads, for there they have a better opportunity for reincarnation, since everything is full of souls awaiting their chance. They hold a lookout for bodily mothers into whom they can slip from earth navels, which are caves with a rock on them. Young girls flee from these places or cover themselves up, limping past them on canes, pretending they are aged in order to escape unnoticed. Similar habits exist with the Hurons, Algonquians, and some West African tribes.

The man, at the very most, serves as an opener to smooth the passage for the spirit. He has nothing to do with the creation of a new being, since nothing new is being created. The whole thing remains a question of abodes, to be settled between spirit and woman, a situation in which she provides the fleshly vessel in whose sap immortal souls can implant themselves according to an entirely regular, subterranean cycle within the state of death, which has several gradations. Thus they can have themselves borne again and assume bodies. Children never die deeply, especially the infants who have never had a full life. After a very shallow death course, they slide upward again. An Australian woman therefore kills her baby with all the simplicity with which a European woman tells hers, "Go away, you bother me." She knows it will come back soon.

There is no refined culture without a trace of this animism. "Through Plato's earth gullet, roaring with birth, the souls rise and set, moving down when they come from Life and moving back up with a new destiny that they have been allotted." Since the majority of aboriginal peoples are totem races, they believe that these souls come from their proper totem, the great ancestral soul. They are related with this soul, not only physically but also in a profoundly magical way. The totem itself may be anything whatever: an animal, a stone, a plant, a part of the sky, a direction, rain or a rainbow, a fixed or a falling star. Having the same totem means an extremely strong, external tie as well as identity of substance, something so fundamental that its members are united inseparably in a living organism and are differentiated from all other people for all eternity. The original term *ototeman* is derived from the Ojibways and includes the totem animal as well as every member of the clan. The term, literally translated, means "derivation in the female line." The word "ebussia" in the Fanti language of the Gold Coast also signifies the totem animal as well as the maternal family. In Assam, there is another great mother clan with a female hearth totem, probably one of the oldest in existence.

Animism and immaculate conception apparently belong together. In countless versions, they are encountered with most peoples. Those peoples whose nature guided them beyond animism to the creation of myths and advanced cultures usually attributed their origins to parthenogenesis. This was done most boldly by the Indo-Europeans.

"In the beginning was the Word." In the Vedic nature religion, the goddess *Vac* occupies the place of this creative word, from which the Platonic ideas, the original concepts of all things emerge. *Vac* means language. She is not the male sacred spirit, which disgorges itself through the usual "fiery tongues"; rather, she is the maternal mouth cavity which forms and awakens the living word without being touched by a tongue as paternal phallus. In a hymn, the goddess says of herself: "I was pregnant with omnipotence; I dwell in the waters of the depth, spread thence throughout all creatures and touch the sky with my crown. I roar through all of creation like a gust of wind, over the skies and over the earth."

The axiom of the living word stands imperturbably, beginning with the sublime limits of metaphysical speculation, through all the strata of the soul, to the practices of witches and medicine men, in all the more gifted races of the five continents and in all realistic times. Word creation is equated with world creation, evocation of form. At the same time, it is a spell and an incantation, and as such, it is necromancy and poetry.

Possessing the creative word and thereby being enabled to call things by their proper names means acting upon their original ideas and literally *evoking* them; it means exercising the most awesome magic power for good or evil; it means changing things in their very nature. Calling gods and demons by their proper names means subjecting them to one's will; calling the dead by their proper names means pulling the dead back from their free dissolution; calling any creatures by their correct names means forcing them to appear in their true nature. "Oh, how good that no one knows that my name is Rumpelstilzkin." Name is equal to substance. Things that have no name do not exist. Therefore the West African Yoruba inquires through his priest which one of his deceased ancestors has the intention of dwelling in the new-born babe, so that it may get his name. Only through the identical name can ancestor and progeny become the same person.

The Christian receives his name through the sacred rite of baptism; monks and nuns get their spiritual names when they enter their orders; lovers all over the world find new names for each other. Every author is unpleasantly familiar with the fact that no fictional character acquires a credible life for him before he has found the only right name for him. Until then, one cannot do a thing with the character; it remains the dullest construction, neither radiates nor agitates, regardless of how true it may ring otherwise.

When physics speaks of a "center of gravity," "electrons," or "quanta," that also is an incantation and a spell. As Spengler says, "Essentially nothing has changed, starting with the name-spell of the savage and extending to the natural science of our times, which subjugates things or puts them under a spell by coining names or technical expressions for them."

Conversely, if one eradicates the name, one wipes out the

creature with it. In many primitive peoples, each person has two names, one apparent name and one real name, which, in order to prevent its misuse, is kept secret from all but the members of the immediate family, for if this living name were to be carved on mortal matter, such as a leaf, and then exorcized and buried by an ill-wisher, the bearer of the name would waste away at the same time as the decaying letters. Every American Indian believed that whatever happened to his name would also happen to him. If a Kaffir child has an inclination toward theft, his name is repeatedly spoken into the steam of cleansing magic herbs; the child, who is not allowed to learn anything of this procedure, is then considered completely cured of its aberration. An Irish bard, on the other hand, was unsuccessful in casting the spell of death upon a king of Ulster because the king's name could not be scanned correctly according to any known meter. The meter is considered a spell-casting pattern. A name, once it is scanned according to this pattern, lies ready for further magic treatment. Icelandic minstrels, for this reason, were subject to strict laws, for through their language they were able to muster that immeasurable power which came with forming original words and, with them, new ways of combining the cosmic net of forces. In Sumatra, the priestesses have the honorary title "sihoro," which means "word." In the Cabbala, too, the practice of magic is considered the same as influencing ideas through purposeful words and concepts.

In the Indo-European nature religion, the goddess *Vac* is that first, inscrutable word which evokes the eternal ideas themselves. Therefore, she is said to be "surrounded by pictures of all creation at the deepest, very deepest abyss." When Goethe understood the original word "mothers" in this sense, he said to Eckermann that he could not help a strange shudder.

II

THE BLACK AND WHITE
EGG MOTHERS

THE WHITE MOTHER

If one penetrates that entire symposium of Olympian department heads, the superficial, enlightened, and sentimental crowd of gods, and reaches the realm of darkness, this change in strata leads into a more profound, more soul-filled frame of reference, to the single Great Goddess derived from the moon. The whole family of gods are her progeny.

This original Aphrodite has many names: Rhea, Neith, Demeter, Ishtar, Shing Moo, Cybele, Agdistis, Bona Dea, Ana Perennia, Cailleach Bhiarach, Fir Dea, Bu Anu, Anaitis, Bellona, Astarte, Harmonia, Unakuagsak, and Tetevinan are only some of them. The Dravida, the original agrarians inhabiting India, simply called her Ma Mata, which means Mother, or called her "black soil replete with darkness" (*homo, cf.* humus). This infantile word for the maternal breast is repeated in related names of the most diverse languages: Jesus' mother is named Mary, and Buddha's mother is called Maya. The antiagrarian Aryans, Semites, and Central Asiatics worship her as the egg of heaven, the female constellation, which is the moon. The dreams emanating from her breast, silvery and gentle, flow into the plants breathing at night, overflow, and not infrequently become an intoxicating ritual beverage. Thus the *soma* of the Hindus is a moon vine, grown by the nocturnal, uterine light, as was the Celtic mistletoe potion. Sedna or Unakuagsak, the Great Mother of the Eskimos, is active as a cosmic force, just like the Great Mother of New Zealand and Brazil. "Ebb and tide, waxing and waning, decomposition of the flesh, fermentation and alteration of the wines, phosphorescence, the rotting of the wood, incubation, easy births are due to her."

Under the name of Isis, she glides through the upper, fertilizing waters of Egypt on her heavenly bark, the lunar sickle. As the great North Goddess, she rides on the wagons of the nomads or drifts on her ship, rolling along on spoked wheels and propelled by weavers, herself the great weaver. The ship going over land, an egg that has been set in motion and rolls along, lifted out of its dreamy waters, this symbol accompanies the most ancient mother religions of Babylonian, Hindu, Egyptian, and Old Norse antiquity and extends throughout the Middle Ages, surviving into our carnival floats. It is the shrove-tide float, the "fool's cart," surrounded by an orgiastic crowd. Tacitus saw a Suebian goddess venerated in the shape of a rolling ship and the goddess Nerthus on her ship wagon, adorned with brightly colored cloth and pulled by milky white cows, accompanied by seven Germanic tribes on their cultic processions.

In Ireland, the great mother religion is a forest and moon cult. Its intoxicating beverage, "sticky as the libido," oozes out of the glassy mistletoe, which at certain phases of the moon was cut with a silver sickle by Druid priestesses or priests in female garments. In honor of this goddess, all Celtic tribes had adopted the lunar year and divided it into nights, not days. The Dea Syria fell out of her own moon egg from the sky into the Euphrates, was rolled on land by the fish, and incubated by the pigeons. The Arabic great mother was called *Al-Uzza*. Her shrine, the Ka'abah, was guarded in pre-Islamic times by the priestesses of Mecca; she herself was venerated in the shape of a black stone (moon egg).

The great mother of Mexico was called the Ancestress Tonantzin, also the Earthquake Mother Thalli-Yjolta ("beating heart of the earth"), or the Maize Mother Centectl. She is black and white, like the antique mystery eggs, like the Erinyes, the Indian (Hindu) Aphrodite, like everything chthonial or connected with the depths of the earth. In her temple she was venerated in the shape of a squatting, green giant frog, cut out of a single, huge emerald: the totem animal of creation in (or from) the quagmire. The Caribs, when there is an earthquake, say, "The Great Mother dances." Everywhere she appeared in a dual role, as earth and moon; the two together comprised a single system of reference of a predominantly feminine nature, the moon representing the spiritual; the earth, the material ("earthy") element. The body, after all, is a form of the soul. "In the moon the souls dissolve like the bodies decomposing in the earth." Ishtar, the Great Mother of Babylon, was both at the same time. She was the uterus at rest, which was the earth, around which the entire cosmos rotated. Her belt was the zodiac, she was the morning and the evening star, the creatress of all things, the great huntress, the mistress of battle, the queen of heaven and earth, the horned moon goddess, mother of gods and men, and was venerated almost monotheistically. Sumerian and, after them, Babylonian queens were considered representatives of Ishtar. The Babylonian kings were called spouses of the queen of heaven.

Originally, the great life mothers were all moon women. Where agriculture prevailed, they were limited to the role of Mother Earth granting the harvest. Primarily, however, they were living destiny itself. Their worship was, therefore, not restricted to a regularly fertilized soil or a maternal, original morass. It was connected with the female egg, with which all moon women were associated. Even in their tellurian shape, they wore the lunar crescent insignia as sacred virgins. All of them remained virgins, which was to say *unmarried, not chaste*. Priests serving them had to carry on female mimicry: the priests of Ishtar, Dea Syria, and Artemis of Ephesus, and the moon priests of Africa and Asia were eunuchs. The priests of the Great Mother of Mexico were very aged men. The practice of the religion of the primordial Great Mother was an exclusively female office, like necromancy, prophecy, direction of natural forces, and magic. If a man was to participate, he might do so only after surrendering his gender and adopting the other, or in an androgynous form.

Everywhere the Great Mother existed from the beginning as a given quantity. Male gods, on the other hand, had a childhood, broke out of their dark enclosure as dependent creatures to face the light, like young males in lower forms of life who parthenogenetically emerge from the grown mother animal. Half the gods of Asia Minor were created this way: timeless mother, childish son. The purest form of it appeared in Crete. The Minoan culture, one of the most original and refined in the world, in some fifteen hundred years of prosperity did not have a single independent god, only a Great Mother. On some cameos and rings of the third pre-Christian millennium, she was portrayed with a dwarflike creature beside her, son and husband at the same time. The thing looks like a termite queen and her tiny prince consort.

The budding Greek civilization retained Rhea as the Great Mother and the only adult goddess, accompanied only by some dactyls, finger stalls, or minute phalli. No man was attached to them as yet. They were first conceived only as a male principle without personality, the naked, short-lived principle—no more. Long after the world was full of grown gods, there still abounded the gnomes, heroic dwarfs, and demoniacal blacksmiths who hammer and forge their material on a simmering inner fire with muted blows. Deep down there, the dactyls taught the Great Mother the art of metallurgy. Even Golden Aphrodite, not at all an Earth-Mother type by the light of day, took limping Hephaestos, an unprepossessing blacksmith, for an underworld husband, while up above she married the fully developed war god Ares. Even today, the Gretna Green blacksmiths hammer together couples in a hurry. This craft is always entrusted to a male, demoniacal creature. There is about it a lowly, fiery magic conducive to secret associations and clubs. Even in African matriarchal areas with female chiefs, the blacksmith's occupation is exercised exclusively by the men.

Slowly the powers of the gods underwent a transition. At first, the male appeared only as an adjunct to the Great Mother. Later, he became the lord of storms and the moon, for, just as the dactyls rose from the earth, so the male god emerged from the female substance of the moon. All these males, only half developed, followed the Great Goddess as a wild, servile entourage. Even Dionysos, "His phallic lordship," the seducer of women in women's clothing and with a hermaphroditic body, was nothing but the leader of her followers, whereas the dactyls were the lowest in their ranks.

Moon gods remain without a purpose in themselves, destined to serve the female with a strictly physical virility. Odin, too, originally was a moon and wind god, the stormy flagella cilium of insurrection in an expectant air cavity. That explains why he—as late as in Wagner's operas—always appears in a hail storm, while the naïve spectator might think that, if someone is a god, he could at least make some decent weather for himself.

Everywhere and always, the Great Mother is served voluntarily, with awe, intoxication, gratitude, respect, ecstasy, as the original source of all creation. From her, prosperity, love, happiness, and good fortune well up. All festivals of orgiastic intoxication are traceable to earth women and original Aphrodites, mysteries as well as carnivals. She is a serious ordainer of order and a principle of joy at the same time. She is natural law and justice, because she incessantly gives to her children from her plenty. Whoever violates her in any form at the same time violates himself, commits an outrage against creation, and must inexorably perish. Demeter, Themis, Dike, Poine, Nemesis, Erinys, and Justitia are the bearers of an ancient order, never completely replaced by the later, man-made law. Although Osiris, as the judge of the dead, tells the verdict, a goddess with a never-erring scale weighs the hearts for him. The male civil law needs a search and a determination of the proper law that applies; female, natural law is the law itself, donates itself, and permits no appeal from its findings.

The goddess of a hundred names, the only one, the white mother, the incomprehensible giver gives nutriment to all —even Death.

THE BLACK MOTHER

"The belly caves in, the convolutions of the intestines enter its contours, the last feeling escapes into the navel and wants to leave it, too, in order to return to the mother's body. The road has been cut off—how horrible!—and the other road is death." (H. H. Jahnn)

Yes, she prepares food for the all-consuming time, nothing else. She drives defenseless babes from their beautiful protection into the irreversible, into the chain of "Never more's," and does so much too cruelly for anyone to complain. Being born means being dragged out of the small child and being imprisoned in a disgusting old thing, being pulled by one's hair and nerves in only one direction, without a respite, without pity, where happiness and duration exclude one another and any victory, no matter how hotly contested, must end in the cold defeat of lying down to die.

That is what is meant by the Great Mother's black-and-white face, the black-and-white moon of Persia, and the vulture on Neith's head bearing down to devour the world carcass, everything that has outstayed its time, in order that it might not remain too long. Great Mother is not a name reserved for Aphrodite and Demeter, Bona Dea, Fortuna, and Abundantia, who gave life and nutriment: she also appears as the child-devouring Mara, as Lamia, as the frightful Kali, the fishy eyed Durga, the black Humus, Hecate, as the evil huntress Diana, chasing down and impaling the sacrificial boy, as Ampusa, who drifts about as a blood bubble with one leg of iron, the other of ass's dung. She is the dragon house of all puberty rites, the evil ancestress Hine-nui-te-po of New Zealand, a maternal mouth that spits out and sucks back in forever.

At the same time, she is Mater Dolorosa, immortal mother of a mortal son. The world is full of wailing Great Mothers from Thrace to Samarkand, from India to the Nile, whether the son is named Tammus, Attis, Adonis, Dionysos, Iasion, Ruadan, or Christ. All noble resins, frankincense, and amber are called tears of the earth goddesses for their mortal child. The thing they have created, Creation, is usually symbolized by a tree. In Bengal, the "son" in the shape of a sacrificial tree is adorned with flowers, fruit, and burning lights like a Christmas tree, carried to the river by youths, and surrendered to the water to dance on, where it is swept along by the current to be drowned elsewhere. Attis was worshipped in the shape of a violet-lined pine tree. The Sumerians some 6,000 years ago called the "true son" Damuzi, or Wanderer, "good shepherd," son and lover of Ishtar; he also drowns, carried off by the black mother into the underworld, while her white face above floats in tears.

Wherever the sons later appear in the guise of grain gods, the death is followed by a festival of resurrection; much later, in Greek classical times, when incest became a punishable offense, the death of the sons was reinterpreted as punishment for their love relationship to their mothers. Anaitis of Nineveh, however—mother of life and death at the same time—stuffs her son back inside of herself in a giant orgy of fire. Every year, the most beautiful youth was selected for her,

> a luxuriant figure of semifeminine shape, his white face painted with psimythion, his eyebrows and lashes with stimmi, adorned with golden bracelets, rings, and earrings, dressed in a bright-red, transparent garment, his hands clutching his cup and his double axe, surrounded by women, sitting under a purple canopy—that is how he is exhibited to the people. After one day and one night of orgiastic intoxication, there was a different kind of show, when this splendid person was to be seen on a vast bed of precious woods, covered by carpets woven with gold, and laden with all kinds of incense and aromas, which was set afire, while countless masses of people howled and shrill music provided a deafening noise. An immense pillar of fire then rose toward the skies and flooded half of Nineveh with smoke and fragrance. (O. K. Müller)

The problem of immortality for the son consists in being born through the body of the black, as he was through the body of the white, Great Mother. Once his problem has been solved, she is no more to him than a dark, soft portal of eternal resurrection. "Earth, though, was consistent this night, too."

The Polynesian Maui myths in their many variables have no other theme than this "going through the Mother twice" (Jung). There, the hero's maternal enemy is the evil ancestress Hine-nui-te-po. He bravely climbs into her in order to destroy her from inside, but prior to doing so, he warns his "little birds" or wishful thoughts that they are not to laugh, the time for jubilation is not to come until he has happily come out again. But the "little birds" laugh too early and too loudly, the evil old woman awakens and closes her mouth. To the right and to the left, Maui's legs fall out of the corners of her mouth. The resurrection is a failure. Mysticism, religion, philosophy, myths, and fairy tales all have the same motif, the dual aspect of the black-and-white Mother. In the myths of the Eskimos and of the North American Indians, in Mexico, in the Sahara, and along the Congo, everywhere and for all races death has come into the world through the woman. They do not know why, but they know it from the observation of Nature.

Still, is she evil, the great, final one? Is she not also the yearning of the born infant? "The yearning for the Holy Night," for vanishing out of the tortuous chase of the eternal wakeful "Onward" into the deep return, into the dreamless rest of Nirvana? For the person tired onto death, the black-and-white mothers become interchangeable. The "good" one was "evil"; the "bad" one becomes "good." The dead are called Demetrians: squatting in the embryo position, they are placed into the earth, the realm of Demeter. "Like the new-born babe, they pull their thighs up to their bellies and are bedded back into their maternal grounds." Their souls return home for a reunion with the great earth soul.

THE GREAT WEAVER

All mother goddesses spin and weave. In their concealed workshops, they weave veins, fibers, and nerve strands into the miraculous substance of the live body. Everything that is comes out of them: they weave the world tapestry out of genesis and demise, "threads appearing and disappearing rhythmically." Maja and Dea Syria weave them into the veil of illusion, Harmonia weaves the starry sky, and Arachne spins all the romantic entanglements of gods and men into her net.

When the mysterious weaver proclaims her work, she is projected into time as a triple person, corresponding to the past, present, and future, and called Nornes, Fates, or Moira. They are called Graces, if they weave good things; Erinyes, if they weave bad ones. Ilithia, the midwife, is sometimes called the "good weaver," and weavers pull the cart of the wandering North Goddess in the shape of a ship. Knitting, knotting, interlacing, and entwining belong to the female realm in Nature, but so does entanglement in a magic plot or in the poisonous shirt of Nessus and the unraveling of anything that is completed. At night she must unravel what she has woven in the daytime, "so that eternal freshness be guaranteed for the cloth, which becomes possible only through eternal death." The weaving of garments was a ritual act with all cultured peoples and still occupies this place with primitive nations today, a secret guarded by the women and entrusted especially to the priestesses. It was considered a female invention and a kind of projection of the sex organ, for the labia of the vulva resemble the flax comb or the weaver's reed, whose teeth separate the individual threads. This comb is everywhere an object of religious worship and an ancient symbol of woman. Persian and Turkish prayer rugs bear this imprint on the "East" side, where the good wishes are recorded, woven into the pattern as an ornament; the pattern repeats as many combs as the donor of the rug wants the recipient to have wives.

A relationship to the weaving of the earth mothers is borne by everything woven, victors' shirts as well as shrouds. Black-and-white cloths wrap the deceased like umbilical cords into the hereafter, so that the thread of Fate may not tear and something might be ready for the great weaver woman to grasp and continue weaving. And whoever was initiated into the Eleusinian Mysteries of Demeter always wore the sacred thread around his hand and around one ankle, a visible sign of that immortality which his visual instruction had conferred upon him there.

The woman is the possessor of the most secret arts of knotting which is practiced by almost all nations even today as magic against sickness and any kind of misfortune. (It is most commonly used as a cure for warts.) The effect is due to the wrapping and stopping of the running thread: Fate is sealed off at the vulnerable points in its course, stopped, turned, or averted. Even the rational man of civilization wears an amulet or protective knot against diseases of the throat to this very day, and that is the necktie, for that was its original intent. For modern graphology, everything that is looped in the letters is connected with the sexual and fateful sides of a person's character; at these crossings one may best see the relationship of the writer to the great weaver woman.

All knowledge of Fate comes from the female depths; none of the surface powers knows it. Whoever wants to ask about Fate must go down to the woman. This is the reason for the

female predominance in the realm of the mysteries. There
never were mysteries of Zeus. Of the female mysteries of
Eleusis, Adesius wrote to the Emperor Julian: "Once you
have participated in the mysteries, you will feel ashamed to
have been born a mere man." In a fragment by Pindar, it is
said of them:

> Happy he who has seen that communion under the
> earth.
> He knows the end of Life and also the god-given
> beginning.

At every point where the earth is cleft apart to form a female flax comb, the oracles come forth. From that point, the
young temples of the supernatural, profane gods rise in
Athens, Delphi, Sparta, and Dodona. The Areopagus also
stood above the sacred ravine of the Erinyes. Whoever was
acquitted sacrificed to "the Honorable Ones" on the spot,
for they accused him and they acquitted him. Even Delphi,
the major stronghold of the male, spiritual god, was built
around the ancient navel stone of the Earth Goddess Gaea.
In the navel itself, a domed building in the middle of the
temple of Apollo, there lay Gaea's son, the earth spirit Python,
in his grave. Pythia, a woman, prophesied while bent over the
steam of the female declivity. Plutarch was informed by a
Delphic priest that this oracle in the house of the sun god
was inspired only at night, when the moon shone. The Moira,
too, had their shrine there. They were called "The Three."

III

MATRIARCHY

A female-oriented morality is the natural consequence of a philosophical climate tending to surround the female potential with the totality of power, where the rise and fall of civilizations is considered to be determined by goddesses of destiny, wooed by the living and the dead, whose fate they decide. A cosmic mood, taut and trembling with the symbolics of motherhood, could not remain a mere belief without formal expression. Rather, such a mood penetrates all levels of consciousness. The religious structure of every era contains its most vital and most fundamentally true elements. This religious structure confers the realities of power. Veneration of woman as a goddess would have been incompatible with making her a slave on earth.

Still, several thousand years elapsed before someone understood these facts and was able to draw from them all the logical inferences. Naturally, I here mean Bachofen. This gentle, corpulent Basel patrician, with the wonderfully rounded child's mouth, with a dozen million Swiss francs, many honorary titles, and an almost unbelievable understanding, in his profound, inner loneliness discovered the female era at the lower seam of history, with its sacerdotal, political, and economic female dominion. He proved its existence himself for fourteen regions, countries and city-states: Lycia, Athens, Crete, Lemnos, Egypt, Tibet, Central Asia, India, Orchomenos, Locris, Elis, Mantinea, Lesbos, and Cantabria. He also predicted proof for similar conditions for a majority of the greater part of the earth, and he was borne out.

As a scholar primarily interested in comparative law, he named his rediscovery "matriarchy" for its most significant legal characteristic. This institution ignored the male's role in the child's procreation and traced descent solely from the maternal line. "Descent" is here used in the literal sense, "to come from." Genealogy, therefore, was strictly feminine. There was no difference between children born inside or outside of wedlock, for all children inherited their mother's class and bore her name or that of her clan. Property also was inherited solely in the feminine line: it passed from the mother to her daughters, and so on. The sons received nothing, though occasionally their sisters gave them a dowry when they got married. They could not inherit anything from their bodily father, because he was not considered related to them. Whatever he captured or earned in his lifetime was logically bequeathed to his uterine clan through the common mother, or through her to the children of his sisters. These nephews and nieces were considered much more closely related to him than to their own fathers. During the transition between matriarchal and patriarchal law, the mother's brother was the only man who was accorded any influence upon the feminine clan. Even the extremely patriarchal Roman law still recognized a sharp distinction between the two uncles, the father's brother, or *patruus,* and the mother's brother, or *avunculus,* which means something like "little ancestor."

That is what, in sober outline, the structure of matriarchy is like. But this is only scratching the surface. It has been rightly claimed that Bachofen was "perhaps the greatest discoverer of primeval consciousness, with reference to whose dissertations on cult and myth all religious tenets, without exception, appear to be dilutions and disintegrations of an original source."

There have always been two kinds of research men, prophets and thinkers. Bachofen was both, which made him an unprecedented anthropologist. For the divining rod called intuition only indicates those spots at an as yet unknown depth where the mind may apply the sensitive and deliberate technique of discovery. The divining rod knocks where deep sifting may prove worth while. Bachofen's wonderful intuition always started divining precisely in those areas located between the specialized disciplines and normally fenced out by all their neighbors, such as archeologists, philologists, cultural historians, and researchers into mythology. They, strictly limiting themselves to their own fields, tended to cover the intervals with the debris of their excavations. But Bachofen proceeded step by step, according to the strict rules of research, with a purposeful march into the unknown. His precise methods then led into wide areas of new spiritual depths completely unknown to the superficial protagonists of extensive, rather than intensive, work. He had to steel himself to tolerate solitude and complete independence from the opinions of his contemporaries, he needed to be "adamant in the face of sarcasm and doubt, those immature fruits of wisdom."

He was fighting the ideal of "critical examination of sources," which reigned supreme in the historical sciences in his times (the latter nineteenth century). In examining their sources, these historians tended to forget that they, too, were subject to the fashionable prejudices of their times, as was pointed out by Bossier* about his fellow historian Théodor Mommsen and Mommsen's disciples. If all ages went through history with this process of elimination, nothing would remain of history but empty dates. The raids of this rationalism, above all, eliminated that "fantastic bric-a-brac" called tradition and threw these useless notes on the trash pile as incredible, immaterial, or "insignificant anomalies"— a practice which thoroughly angered the otherwise so gentle Bachofen. In order to discredit any materials as historical evidence, one merely condemned them as "legendary" or, still worse, as "mythical." Whatever was disgraced by this dunce's cap became untouchable for anybody who wanted to be taken seriously.[1]

Ingenious outsiders then brought about the victory of the legends all along the line. The book of fairy tales has long been considered the Baedeker of the archeologist, who in his turn obtains new material for the historian. Whoever wants to find something solid digs out the core of myths. It began with Schliemann. His unerring judgment, disregarding all

---

* Where possible the editor–translator attempted to supply initials for all sources cited. In many instances it was not possible to establish this data.

[1] In the original work, the passages condemning nineteenth-century scholarship and heaping imprecations upon Bachofen's enemies are considerably longer.

ridicule, took the Homeric tradition seriously, and he found
the entire Mycenaean-Pelasgian stratum. Arthur Evans took
King Minos, Daedalus, and the labyrinth seriously and bared
a whole new civilization with the Cretan excavations. No
serious scholar of today is prevented from looking for the
residence of the hero of the Gilgamesh epic by the legendary
assertion that he was two thirds god and one third man, that
he fought with scorpion people, went to the underworld, and
almost burst through the brazen bars of the nether kingdom
because of an erotic difference with the goddess Ishtar.

Just as the mammals seem boring to modern biologists
spoiled by the unlimited potentialities of the lower realms
of microbiology, so anyone who has come under the spell
of the creative shudder abounding in nascent pre-history
tends to deem the upper-level, firmed-up history rather dry.
This is especially true of anyone studying the great cultured
peoples at that transitional stage before they adopted ration-
ality and enter the well-illuminated part of their fate. For
those peoples had the most awesome pre-history; otherwise,
their later development would not have been as far-
reaching.

It is hardly possible to exaggerate the bright contents or
the many gradations of this anterior past. Probably, however, history itself, or at least a story preserved in tradition,
is much older than seemed possible not many years ago. One
should not regard as mere manufacture of nymbus the
claim of the Egyptians that their dynasties reach back 28,-
000 years before Menes, or that Sumerian assertion according to which Sumer had 64,000 years of uninterrupted
history, perhaps even 400,000 years before the Great Flood.
The kingdoms of Kish and Uruk, founded after the flood,
are supposed to have been governed by demigod kings for
some 20,000 years. From about 5000 B.C. on, the rulers are
listed without many gaps. Around 4000 B.C. came the invasion of the Semites, which disrupted the homogeneity of
the population, and around 3000 B.C. the realm was divided
into Sumer and Akkad. Then came the end.[2] (Ungnad)

----

[2] The more recent historical research has tended to reduce rather
than increase the lifespans of the more ancient kingdoms. Atomic
physics has given us the radioactive clock, whose workings enable

Human civilization is proved to have existed in the Old Stone Age. The Aurignac level goes back some 40,000 years; the Swedish rock pictures are tens of thousands of years old, and the newly discovered South African sculptures from the Paleolithic era date back some 30,000 years, although they show several different styles and must be considered the culmination of a long development.

There is, then, always a continuation, never a beginning, never a mere cause, but everywhere the consequences. The true scientific quest, however, does not end with the answer to the question What? but is answered only with the answer to the question Whence? and may then answer the question Whither? from that information. Bachofen, the sovereign scholar in the intangible realm of significance, hit upon a layer where apparently a total change of polarities had occurred not long ago at the beginning of the history of Egypt and Asia Minor, and especially in Greece, the Greek islands, and Rome. This change had not been a change between classes or races, but had been a change of the basic polarities themselves, changing the entire view of Nature and the heavenly bodies. The moon was overthrown, the sun enthroned; night and day, left and right, even and uneven, the first-born and the last-born exchanged places.

This was the most distinct possible incision between the earlier and the later eon. The old ways were extinguished in a compulsive forgetfulness. But a terrible spiritual tempest

---

us to date rather exactly archeological findings. According to it, the Sumerians took over an already flourishing civilization from some other, unknown people around 3000 B.C., although those other people probably date back to around 5000 B.C. The Semitic Akkadians conquered the Sumerians about 2350 B.C., and a new wave of Semitic invasions founded the Hammurabi kingdom about 1800 B.C., followed by the invasion of the Kassites about a century later.

Egyptian civilization was roughly contemporaneous. The gradual enlargement of the tiny political units culminates in 3000 B.C. with the unification of Upper and Lower Egypt, and the Old Kingdom, which built the huge pyramids, began at that time. The 28,000-year history of the chronicles, the author's objections notwithstanding, cannot be regarded as historically sound. (data according to Ferguson-Bruun, *A Survey of European History*, 3d edition, 1962)

continued to glow in the waning myth, like a vanishing thundercloud disappearing at the horizon, still sending out flashes of lightning from afar.

Alien legal remnants are scattered throughout our tradition, taboo and misplaced in the logical, polished, classical order of our times. Loose ends of customs, tying into nothing apparent, are stubbornly retained at ancient festivals, all sorts of seemingly eerie nonsense which, however, is connected somehow with the makings of national hero worship. In the midst of the strictest patriarchy, there are demigods, presumably one's ancestors, who trace their lineage only to their mothers. The wedded state, dominated by men, is called *matri*mony, not *patri*mony. Respectable people, such as the Cretans, oddly enough, say "motherland" rather than "fatherland." And why is it that in ancient Rome, where everything good was associated with the right side, the popular oracle interpreted the flight of the birds so as to have favorable omens coming from the left?

Furthermore, the woman is politically without rights in the classical period. Yet tradition had it that fighting armies in ancient Greece were separated by the *matrons* of Elis, who were obeyed without protest by both armies. When one gathers up all the evidence of this kind, together with the acknowledged history of other barbaric nations, it seems almost incredible that the times of the matriarchy could ever have been doubted: anyone could read in Hannibal's treaty with the Gauls the stipulation that, in case of disputes, the interpretation on the intent of the treaty was to be made by a court of Gallic *matrons*. "The exercise of supreme jurisdiction by matrons always is the part of the female dominance which is preserved longest. It is traceable to the respect for inscrutable authority that only surrounds old women, and which was later perverted into the fear of witches."

Bachofen, still all alone with his discovery, was amazed to find the evidence of female greatness in legend and myth. In Homeric poetry, he meets with sovereign queens in no fewer than five kingdoms. The sharp contrast between them and the prevailing system proves such features to be original and genuine; for a later age would never have added them out of the imagination, since the line of sensitivity removed itself from that tradition. Here the psychoanalytic interpretation is wrong when it tries to interpret the "mythical" rule of "Great Mothers" as a fantasied "Ersatz" for forbidden incest, for the existence of the queens has been proved factual since such statements were first made.

Bachofen pursued every change in legend, where an alteration is attempted, not in the events transpiring but in their significance. He finds the same person judged differently for one and the same deed, "innocent or criminous, praised and abhorred." If one views all the material from a false perspective, it is a useless pile of contradictory fragments; if one views it correctly, it fits into a single cast. One finds that female predominance entails a preference for the left side, for even numbers, for black, white, red, for night, for the moon, for unforgiveableness of matricide, and for the last-born; whereas male predominance means a preference for the right side, blue and yellow, uneven numbers, the day, the sun, atonability of matricide, and primogeniture. When a people changes over from one system to the other, all the symbols of the style of living also must be changed. The cosmos changes, from the sidereal tent to the smallest gesture. With minor deviations, this is applicable to most peoples and most times, because matriarchy does not seem to be tied to a certain race or epoch but rather to a certain frame of mind. Some races never change this frame of mind; some, early; some, late; others, too late. For each one, however, the decisive event in its history lies in the manner in which the change is brought about and in what shocks it entails.

At times, the myths themselves provided a vivid enlightenment on the conflict of the two systems when patriarchy replaced matriarchy. Bachofen found such a source of enlightenment in the Greek treatment of the Orestes legend, even in the late form of the Aeschylus trilogy. Here was a classic point of friction between maternal and paternal predominance, old and new psychology, the divine and the underworld, the great egg mothers and the Apollo-Athena system.

Orestes had killed his mother in order to avenge his father. Who was the more important of the two? According to the old, tellurian law of the Erinyes, that avenging murder ordered by Apollo was the only sin unforgivable for all eternity.

The exposition of the Eumenides, given at the beginning, reveals a concrete picture of this deep conflict: There lies Orestes, embracing Apollo's altar, harried by the Erinyes to the point of madness, at the only point not subject to the dictates of the earth. The Erinyes outside wait, their snake hair hissing from time to time, until their victim must leave, so that they may chase him to death. Athena appears just in time to arrange for the harried man to have a trial at the Areopagus. The most respected citizens are to decide his fate. Apollo, who ordered the deed, leads the defense. When the Erinyes shriek their accusations, the desperate Orestes screams, "Why do you pursue only me? Why did you not persecute Clytemnestra in her life?" But the Erinyes, and with them the matriarchy, answer, "She was not related by blood to the man she slew." For them, only a uterine relationship, through the female body and female blood, can matter.

A husband is a strange man. Agamemnon had infamously murdered Iphigenia, the daughter of Clytemnestra's body and her blood. Clytemnestra only fulfills Nemesis' command by taking vengeance on him for the slain girl. To her, that is not only her right but her supreme duty. For this reason, the Erinyes are on her side but are hostile to Orestes, who has committed the most gruesome crime against creative Nature by killing his mother to avenge his father. According to the matriarchy, Agamemnon always remained a strange man, even to his wife.

The opposite theory is advocated by Apollo, who addresses the judges in defense of the new, patriarchal law of the sun cult:

> Not the mother is the creatress of the child,
> She only bears and nurtures awakened life.
> The father creates, she keeps the fruit,
> As a favor for her friend, if no god intercedes.

Since the verdicts of the judges are equal in number on both sides, the tie is broken by Athena, "the motherless daughter of Zeus' head, the even daughter, the trembling lightning of her father," who speaks, while casting her ballot, these words:

> My task it is to render the last verdict,
> And I cast this stone for Orestes,
> For I did not have a mother who bore me;
> No, all my heart praises the male,
> May Orestes win over your tied vote.

This acquittal proclaims the downfall of the matriarchy and the victory of the Olympian over the chthonial world. Only the Erinys rises to utter this curse:

> Woe, that I must suffer this!
> Woe, I must hide beneath the earth, I, the wise one!
> O, new gods, ye overrun old law, ancient justice,
> Ye tear them, in overturning them, out of my hand,
> And I, covered with shame, righteously indignant,
> In vengeance I seed the soil with poison
> That dripped from my heart.

That, however, signifies bad harvests, miscarriages, and death. Erinys is the creative as well as the avenging, original power. The woman, who assumes the role and functions of the soil, is of the same, maternal substance as Erinys. The unavenged matricide hits her in the heart, and so, all of Nature rises in vengeance for broken matriarchal law. Nature herself has been violated: the order of things, the law of Nature, has been shaken and overthrown. But once Nature has been upset, shaken, and violated, the process of birth has been disturbed, and plants, animals, and people, as well as the unborn babe in his mother's body, spoil like the grain in the field. No victory of the sterile powers of heaven can avert this catastrophe. For "just as one can hope for no forgiveness from the religion of the Holy Ghost if one has committed the sin against the Holy Ghost, the religion of material strength, of the motherhood of earth knows no mercy for the sin against its principle." (Bachofen)

> The new customs will overthrow everything,
> If the guilt of the godless matricide
> May win out before the law.

Athena, the wise one, begs, flatters, mediates, and concili-
ates. She wants Erinys to be the co-ruler over the country
at her side:

> In an honorable dwelling,
> Near the temple of Erechtheus, thou wilt in future
> Be highly honored of men and of women,
> As no other country ever honored thee.

After this encouragement, the ancient goddess takes back her
curse, so that

> . . . the seeds shall not miserably perish in failure,
> The cherished place of pasture
> May feed in its time by the earth's green plant
> Sheep glad and full, twin lambs all around them.

The Orestes legend openly reveals the change in cultures
from the material rule of the mothers to the intellectual rule
of the fathers, which demonstrates its difference from the
parthenogenetic principle in the Roman system of adopting
sons. There can be nothing more opposed to the old social
system than the change into a son of a total stranger, completely ignoring all of his hereditary qualities.

The radical change into the Apollonian principle may be
carried out only by the man Orestes. Such a woman as Electra
is not permitted to carry it out, despite her hatred of her
mother and her closeness to her father. "The age that we
know was created by the spirit, which is always Man."

As long as the original Great Mother occupies the peak
of creation from whose lap all of Life is born, she punishes
any transgression of the matriarchal laws with infertility, crop
failure, pestilence, and worse. This fate that is worse is well
described in the Gilgamesh Epic in the passage describing
the wrath of Ishtar and the primordial fear in the myths of all
nations that there might be more dead than live people, so
that the black-and-white mother would become entirely
black.

> To Kurungea, the somber country,
> Ishtar, the moon god's daughter, directed her steps,
> To the land without return, the land known to thee,
> To the road whose course does not turn,

To the house of putrefaction,
Where they eat dung, where they drink dust,
Where they dwell in darkness, seeing no light.
They are clad, like birds, in feathery dress.
When Ishtar reached the gate of Kurungea,
She spake these words to the watchman:
Keeper of the threshold, open thy gate!
If thou dost not open, I shall smash the gates,
I shall break the bars, splinter the stakes,
Lift the doors from their hinges,
I shall guide up the dead, that they eat and live.
The dead shall eat the living,
Crowd around the live people,
That there may be more dead than living men.

"Stop. Do not smash the gate," answers the keeper of the
threshold. "I will go and announce thy name to Queen
Eresh-Kigal." He goes and tells Eresh-Kigal, "Lo, thy sister
Ishtar stands at the gate, she who conducts the great orgies,
who stirs up the waters before Ea, the Lord." When Eresh-
Kigal hears this, her face becomes pale. "Go, keeper of the
threshold, open the gate. Treat her according to the laws."
He goes and opens the gate for Ishtar. "Enter, mistress. May
the underworld receive thee with joy. The palace of Kurungea welcomes thee." At each one of the seven gates of the
realm of the dead, he takes one of her amulets: her kerchief,
her earrings, the chains from around her neck, the jewel from
her breast, the birthstone belt from her hips, the bracelets of
her arms and legs, the loincloth from her abdomen. Thus he
takes away her magic powers, so that she sinks into the sleep
of the underworld. Thereby, however, the power of love in
the world above is also put to sleep.

After the mistress Ishtar descended to Kurungea
The bull no longer mounts the cow,
The lord no longer bends down to the slave-girl,
The man sleeps at his place alone, as does the woman.

Even the jackass will not make love any longer. A joyless
cosmos begs for the return of the mistress Ishtar despite all
her cruelty and willfulness.

After every change in systems, those of the deposed figures
who, for some reason or other, cannot be liquidated, are put

in jail or driven into exile. By the same token, the change in
the interpretation of legends places the former upper classes
in some kind of hellish dungeon and compulsively arranges
for a fitting, eternal punishment for precisely the characteristics that had previously given them their standing.

In Hades, too, there was this sort of an aristocratic prison
colony, led by Tantalus and the Danaïds, the representatives
of the ancient matriarchy. The Danaïd myth belongs to a
whole group of blood weddings at which the girls, forced
into the wedding night, kill their husbands, with only one of
them sparing her mate. In the original myths, the nonmurder-
ess was the only contemptible one of the lot, but later she
became the praiseworthy exception.

This pattern, with some exceptions, also applies to the
Lemnos wedding, which belongs to Bachofen's discoveries.
On the women's isle of Lemnos, as in all matriarchies, the
women selected their husbands, who in turn were obligated
to remain faithful. Sexual fidelity in the predominance of
either sex is almost always required by the ruling gender of
the dominated one. This makes up the local sexual mores.
Daudet's maxim "tue-la" may be altered into "tue-le." Either
one is an extreme form of sexual possessiveness.

In Lemnos, the catastrophe begins when the women of the
island, whose beauty and glamour were famous, neglected
the service of Aphrodite. The goddess leaves them their
beauty but punishes them by inflicting upon them dysosmia,
which we should call a lack of sex appeal today. In sheer dis-
gust, their men acquire some Thracian girl prisoners as slaves.
The Lemnic women then kill them all, including their con-
cubines, during their wedding night. According to matriarchal
law, that deed was defense of their self-respect as well as a
defense of the interests of the state. Only Hypsipyle, the
king's daughter, spares her father Thoas. In the patriarchal
legend of the Argonauts, the heroes then land on the entirely
manless island. Jason forms a liaison with Hypsipyle, and his
associates take the other women. The sense of the legend
now is altered: the Lemnos women suffer pangs of remorse,
mend their ways, and, as a symbol of this change, they name
their children—after their fathers. (Apollodorus)

The fate of the Danaïds gives more clues and is more succinctly to the point. The Danaïds never regret their action. A free disposition over one's own person is an original right in a matriarchal society. The sons of Aegyptus (their husbands) cynically break with that right when they marry the fifty daughters of Danaüs, not for love but in order to acquire political control, since inheritance always goes with the daughters. The fifty girls therefore are the victims of compulsion. Aeschylus, though living in a patriarchal society, permitted himself the liberty of confronting his audience with the unadulterated legend, largely because of the stage effect. His "seekers of protection" retain all the contrasts, starting with the "dovelike trembling of the frightened girls" and going to the moment when, dancing and shuddering for the satisfaction of their triumph, they emerge from their violators' bedchambers in the morning in order to sing about their handiwork. Only one traitress dwells among them: Hypermnestra infamously spared Lynceus, and for this reason the delinquent is manacled and placed before a court of justice.

Hercules is supposed to be a descendant of this converted Amazon in the thirteenth generation. He is the mysogynous sun-hero who resolves never to rest until the last matriarchy has been wiped off this earth. Bachofen sees a relationship to this resolution in the disgrace inflicted upon his ancestress. That Danaïd breaking faith with her family had offended against matriarchal law.

IV

THE CHANGING FACE
OF THE MATRIARCHY

Based on a justifiable consciousness of his great culture, the European used to reason that woman, who as not entirely the equal of man according to his own law, must be far worse off in societies of a lower level, especially in "primitive" nations. But nothing could be further from the truth. With only the exception of parts of Melanesia and of the Australian aborigines, where she is suppressed, woman in aboriginal civilizations is freer, more powerful, and, above all, economically far more secure.

If one sees her perform heavy labor while the male lounges about or putters around the house, it is because he is not permitted to perform or decide important things. The woman is usually voluntarily doing the work on her own property. Conforming to matrilocal custom, the male has followed her to her home, where, up to a certain degree, he remains a guest, alien to his wife's clan. In primitive society, conjugal ties almost always are superseded by the bonds of the clan. The man, though forced to marry outside his own clan by the law of exogamy, remains instinctively loyal to his own clan. That clan is embodied in his mother, who usually has breast-fed him until his fourth year. Observers are filled with astonishment at this magic loyalty. Such a pristine force remains incomprehensible for our superficial levels of feeling.

Primitive man has little in common with his spouse. He only visits her. She also controls the children, who usually have little consideration for their father. The male accords first place in his affections to his mother and second place to his uterine sisters, even if he lives separately from them. G. Schweinfurth reports: "In the lowest human societies, there is a bond between mother and child that lasts all through life, even though the father may remain a stranger. To a Negro, the greatest insult is a disparaging remark about his mother. Even the patriarchal Hereros will save their mothers first in case of danger." The Dyaks, dreaded head-hunters of North Borneo, acknowledge no duties toward their fathers, but their mothers remain sacred. Although in Melanesia women are suppressed in other ways, whoever wants to hire a ship's crew, even for as little as a week's time, often is told by gray-haired men in their forties that they would like to go along but first will have to ask their mothers for permission. (J. Chalmers and W. Gill)

When some of the most agile Aleutians were invited to St. Petersburg to show off their arts on the Neva, they earned a great deal of money and were spoiled immeasurably, but, despite all pleas, they refused to stay on the grounds that they could not leave their mothers alone any longer. (J. Weniaminoff, *Character Traits of the Aleutians of the Fox Islands*) The guide of Cameron's African safari took the expedition for a hundred-mile detour just to see his mother; another native did not dare to make a farewell visit to his mother for fear of breaking his contract: "If I had seen her again, I could not leave," the man said, with tears in his eyes. Similar things are reported about the bushmen, and the Hottentots are completely subject to their mothers' wishes. The greatest oath of a Herero is, "by my mother's tears." The Iroquois consider it a horrible and unprecedented crime for a son to rebel against his mother. The same deep ties connect mother and daughter. Always and everywhere, the women live together. The company of the wedded husband is sought out only at times, while his meddling is frowned upon.

Old women are revered everywhere, even if they are not the mother. In Africa, old women frequently are spoiled by the men. Everyone tries to please them. Whenever things go topsyturvy in the Australian bush, the men elect an old woman to be "grandmother" and mediate disputes, regulate war and peace, and be an inviolate arbiter, who may even take their spears away—the same Australians who otherwise esteem women so little. J. G. Fletcher Moore, as well as Spencer and Gillen, deduce from early myths and certain indications in the Australian religions that this "grandmother" is the remnant of a female domination that has long been forgotten and in resentment against which the women are kept strictly away from important ceremonies.

But what is a female dominion? Where is it or where was one? How does it come about, how is it reinforced, and how is it overthrown?

Dr. M. Vaerting and Schulte-Vaerting researched "female characteristics in matriarchies and male characteristics in the matriarchy." Justifiably, they compared the sexes only under identical conditions: males in patriarchies with females in matriarchies, that is, both genders under favorable conditions; and males in matriarchies and females in patriarchies, that is both genders under *un*favorable conditions. Finally, they examined the situation in cases of equality in order to ascertain what are the natural peculiarities of each.

At first glance, their findings are astonishing. The traits are often inverted. The Vaertings are of the opinion that many traits considered "typically" masculine or feminine merely are the result of the predominance of one gender, and that these characteristics are often grotesquely inverted when the conditions of dominance are exchanged. First of all, there is the division of labor: the *dominated* sex "belongs in the house," has to cook, rear the children, develop shyness and delicacy, adorn itself, and conform to its supreme duty of obedience. The *dominant* sex monopolizes business outside the home, establishes a reputation for intellectual superiority, and demands that the intellectually inferior sex have youth and beauty; this condition is accepted as "natural" by the dominated sex, too. It was shown in this manner that feminine "frailness and need for protection" are not the cause but the consequence of the male-dictated division of labor. The Vaertings' investigations have made a number of additions to Bachofen's characteristics of matriarchy:

1. The female family name is retained, while the male one vanishes; the children of a noblewoman remain nobles, even if the father be slave, while the children of a nobleman with a slave girl are slaves.

2. The children follow the female line; their father is not related to them; what he acquires is inherited by his uterine clan, that is, by the sons and daughters of his sisters.

3. Movable and immovable property remains in the hands of the woman and is inherited by or through her daughters; the sons inherit nothing but may receive a dowry and are occasionally married off by their mothers or sisters. Where a chief's office is heritable, for example, it cannot be bequeathed to a son, but only to a sister's son.

4. The difference between legitimate and illegitimate birth disappears.

5. The woman becomes the wooer.

The characteristics of matriarchy found by the Vaertings concern many different areas. Above all, the woman possesses free disposition over her body and may interrupt pregnancy whenever she wishes or prevent it altogether. Female children are preferred, because they continue the family, which boys cannot. The boys sometimes are killed, as were the girls in patriarchal China. Physically, the woman is stronger and more agile than the man because of the greater freedom of activity outside the house, while the man puts on fat, becomes a "housewife," and will not take his eyes off the children. Meiners says of the Kamchatkans that they are so domestic that they dislike being away from home for a single day. "But if Kamchatkan men are forced outside the house, they persuade their wives to travel along with them, since they cannot live without them." According to Westermarck, the Encounter Bay tribe believes that paternal care is indispensable, for which reason women prefer to kill immediately any babies born after their fathers' death.

In the female state, domestic work is beneath the woman's dignity, just as it is beneath the man's dignity in a male-dominated society. In the realm of sex, even Bachofen knew that she was the wooer; now it is established that the male must preserve an attitude of demure coyness. In marriage, obedience is demanded of him, as was specified in the marriage contracts of ancient Egypt. He also must remain faithful, while the wife remains unencumbered. She also retains the right of divorce and repudiation. Bachelors are subject to the same ridicule as old maids in male-dominated society.

The man, as the wooed partner who must be erotically enticing in order to be chosen, becomes vain and conscious of his appearance, which he can also cultivate better because of his greater leisure. The working woman, whose brains are what really matter, remains simple and unadorned. Strabo tells us that in Libya, an important center of matriarchy in his time, the men put waves in their hair, "wore a great many golden trinkets, and were diligent in brushing their teeth and cutting their nails. Their coiffures were so artificial that one seldom saw them taking a walk, because they wanted their coiffures to remain undamaged." The men of Tana (Hebrides) wear their hair twelve to eighteen inches long and part it into six or seven hundred little locks or braids. According to Tacitus, the Germanic men dyed their hair. North American Indians let their hair grow down to their feet. The Egyptian called a wife "she who clothes her husband." He had to have two garments, while she owned only one and gave herself a much simpler appearance.

In a women's realm, the male youth is the ideal of beauty and is usually married to a much older woman, just as in the male-dominated society a mature man marries a younger woman, without anyone's thinking this offensive. Phallus cult is as common in a female-dominated society as Venus cult in a male-dominated one. As for religion in a society with one sex dominating another, the main divinities always are of the dominant sex, while the sexual divinities are of the other gender.

In the socioeconomic area, communism is characteristic of the beginning of a matriarchal clan. After the advancement to the private-property concept, the woman possesses sole rights to property, just as the male has in a male-governed state. "The prevailing sex always secures freedom and dominion by supporting the dominated sex," that is, by assigning to it the passive role in this house while giving itself the most important and decisive affairs outside the home.

By way of contrast to a male-dominated society, a matriarchy considers fear of death an admirable quality, because a life, given birth by woman in pain, must needs appear to her as the most valuable possession. In the sexual realm, the tyranny of woman over man is never as complete as the converse sometimes is; there are only a few instances of anything like male prostitution, if for no other reason than because the male organ limits this possibility. Female prostitution is lacking entirely. Polygamy is considered typically patriarchal; polyandry is an indication of matriarchy (with some exceptions).

Certain telling objections could be raised against this impressive list. In the case of some characteristics, the causes must be attributed at least in part to race, civilization, the historical era, and purely dynastic matters. Some other assertions cannot be substantiated at all, notably the domesticity angle. In the case of some very strict matriarchies, the exact opposite is the law: the man is not allowed in the house and even must take his meals somewhere else, living at the fringes of the female clan only as a provider of meat, taking his orders from his wife's clan, while never entering the house except as a guest. If one recalls the symbolic significance of the house and the exclusiveness with which the women build their houses in mother clans, one can hardly be surprised if the male is admitted to it only for his most obvious function. "Visitational marriage" is the rule precisely in the great mother societies, with the North American Indians, the Sioux, the Algonquians, Ojibways, Delawares, Mohicans, Iroquois, as well as the Bororos of central Brazil, Caribs, and certain groups among the Borneo Malays and the Hottentots.

Of the Hottentots it is said: "The women always have occupied a position bordering on despotism, while the man has nothing to say. Female rule is unlimited." (F. Hahn, Tsui-Goam, as well as Jakobowsky, and M. Poix) The culturally least advanced, matriarchally most extreme Indian tribe, the Seri, permit only the brother to share the woman's hut, not the husband, and he has to pass an extremely demanding entrance examination before a college of matrons before he may join the female's clan.

The Vaertings' chief example, Egypt, partly backfires on them. Miles of reliefs show the man "outside the house" in busy employment. The army and the medical profession were exclusively male. What the medical profession signifies in Egypt Herodotus explains: "In their country, everything is crowded with physicians; some work as physicians for the eyes, others for the head, others for the teeth, others for the abdomen, and still others for invisible diseases." Diodorus reports: "On military campaigns as well as journeys inside the country's borders, all enjoy free medical care, for the physicians receive a salary from the state." It seems somewhat surprising that in Egypt men carried on the medical profession, which in other realms was a carefully guarded female monopoly.

Egypt conforms even less to the pattern of "prevalent male vanity and consciousness of appearance." The predominant Egyptian woman was not characterized by a lack of adornment or by simplicity. One of the earliest predynastic pieces of evidence connects a female name with a pomade to stimulate the growth of hair, and further ample evidence of diligent body culture comes from the graves of women. The equipment of a modern New York beauty parlor would be put to shame by the make-up pencils, eyelash salves, lip pomades, hair dyes, and manicuring equipment of those old Egyptians, who even practiced the slitting of the eyelids for extending the eye sideways. The quality of their sandals for women was famous. Although neither sex wore much clothing, the female garment was carefully pleated and draped. A walk through the Cairo Museum will convince anyone of the quality of their jewelry.

Despite a thoroughgoing male predominance in their realms, satraps, oriental rulers, Moguls, khans, Hindu princes, and Greek as well as Roman gallants were just as greatly polished and decked out, bejeweled, rubbed down and massaged as any men in a matriarchy. As for the dying of hair, we still have the bleaching recipe of Cesare Borgia, who was anything but effeminate. Although the Teutonic males bleached their hair, they did not live under gynocracy either, for Lamprecht merely proved a matriarchal legal system prevailing among them, no more; such an assumption would also be contradicted by the strong homosexuality, of which so much has been written. Diodorus says of them: "Although their women are well-proportioned, they pay little attention to them. They are driven instead, as though by a crazy compulsion, to the embraces of fellow males. Far from seeing a disgrace in this, they rather consider it dishonorable for a man not to accept the proffered favors of another."

Polygamy, too, has become a questionable symbol of patriarchy, for women everywhere not only tolerate but even favor it. When a Fula wife, one of five, was asked whether she would not rather be the only one, she winced at the idea and stated that her arrangement was more amusing and convenient, since she could not entertain her husband all by herself, so that the conversation of the others was a relief (as reported by Briffault). This African lady had the motto, "The more wives, the better." Miss Kingsley reported knowing a number of men who would have preferred having only one wife and spending their money in civilized fashion, but whose wives would not hear of it and hated the missionaries for preaching monogamy; they would be ashamed of a sentimental husband. Women seem naturally gifted for the arts of erotic freedom. Matriarchal society, therefore, exercises great sexual tolerance. The male harems of African princesses are more of a dynastic symptom, with their death penalty for infidelity: it is the disloyalty toward the sovereign that is punished, either in a male or a female slave.

Polyandry, on the other hand, may be due to the most diverse causes. In Tibet, where the bride also marries all of her brothers-in-law, this seems to be a residue of ancient group marriages, though the women do eagerly maintain the institution. On the other hand, the same group marriage may be the origin of the custom of the matriarchal American Indians in which a man marries first the oldest sister and then all of the younger ones, as they become nubile.

Finally, prostitution is not considered a disgrace anywhere outside of Europe. One might almost risk the postulate "sacred prostitution—unsanctioned marriage." It was precisely in the most highly cultured female realms, in Egypt, Lydia, pre-Aryan India, and Sumeria, where males and females enjoyed equal rights, that there was temple prostitution from which no lady, no matter how high she was in rank, could abstain. Any woman had to submit to any stranger who desired her during certain festivals, for there was always the god that might have assumed the guise of that stranger.

It simply is not possible to exclude spirit, mind, and instincts as the sources of behavior of so many diverse origins and to deduce the patterns of behavior only from domination or being dominated. Of the Vaertings' characteristics of female-dominated society, only these, then, remain:

1. Freedom of interrupting pregnancy, that is, the culture of giving birth or not giving birth according to the woman's decision.

2. The wedding of the older woman with the younger man.

3. In a female-dominated realm, the beautiful youths call the tune; in a male-dominated one, the beautiful girls.

The Vaertings very justifiably classified "gallantry" as typical patriarchal. The famous "dixhuitième," the French female century, was the opposite of gynocracy, for the woman could rise only by the favors of a man and to the extent that she pleased him, and she fell from grace as soon as she lost his favor.

V
THE SYMBOL

THE EGG

What is a symbol of Nature? No one has ever defined one, for one can do anything with it. One can unfold it into a myth, a religion, a philosophy, or an art or into all of reality. Only one thing is impossible: one cannot explain it, for it belongs to neither the linguistic nor the conceptual form of communication. Nor can a symbol be "sought" or "found"; it can only be perceived. That makes it different from an allegory, which is founded on a concept. For the concept, one then tries to find the proper allegorical image, which is an entirely rational, aesthetical process. For that reason, an allegory can contain no more than the thought that was put into it.

The symbol, on the other hand, stimulates thought but is incapable of rationalization. Symbolism is compulsive; allegory is voluntary. That, of course, does not explain symbolism to a person who is not susceptible to its powers. Symbols have been defined as "an immense emotional experience, contemplated in the shape of an image," or as something received by the eye in a creative state of intoxication. Probably the symbol once was the wordless mother tongue of a magic human race. The magic person is one who, when seeing a thunderstorm, feels "the sulphur flashes of pink lightning," while the technical person thinks, "an enormous wastage of electric current."

Only five or six great poets, whose words sprang directly from experience and contain the magic of sound, sometimes succeed in transporting something of symbolic content into their language. Paul Claudel, the chthonial genius of lead and ether, once summoned words for a tree that were first dipped into this primordial substance. If a human race insensitive to symbols no longer perceives what a tree is, it belongs to the *"lasciate ogni speranza"* type and would be better off mounted as a rationalized machine cog on a concrete socket. Goldhaupt, the hero of the piece, has interred his dearest possession into the black mother earth, a thing with a child's face, like an acquired fairy godmother. It is night. His heart is as heavy as a stone at the end of a rope. The storm whips a mask of rain into his face. Arid thorns tremble beneath an iron sky. Roving over the bitter earth, he loses his way more and more. "We are losing our way more and more," says Cebes, the boy-admirer.

> *Simon Angel* (called Goldhaupt): Do you see? I was
> Never concerned, with no human being,
> Whether young or old, about that which he bore inside
>   of him.
> But a tree was my father and my teacher,
> For sometimes, when a child, I was seized by a dark
>   despair,
> When any company became abhorrent, the common air
>   would choke me,
> I had to withdraw to solitude, nurture my melancholy in
>   secret,
> And I felt how it grew inside of me.
> I met this tree and embraced it,
> Put my arms around it, as if it were an oldfashioned
>   man.
> For before I was born it was here, and still will be
> When I have long been gone. Its time has another
>   measure.
> *Cebes:* And what did that tree teach you?
> *Simon:* Now, in this hour of anguish, now it may be,
> That I find it again!
> (And they reach the trunk of a tree, a very large tree.)
> O Tree, receive me! Alone I departed from the protec-
>   tion of thy branches,
> And now, all alone, I return to thee, my firm-grown
>   father!
> Receive me back into thy shade, O Son of this Earth!
> O wood! In this hour of greatest need! In thy murmurs
> Tell me that word that is I and whose terrible drive
> I sense within me! Thou art entirely durable urge,

Life's constant Upwards from soulless, original matter.
How thou sucklest from the earth, Old One,
Deeply submerged, sendest everywhere thy roots strong
    and fine!
And how thou strivest upward toward the skies! How
    thou
Condensest entirely in the pressure of thy breath, a giant
    leaf,
Figure of fire! The inexhaustible earth, clasped by the
    roots of thy being,
And the boundless sky with the sun and the rotating
    stars,
Whereon thou attachest with this mouth from the omni-
    presence of thy arms,
With this lip of thy body, and which thou seizest with
    all that breathes in thee,
The earth and all the sky, they must be there for thee to
    stand upright!
O, might I, too, stand upright! May my soul never perish!
May I not waste this fountain sap, this inner dew, this
    inwardness,
Whose bearer I am, in useful chunks of green and
    flowers!
May I grow consistently! May I remain straight,
    a unifier! . . .
Cebes: Simon, you cannot leave like this. Have you per-
    ceived
Nothing under this tree of wisdom? If
Truly a law has been planted into your heart,
If some kind of law and a superhuman will pushes you
As though with a knee into the midst of us poor ones,
Remember me.
Goldhaupt: A specter rushed over me, and I tremble like
    a pole.
I have received a power, strict and wild!
This is the furor of Man, and nothing of Woman is within
    me.
O work, work, work! Who gives me the strength for
    deeds?
                (He flings himself prostrate on the ground.)
O Night! Mother!
Crush me and fill my eyes with sand!
Mother, why hast thou slit my eyelids

Through the middle? Mother, I am alone! Mother,
Why dost thou force me to live?
I would rather the dewy earth never
Turned red in the East again.
I cannot! See me, me, thy child!
Now I lean against thy breast.
Night, maternal night! Earth! Earth!
                    (He faints.)

In the morning, he rises and continues his heroic, armored victor's life until he meets with an Alexandrine downfall at the gates of the Caucasus.

His first teacher on his road was a tree, a father still firmly rooted in the soil, a son of Mother Earth not yet liberated, his roots entwined all through the earth, but replete throughout his body with the essence of air, sun, and stars. This tree is his prophet: "In thy murmurs tell me that word that is I and whose terrible drive I sense within me. Thou art entirely durable urge, thy life's constant Upwards from soulless original matter."

The tree serves as example to him: "The earth and all the sky, they must be there for thee to stand upright! O, might I, too, stand upright! May my soul never perish! May I not waste this fountain sap, this inner dew, this inwardness, whose bearer I am, in useless chunks of green and flowers! May I grow consistently! May I remain straight, a unifier!"

The earth is in agreement. The Great Mother likes it, when first the upper body of a plant wrests free of her, and if later four-legged creatures freely run around on her or others lift themselves into the heavens on their wings. These are mere images existent on the plant mother, reflections of that which the female element has accomplished by forming the flagella cilium and releasing the male out of herself. With the male, there came the restlessness of the world, the aggressive, mobile, progressive, the element shining into infinity, the "Golden Heads" (a pun on *Goldhaupt*) of all times and all shapes, with their cry. "This is the furor of Man, and nothing of Woman is within me!"

It is hardly worth mentioning that such an absoluteness and exclusiveness of one sexual principle or the other can only be accepted as "ideas." In reality, every person, from the anatomical perspective, is a bisexual creature. A "hundred percent" man could not exist even in North America, where this trite phrase comes from. Even the most emphatically masculine he-man still has the feminine nipples on his chest and bears a vagina in the guise of the scrotum seam on his person, just as the most oversexed housewife has a remainder of the penis in the shape of the clitoris. In the case of a living specimen, we are always dealing with the domination of one trend or the other, a domination which varies a good deal within one and the same lifespan. It is said that too many female hormones in the man predispose him for cancer. Why is that disease called cancer, as is the sign of the zodiac whose magic quality subordinates it to the moon? It is a strange verbal intuition.

The tree, a motionless "son" halfway on the evolution toward "Goldhaupt," belongs to both realms, the lower as well as the upper. A simplified sign of the tree is the cross +, which may be considered the "crossing" of the two sexual potentials. In the Venus sign ♀ the tree of life is still attached to the uterus. In the male sign of Mars ♂ that point has already been passed, and the male is proceeding to the right side, the "male" direction. In Christianity, the tree becomes the torture cross of the world. In the spoked wheel of the swastika 卐 the tree has acquired feet, to symbolize the sequence of events racing through time. The tree is still chthonial but no longer female, belongs to the cult of all Great Mothers, and, like them, is sacred. Priests and priestesses are married to a sacred tree, the old Teutons adorned it with golden chains and crowns and held their councils under trees; entire Germanic nations boasted that they were descended from oaks.

The wall is on the same level of symbolism. "It is, like the trees, an offspring of Mother Earth and in constant, firm communication with the mother's body even after birth." The Nature Mothers wear wall-crowns upon their heads. In most languages, city names are feminine. Even in Rome, *Roma aeterna* remained feminine, although the *urbs* was the main protagonist of masculine predominance.

The tree as well as the wall grow into the light like male potency. One says of them *"excitare muros,"* to awaken the sleeping walls. The thing that is awakened is sleeping masculinity. "With the sound of brazen trumpets, one destroys the walls of cities to be conquered. What is reported of Jericho is repeated by the Romans: the walls of Alba are torn down by the blaring of the trumpets, and Mummius tore a hole in the Corinthian fortifications by the same ritual custom. But what the trumpets destroyed must also have been built by trumpets. Ancient jurisprudence on many occasions maintains the principle that origin and destruction must be in perfect harmony." The walls of Thebes built themselves independently at the sound of the trumpet of Amphitryon. The brazen trumpet is always a phallic symbol. "It calls the bull Dionysos out of the procreative waves of the sea and lures Achilles out of the female disguise."

In the tree and the wall, the male principle has acquired visible existence. That is why phallus and snake are so frequently portrayed on walls, not for the sake of obscenity but in a sense of sanctity. They anoint the wall, protect it against profanation, so that no one should desecrate it with excrements. On the walls, one wrote down the fate of the world, and it was generally customary to carve the laws on walls. The walls proclaim the law of the earth above the soil and in a shape of immutability.

Symbols are the key figures to the entire creative view of the world. Bachofen discovered that the things which the gods hold in their hands—be it a black-and-white egg in their left hands or a staff with a snake in their right hands—are no mere appendages or attributes but rather the symbolic, magic origin to which they themselves are traced. Myths, customs, religions, art, and culture unfold out of that origin, where they lay enclosed in an incomprehensible condensation. They become liberated energy of crumbling symbols, which disintegrate to form both music *and* gods. Therefore, even myths alone do not suffice to point up the age of female predominance. That era is comprehended only in the egg symbol, which all great races venerated in an identical, original meaning at a definable point in their cultural history.

A good part of human annals is comprised of the things that each race made out of the symbol, things of varying strength and beauty. A majority of the five hundred pages of

Bachofen's "grave symbolism" are filled with the things that antiquity made out of those symbols. A single, brief example may suffice here: the play of the circles, the egg surrounded by its own creation. The egg symbol is found wherever people celebrate a serious occasion of irreversible consequence, such as birth, wedding, and death. In mosques, it is suspended from the domes on strings. It stands in Peruvian temples, made of pure gold. It rests alongside the dead, black underneath, white on top. It is active in all mysteries, in jurisprudence, and in the liberation of slaves. It is separated into its component parts most beautifully in circus games, which originally were held in memory of fallen heroes and were nothing but "rotation around the egg."

Peace and equilibrium prevail within the original egg itself. The seeds of all things still rest in it without reference to time. Visible creation only breaks out the fractured shell in the conflict of restless motion. Two forces, antagonistic and yet headed toward the same goal, rule the earth and ensure the progress of things by their interaction. The first "romantic" dualist was old Empedocles with his polaric forces of love and hatred which cause two original storm centers in the chaos. Sigmund Freud, with his polaric pair of sex and death urges, will not be the last one.

In the legend of the Dioscuroi, the "two" break out of the Leda-Nemesis egg in the shape of a gigantic pair of twins who steer their chariot. Each of them still wears his half of the egg upon his head as a round hat. Flying along the skies with their vehicle, "the wings of an egg," they alternately bring up day and night.

Every step has its own Dioscuroi. In the body, the nerves of life are arranged in pairs or opposites by association with the sympathetic or parasympathetic nerve system. In psychology, the "two" are introversion and extraversion, in which all psychic events pulsate as development or aggregation. For the spirit, we have the antinomies of pure reason as the pair of contrasts in which all ratiocination must necessarily proceed. Dualism and division into pairs, complementing through interaction, always are the contents of the egg, once they are revealed.

As for their relationship to the races, the egg appears there again. In the oval (*egg*-shaped) circus, there are five, seven, or ten pillars of wood, each of which has an egg on it. After every lap around the meta (goal stone) completed by the chariots, an egg is removed from one of the pillars. The egg is beginning and end of every lap, older than the quadrigas which burst out from their stalls with their inimitable enthusiasm like the chariot of the Dioscuroi from the Nemesis egg. "They keep step with each other in their race. It is their doubled exertion, directed at the same goal, which gives them their unconquerable speed. . . ."

> Fast like arrows, the victorious team of horses flies forward, and fast like arrows is the course of the world of phenomena. The celerity with which the two forces transport Creation is expressed by the speed of the double team. In the progress of movement, the quadriga constantly returns to its point of origin, like the circle losing its end in its beginning. If one of the two forces drives ahead, the other one turns around and completes the circle. The completion of every existence is a return to its beginning, and every departure from the point of origin carries with it a renewed approach to it. The two directions are as inexplicably connected as the two forces to which they correspond. . . . The laps described by the chariots are the image of this circulatory movement. The chariots surround the goal-stones at high speed in order to return to their point of origin and then again to move along the same path.

. . . Thus, two things are illustrated: first, the connection between the egg and the circus chariot race, and second, the relationship between the completion of each individual lap and

> the removal of one egg. Each return to the point of origin completes the cycle of one existence and begins another. The progeny of one egg has taken rise, grown, and disappeared, and another takes its place.

This law of being was always enacted as a race in honor of a great person's demise. The first Olympic Games, according to the legend, were begun by Endymion. His tombstone was a meta (according to Pausanias). He had finished; others might now begin where he had ended. But, if motion is the most profound law of living, the fastest one also was the most vital one. All demigods were well-known runners, as, for example, "swift-footed" Achilles. For fame and fate of the mortal is not an asinine and contrary need for continuous spurring but rather a need to rush from deed to deed according to one's destiny. Demigods, races, and horses are always closely connected with running water, as, for instance, the Isthmian Games, which were dedicated to Poseidon, the potently creative floodwaters coursing around the earth with white spray horses.

But everything turned on the egg. "In the humid valley between the Aventine and the Palatine Hills of early Rome, there was the service of Murcia, an Aphrodite-like Great Mother, along with her demoniacal son-lover. The fertile meadows bore the divine stone called metae Murciae, or 'goal stone of Murcia.' It was there that (King) Tarquin founded his circus." "The connection of the races with the water, with rivers, swamps, humid, grassy dales is apparent everywhere, including Rome; it was for this reason that the dolphin appears as the symbol of the games." The frame of reference in which these concepts moved also dominated all other parts of the circus and the shrines, cults, and institutions connected therewith.

> The natural force, with its feminine-passive and masculine-active potentials, in its dual expression as a vitalizing and a destructive power, found in the Roman circus a representation so perfect and so varied that the circus was considered a veritable pantheon and was designated by the Church Fathers as unclean and strictly to be avoided by all the faithful.

Early man vibrated in every fiber before the reality of the pair of fraternal powers, hostile yet compensating each other. For his feeling, any active form of life rests upon the great "two" as much as a matter of course as the human body is carried by its two legs. Therefore, we have the dual reign of Romulus and Remus and of Oedipus' sons, on whose altar a flame divides itself in two eternally opposite directions, the rule of two Roman consuls, two Spartan kings, and the dual queens of the Amazon kingdoms, as well as the twin heads of

many magistracies. Any instinct for reality unwittingly leans
toward the "two." Even old John D. Rockefeller organized his
Standard Oil Company on this basis: each of the four divisions
of Standard Oil was headed by two directors in charge; they
were oil production, transportation, manufacture, and sales.

A centrifugal emergence from the womb is indicated also
by the frequent dual reigns of brother and sister in the most
opposite corners of the earth. Where, on the other hand, the
power of the egg prevails, there always is a matron as the
spiritual and secular chieftain at the same time, as for example, in the Great Mother clans of the North American Indians
in former days, and as may still be found in Assam and some
parts of Africa. It is impossible to trace at this point to what
extent the male autocracy, the "fatherhood" of king or tyrant,
might be considered a counter piece or imitation of the original, matriarchal family.

Under the domination of the egg, one usually finds a prev-
alence of peaceful, uterine life, satiated, comfortable, com-
placent, though determined in its defense against outsiders.
A matriarchal realm hardly knows such a thing as a war of
conquest, although the defense of the domestic egg is stal-
wart and brave. In some ways, such a society always remains
an introverted world subject to the order of the moon, the female goddess, for the Great Mother is a figure associated with
the night. From a strictly astronomical point of view, the sun
rose and set exactly the same way as now, but people were
unconcerned with it. It was believed that even the plants
regulated their growth according to the moon, and the sowing practices were adjusted to lunar phases. The moon determined customs, assemblies, festivals, and the divisions of the
year. Happiness was subject to its rhythm. The night was
preferred for meetings and councils.

All degrees of civilization are compatible with this way of
life, for it dominated high urban cultures, such as the Lycian,
Carian, and Lydian, as well as primitive American Indian
tribes and commerce-plying Tibetans. In the realm of the
maternal egg, everything is still free and equal. Obeying only
the dictates of their blood, people live almost without laws in
a system of magic. With oval magic, the slave had his head
shorn when he was freed, and a new-born baby had an egg

hat put upon his head. Covered with the maternal, original egg, the prenatal condition of freedom was thus recovered.

Even our manner of greeting people still has relevancy to the Leda egg. Whoever has to take off his hat thereby admits inequality, as if he did not dare to assert his fraternity with the other person. That is, of course, exclusively a male greeting. At no place was it customary for women to remove their hats, not even before the ruler or their god. For women are themselves the hat, which is to say, the egg.

According to recent research, ball games also arose from the egg cult, as did the circus races, not from a desire to build up the bodies of the youth. Cricket and football originally are magic practices with the moon egg designed to bring about a speedy convalescence. The Hurons played such a lunar ball game with rules akin to soccer whenever their chieftain became ill. The California Indians also played with balls in order to stimulate the moon in its waxing period, since matriarchal peoples consider the weather, the harvest, and the renewal of life itself dependent upon this waxing of the moon, not upon the masculine sun. These Indians also reported that their ball games had been originated by the "great rabbit," that is, the moon, using its eggs for balls.

With the rise of the patriarchal sun cult in antiquity, the males created a counter egg to the feminine-material one, which was the egg of the phoenix myth, the myrrh egg of immortality. In the great phoenix and Sothis year of the Egyptians with which, after the completion of a great stellar course of destiny, every new epoch begins, the gold-and-purple magic bird appears with an egg in his beak. He places the egg upon the altar of the sun at Heliopolis, a hollow egg formed of myrrh, which is an egg as well as a sarcophagus, for he places his father's carcass inside. In the flaming myrrh, the father carcass is then burned on the sun altar in order to give new life. The rejuvenated phoenix flies out of his ashes into the solar year that begins. Thus the maternal egg form has been retained, but it no longer contains the original cause; the fertilization occurs by contact with the immaterial power of the fire. Here father emerges from sun, son from father, created by the light ray of the sun, immaculately conceived and without a mother.

THE KAURI SHELL

There are signifying and effective symbols: the latter belong to magic; the former, to religion. The egg is one of the most significant symbols. The kauri shell is one of the most potent magical or feminine symbols, strongly desired as a charm and therefore probably the first world currency.

It was considered a small coin for making change and as a symbol of the female sex organ as early as the Stone Age and is still considered such by almost all primitive peoples. It is found in Palaeolithic caves, in pre-dynastic Egypt, in the Iron and Bronze Ages, in the graves of Central Asia, and at Cape Horn. It was attached to the forehead, to arms, and legs, always in pairs—the sacred "two." The commercial traffic between old Egypt and India also was based upon the currency of the Kauri shell. Palaeolithic finds prove it to have been a probable standard coin of the past twenty or thirty thousand years, not because of its real value but because of its symbolic significance. Its similarity in color and shape to the female vulva, its origin from fecund waters, filled with the rhythm of the tides, the moon rhythm which is also the rhythm of the birth organs, make the shell so much an image of the Great Mother that the Melanesian Aphrodite herself is presumed to have come out of the Kauri shell. Its value is purely magical; for the Australian bushmen, who have no means of production, no goods, and no trade, wear this amulet just like the women buried in the ruins of Pompeii.

Ennius calls the kauri shell *matriculus,* which is to say, small matrix. It was also called *porculus* (whence we get porcelain), which was a synonym for vulva. Pottery, shell, and genitalia were associated. In Somaliland, Morocco, Central Asia, India, Japan, China, South America, Australia, the Punjab, the South Seas, and in ancient Tartary, the shell was considered a life-giving charm against sterility, sunburn, the evil eye, menstrual pains, and poverty—almost all evils. It usually was worn on one's belt, near one's genitals, or tied by a protective knot around one's wrist or ankle. It was the only ornament of the totally naked South Sea islanders. The Chinese sewed it into their heavy silk garments.

RIGHT—LEFT

It has long remained an unadmitted truth that early civilizations as well as the current "primitives" all over the world know a good deal more than they could possibly know according to the state of their experimental science. Where formerly one believed them to have been wrong, one has often proved the error to be one of an incomplete science on our part. Edgar Dacqué coined the word "natural insight" for this kind of knowledge. Races with "natural insight" possess an invisible source incomprehensible to reason. All of their actions derive from that source, so that they frequently seem to be proceeding illogically toward a goal that they actually reach.

Everywhere, as far as this may be ascertained, and since time immemorial, the left was the side favored by females; the right, the side favored by males. Respect for one side and derogation of the other is always dictated by the prevailing gender, although the milder female predominance only suggests it.

Ethnologists, folklorists, and theologists are agreed that the right side becomes the preferred side when solar worship enters the stage, whereas a lunar cult and a division according to nights rather than days implies a preference for the left. Christianity, masculine and solar in direction, considers the previously honored left side demoniacal and devilish; the demons have to be driven from it by sacred objects. From the word for "left" we get the German *linkisch* (awkward) and the French *gauche,* which may be used either for "left" or for "awkward." This dual meaning also appears in the dual meaning of the word *right* to mean "on the right side" or "accurate" or "moral." (This pun comes out in English as well as in German.)

Right and left are cosmic characteristics. Even chemistry shows us that certain amalgamations turn polarized light rays to the left, whereas others turn them to the right. The colloid, chaotic, uncrystallized substance here corresponds to the female "left." (Crystal is the "heroic form of matter.") This original dualism pervades the other realms of Nature, for just as there are chemical amalgams that turn polarized light rays to the left, there also are plants that spiral to the left. Wilhelm Fliess was the first scientist to record what all intuitively gifted peoples had known before him, that men with a predominant left side tended to be effeminate.[1] When endocrine secretion changes, the effeminacy of the male always starts on the left side, the masculinity of the female on the right. This fact cannot be explained by the asymmetry of the heart's location on the left side.

Throughout antiquity, it was believed that boys were the products of the right testicle, and that girls were the products of the left one. On the island of Celebes, as in many primitive societies, the woman hands her man his plate from the right, but she always eats from the left side. According to Rockhill's *Land of the Lamas,* the prayer mills in matriarchal Tibet are all turned to the left. In patriarchal France, *gauche* means "awkward," and *sinistre* means "ominous, ill-boding."

In his *Mutterrecht* and his *Gräbersymbolik,* Bachofen pursued detailed investigations of the topic of left and right and its correspondence to matriarchate and patriarchate. He understands the left side as the passive, the right as the active side. "The left hand holds magic powers; the right holds external power." In matriarchal Egypt, it was the left hand of Isis that was supposed to possess magical charms and was carried in processions. Islam changed this image into the left hand of Fatima, the Prophet's daughter, for no religion can get by entirely without the feminine element: even Christianity had to borrow the mistress Ishtar on her moon sickle to join God-Father and God-Son.[2]

After Aphrodite had assisted in saving Theseus from the

---

[1] In German colloquial idiom, the expression *"links,"* or *"linksrum,"* is used to signify homosexuality, although it means "left" or "in the left direction."

[2] Historians have usually tended to identify the enthusiastic worship of the Virgin Mary and her Christ child with the Isis cult of the late Roman Empire, which utilized images of a maternal figure with a small child (originally the younger Horus). Another possible origin of this worship, as Sir James George Frazer points out in *The Golden Bough* (The Macmillan Company, New York, 1956), was the cult of the Phrygian Great Mother and her son-lover Attis. (Editor–translator)

labyrinth, he built an altar for her on the mountains of Delos, consisting of nothing but *left* horns, around which young men danced the crane dance. The Pelopides, as a sign of their maternal descent, carried the Gorgon head on their *left* shoulders.

Since the art of medicine used to be a feminine art, the fourth finger of the *left* hand was called *medicinalis;* it was painted with aromatic substance on the idols. In a deluge legend regarding the origins of the cat, we are informed as follows: Since the pair of mice multiplied most immoderately in the Ark, Noah asked the Lord for assistance. The Lord had a tom cat jump out of the lion's *right* nostril and a cat out of his *left* nostril.

Finally, it seems worth noting that practically all the Madonnas painted or sculptured in the period of real feeling, that is, approximately in the Christian centuries prior to the Renaissance, held the Christ child on their *left* arms.

MORASS AND FIELD

Lewdly, lazily, and uninhibitedly, spawn and oozy animals bubble up from the anonymous moisture. Between patches of bulrush, swollen utricles hang down from the navels of watery flowers. Now and then, a slimy bubble bursts in the tepid, fecund ponds.

In the morass, the male potential remains invisible. One recognized only the maternal substance and its sedge births. That is why the procreation of the morass is the emblem of promiscuous, illicit mingling of the sexes, whereas agriculture is the very image of well-ordered fertilization through matrimony, with an unequivocal, programed, well-grown fruit. Original egg and morass belong together. All animals of the morass, such as frogs, turtles, and ducks, are dedicated to the Great Mother, wherever she is venerated as the goddess embracing everything. The turtle has raised the earth's crust out of the mud and carries it dry on its back. On this crust, there stands Aphrodite, accompanied by sedge boys and nymphs, with bulrush crowns in their hair. At the Lernaic morass, pious sex orgies are celebrated. The Great Mother of Mexico herself squats on her altar in the shape of an emerald, giant frog. In India, Mesopotamia, Asia Minor, Egypt, Italy, and Greece, just to name the most important countries of ancient culture, the cult of the morass is the token of uninhibited, promiscuous intercourse.

"Through the budding lotos, Isis recognizes the adultery of her brother—husband with Nephtis. Homer, according to Heliodorus, saw proof of his illegitimate origin in the reed-like hair of his thighs." (Bachofen) Sari, the Nile reeds, are called Isis' hair. The law of Manu warns all good people not to marry into a family with too much body hair, which attests uninhibited sensuality. According to the inclinations of the author, the morass may appear as a wonderful moisture or a cess pool. The German word *Hure*, meaning "prostitute," is related to the old Teutonic word *Horo, Horon,* which means "slime, filth." The Gallic method of ascertaining paternity evidences a similar attitude: One threw questionable children into the Rhine, and illicit infants would sink into the mud of the riverbed, while legitimate ones would rise to the surface, as Bachofen informs us. The stork, which is a morass bird, should really only bring the illegitimate children.

Morass cults are almost prereligious. They venerate the earth substance itself as primal magic of fertility. For it, all the long-beaked birds wading in the mud, especially the Egyptian heron, were "nature phalli" in animal shape. The first egg mothers, according to Bachofen's *Grave Symbolism,* were portrayed, as were those of the Lycian Harpies' Monument or the sirens, half original egg, half bird with woman's head. The golden duck called Penelops bears a religious similarity to Penelope, one of those eternal weaver women who rip up at night what they have woven in the daytime. Blind promiscuity was still practiced by Lamia, the great hetaera, who hid her head in a sack during the performance of her erotic duties.

Bachofen assumes three main stages of human development, two of which are female-material while the third is masculine-spiritual. The first mother stage with its aphrodisiacal morass religion corresponds to a primordial age of entirely promiscuous mingling of the sexes. Only with the second stage does real matriarchy appear in its full plenitude of power with the institution of matrimony. In the religious sphere, this stage corresponds to the cult of Demeter, with its agricultural symbols, festivals, rites, and especially of legislation. The place formerly occupied by the morass and sedge boys is now taken up by the field with its young grain gods. The anonymous intercourse in obscurity becomes individual, regulated, and apparent because of the work of the plow.

Legal language in matrimonial contracts derives its terms from agronomy, speaking of plowing and cultivating the porium, or female furrow. Sowing and impregnating are identified by the linguistic habits of the time: the Teutons called both *speirein*. The plow tearing up the ground becomes a sacred symbol, as is the phallus, for "wounding is the nature of love." (Plutarch) On the Demeter-dedicated stage, matriarchal dominance reaches its peak. It is the time when *gyne* and *queen* mean the same thing, not only by origin. Mother is the symbol of power. Nobility is reckoned exclusively according to one's female line of descent. Just as all wealth has its roots in matter, all possessions belong to the material woman. Whatever the man acquired with his arms, he voluntarily placed in her lap, for only there will it be certain to bear fruit. This is the foundation of all laws of inheritance in the gynocratic system, for the morass created neither values nor security; it was not noble, in the sense of differentiation, as was the field. Plato says that the seed is often changed into Mother Nature by the soil to which it is entrusted; whereas the land is never changed into the nature of the seed. Old matriarchy is based on this analogy, though nothing was known at the time about sperma or the equal numbers of chromosomes. Animal breeders subscribe to matriarchy: in tracing the lineage of race horses or any other Thoroughbred, major emphasis is placed on the mare, much less on the stallion.

Agriculture and regulated intercourse of the sexes belong to the same philosophy of Life. This fact gives rise to a contrast in female nature, for Aphrodite hates monogamy. She did not endow Helen with all possible attractions to have her wither in the arms of a single man. "Any permanent liaison is an infringement on Aphrodisial precepts and must be atoned." That is, according to Bachofen, the sense of all those sacred sex festivals in those nations that, even at the height of their culture, permitted no woman to withdraw from the orgies. During the transition from the first to the second matriarchal stage, every young girl had to buy her freedom from the ancient laws of Nature before she got married: she had to serve for a specified period as a prostitute, usually at a local temple. Later, this sacrifice was curtailed. In the Nasamonic rites, all the guests enjoyed intercourse; last of all, there came the bridegroom; in other cases, a mere symbolic sacrifice was required, such as the cutting off of the bride's hair.

As a student of comparative law, Bachofen traced the changing laws, including the laws of dowry. Originally, the dowry was the money earned by the prostitution of the body. In the period of sacred prostitution, the money earned in this manner was used as a compensatory payment for the goddess. In the Demeter period, the girl received her dowry and some capital from her family as a token of complete liberation from temple prostitution.

There have been many scholarly objections to Bachofen's theory of the general, promiscuous morass cult. It has been argued that one could not find a complete promiscuity anywhere, least of all in primitive society. Though one formerly thought that the primitives practiced it, it has been discovered that they, too, have religious prohibitions, sometimes subject to more solemn ceremonies than our wedding. "Free love" is never entirely free. As for the morass, it could not very well comprise a religious stage with peoples of the steppe, the desert, the Arctic tundra, or the great mountain ranges.

The "procreation of the morass" in the sense of Bachofen is only an *inner* truth, like most truths. Every procreation essentially is a "procreation of the morass." Wherever this morass, this "wonderful moisture," this cess pool of sin is not completed by other elements of a corporeal and spiritual nature, there we have the cult of the morass, even though the environment geographically belongs to the steppe.

In the gradation of events, the matriarchy of Demeter, according to Bachofen, is the highest step compatible with female predominance. It is then superseded by masculine patriarchy. Spirit stands opposed to matter, day to night, between the antitheses man-woman, no matter if the champions of the sun are called Hercules, Perseus, Achilles, Mithras, Christ, or whatever. With the patriarchate, we enter the real "dawn of the Occident." This Western victory was rendered secure only by the triumph of Rome over Carthage, that city of Dido, with its cult of Astarte and its predilection for hetaera. As for Bachofen's three stages of man, his antithesis of patriarchy versus matriarchy, or spirit versus matter, could also be formulated as the conflict between spirit and soul or gray matter and pineal gland.

The second stage does not follow the first, nor the third the second, by a peaceful replacement. Rather, the old stage is overcome because it overtaxes its resources. The woman, indignant or utterly exhausted because of her incessant sexual misuse in the age of sacred prostitution, wages a protracted fight for a purer life and achieves a regulated marriage. During the agricultural age, she then rises to such an ascendancy that she, in turn, enslaves the man and herself degenerates into an Amazon. During the heroic age, there then follows the male counter revolution, which begins the classical period with Perseus, Hercules, Theseus, and Bellerophon. That period, at least in Europe, results in the final victory of patriarchy through the triumph of Rome.

VI
THE TWO

Goethe once said that Sophocles' *Antigone* was spoiled for him by the fact that the heroine did everything for her brother rather than for a husband or a lover. To his taste, this meant an absence of compulsion, which meant, of tragedy. It was the judgment typical of a patriarchal century, no more: instructive in its narrowness conditioned by the times, precisely because Goethe otherwise was such a cosmopolitan, genial spirit. It shows that the spirit may be expanded at will, because it has nothing to do with temperament, though the axioms of sentiment are rigid, and it is these axioms that are concerned in the problem.

Darius, sensitive to different concepts, had the opposite feeling. The contrast was first reported by Briffault. Herodotus reports that Itaphernes' wife stood sobbing before the king of kings after her husband and her entire clan had been convicted of treason. Darius said he would grant her the life of one of her relatives, so that she should not be all alone. She was to choose one person. "If the king grants me the life of only one person," she replied unhesitatingly, "I'll choose my brother." Darius was so delighted with the reply that he granted her the life of her eldest son, too.

The Persian king felt very close to matriarchy, which considers the brother the only person that counts, and that only because of his uterine relationship. The Iranian tradition of the Persian king contained laws on sacred marriage of brother and sister; Zend Avesta and Ahura Mazda recommend the marriage of siblings as particularly praiseworthy, and Darius' own harem was inhabited by several of his sisters. Such a marriage was considered the most profound relationship between members of opposite sexes. That is why, among the

North American Indians, the sister and not the wife went to meet the returning warrior, and he gave her the best item from among the booty. She was not taboo but sacred. In primitive societies, the sister's authority could be substituted for that of the tribal mother.

In Samoa, the word for sister is *tamasa*, "sacred child." In Polynesia the chief's sister is shown the most ceremonious deference, even where inheritance is in the male lineage. If a Hottentot whips a slave, the victim only has to call out the name of his master's sister to make him cease.

The woman under gynocratic society permits male interference only from a brother, because he shares the honor of the same uterine descent. That is why, in the transitional state between matriarchy and patriarchy, the mother's brother enjoys a preferential position: only he can become a guardian to his nephews and nieces. Wherever the sister does not choose him for a husband, he or his son is considered an ideal mate for her daughter, which is the cause for the very common marriages of uncle and niece or of cousins, as for example, with the West Hamites, Bedouin, and Tuaregs, as well as all in Arabia, where the marriage of brother and sister was the rule in olden times. This was often not done for financial reasons but contrary to their material interests.

Constant incest through the marriage of first cousins was an ideal in large parts of pre-Aryan as well as Aryan India up into the highest castes. *Kanyaka-Purana*, the holy scripture of the Comatis of southern India, prefers such marriages to any other, even if the young people should be black-skinned, ugly, blind in one eye, without brains, and depraved, even if their horoscopes will not fit together and the omens are unfavorable. The marriage of cousins is the rule in Ceylon, among the Singhalese, in Assam, northern Burma, parts of China, Australia, with a number of Mongolian tribes, and in Africa among the Hereros, Ashanti, and many others. Among the Dyaks of North Borneo, brothers and sisters are often married, as is the case also among the Bedouins, the mountain tribes of Java, and others. The purest incest races are everywhere the most handsome and evenly featured and healthiest. Nor is there any apparent decline in fertility.

In this connection, one must consider the reasoning on incest. The marriage of siblings may be considered preferable because it *is*, or because it *is not*, incestuous. Wherever there is much pride in blood and race, the marriage of brother and sister is allowed if they have both parents in common. But in matriarchal societies, the marriage of brother and sister is not considered incestuous if they have only their father in common, because then they are not related. In Plato's ideal society, with its natural law, the marriage of full brothers and sisters was allowed.

Even in the worst gynocracy, such as that of the Beni Amer, where the man is completely enslaved, maltreated, and ridiculed, where he may pay fines for everything and the woman feels ashamed if she helps him in case of illness or mourns at his death, Munzinger reports that "the love of sisters for their brothers is great." In Madagascar, husbands are treated very badly, and there is neither affection nor consideration for them, but the most tender love exists between brother and sister. Among the matriarchal Hamites, as well as among the Tuaregs of North Africa, Frobenius reports that the husbands complained because their wives considered them nothing and their brothers everything.

Arabian ladies during the apex of Moslem civilization emphasized time and again that they deemed their brothers much nobler and better than their lovers; for this reason, it was a special distinction to be called "elder brother" by them. Early Arabian culture, therefore, was not a matriarchy; although there were matriarchal legal forms, society gave preference to the daughters. The domination of women was still there, but the women exercising it had changed. This made it very different from the old women's clans of Assam and Sumatra or the African kingdoms, where a queen dowager comprised the center and cohesive force of society, like a queen bee in her hive.

If we consider Arabia a realm dominated by the beloved sister, and thus some steps removed from true matriarchy, this approach may also go a long way toward explaining the dynastic incest practiced in Peru, Phoenicia, Persia, Caria, Hawaii, Mexico, and especially Egypt, where it was carried on for some five thousand years. Frazer assumes for all these matriarchal realms that ambitious sons married their sisters in order through this connection to make their children the heirs to the throne, because the daughters of the family were the only ones who could inherit. Later, he thinks, the kings locked up the priestess-princesses and made them Vestal virgins in order to shunt them aside.

But how would this have been possible in the beginning, since the female clan held the priesthood and exercised magic power over the people as the most important privilege of gynocracy? How could the women have been locked up when they held the right freely to dispose of their persons? The story of the Danaïds tells us that any violation of this right was punished by immediate death. Dynastic incest, even though it may later have led to violent overthrow and patriarchy, could only have been possible because it was furthered by the women for emotional reasons. The wooing of the brother simply was preferred to any other. Artemisia of Caria would not have been so deeply moved by her widowhood as to renounce her throne and the world if she had been forced into marrying her brother.

In the matriarchy the brother simply is the only man that counts. He never lacks for love and tenderness, even where there is a stranger–husband, who merits little consideration while being used for sexual purposes. It is through dynastic incest, through the state of mind that made old Iranian religion recommend the brother-sister marriage and made American Indians, Samoans, and Hottentots refer to sisters as "beloved women," that the predominance of the sister came about. For the man, his uterine ties were simply advanced by one generation.

VII

CIRCUMCISION

It would seem inconceivable that it might be possible to print more erroneous opinions on paper than one can find in older discussions on circumcision. Since one practically knew only the Jewish form of circumcision and also was convinced that the Jews were a practical and rational people, any of their measures—regardless of what they did and on what level of mental development it might lie—absolutely had to have a practical and rational purpose. That is why circumcision was largely discussed as an aseptic measure, just as their prohibition on the consumption of pork was supposed to protect them against trichina. The more their religious feeling seemed gauged to asepsis and trichinosis, the more it was certain of a condescending recognition.

There was, then, no end of praise for the eminent advantages of a fundamentally hygienic operation, which was clothed in ritual. The concrete advantages were something on which there was less agreement than on their eminence. There were those who claimed that circumcision stimulated the sex drive and others who claimed that it rather inhibited it. But above all, it was supposed to be aseptic. For the practice of artificial defloration and circumcision of females, on the other hand, there were such terms as aping imitation, perverse, disgusting, bestial, and infamous. Briffault very justly observed that, if it were a question of asepsis and cleanliness, female circumcision would be much more commendable than male, and the conscientious removal by Chinese nursemaids of anything that would stand in the way of inner cleanliness and had to be removed some day anyway from the uterus of their charges could be far more easily justified than the senseless maiming of the male organ.

"If the aboriginal custom of artificial defloration and female circumcision had been maintained longer by the Jews
and the Romans than was the case, there would undoubtedly
exist a voluminous medical literature demonstrating the sani-
tary advantages of these practices." Since that, however, was
not the case, the prejudiced medical profession considered
those practices a revolting bit of mischief. Advocates of wom-
en's rights, sensing a whim of male voluptuaries, comically
enough believed that female circumcision was the height of
male brutality toward outraged femininity. Of course, this
was nonsense, too, for it was precisely in the powerful matriarchies that the operation was performed by women on other
women, and it survived in that form to our own times.

The Coptic Christians have long considered female circumcision more important than male, and for aesthetic reasons: the Egyptians—among whom Coptic Christianity is
strong—have considered this operation a female characteristic
for six thousand years. When a Catholic priesthood tried to
outlaw female circumcision, the converts from Coptic Christianity rebelled and married "heretics." The College of Cardi-
nals finally had to send some physicians to Egypt to carry on
an investigation on the spot in order to determine whether
the intimate parts of North African women were too strongly
developed and thus gave justifiable cause for an excision.
Rome once more showed itself to be conciliatory and concluded that a compromise was in order.

The circumcision of girls certainly was no beauty operation
and only seemed such because of long habituation. Like the
circumcision of boys, it belonged to the ritual of almost all
puberty rites, which Frazer calls "the central mystery of primitive society." It was customary not only among primitives
but also in great civilizations such as those of ancient Egypt,
India, Mexico, Arabia, and Babylonia, and, of course, among
the Israelites. Mohammed referred to circumcision as "a duty
for the man and a matter of honor for the woman." The
Arabian tradition would have it that the female form is
older than the male. Briffault quotes his Arab sources: "Sarah
first performed it on Hagar; then Sarah and Abraham circumcised themselves as Allah commanded them."

Strabo reports the practice as current among Jewesses;

Abyssinian Jews used to consider it a custom they had
brought with them from Palestine. The Abyssinians, Egyptians, Arabs, and Nubians practiced the radical form of female circumcision, an operation in which the clitoris, small
labia, and prepuce are sacrificed to the knife, which is also
the form used in many tribes of west, east, and south Africa.
A milder form is practiced as artificial defloration with the
Madagascans, Kamtchatkans, and numerous Indian tribes of
South America, as well as the Malays still today.

Westerners who do not exercise special leadership for
young people during their puberty can hardly appreciate its
importance among other peoples. The unconcealed violence
of the puberty rites makes this period equally as important
as birth and death. Depth psychology has occupied itself
with this central mystery, but has been almost exclusively
hypnotized by the male part. Indeed, the male form seems
more drastic because, as a second birth into a new way of
life, it contains the ritual of "death and resurrection," whereas
the female form only reveals an existing mode of being
through the removal of inhibitions. Uninitiated males do not
count among the human members of the tribe; whoever
might try to dodge the ceremony or might be absent through
some unfortunate circumstances would not be able to marry
and would be considered the equal of dogs and other animals,
and his children would not be members of the tribe.

The question of what a Western cosmopolitan could possibly find interesting in such bloody nonsense committed by
African Negroes or Australian bushmen can best be answered
by the observation that these rites bring out into the open
the vehemence and purposes of an individual's instincts.
These determine his inscrutably intricate fate despite scientific objectivity, automobiles, and air mail—the awesome
forces by which he lives and which are the raw material of
his victories and defeats.

In essence, puberty rites consist of the following: The novices are suddenly separated from the women and children,
their previous environment, and taken out into the forest.
In a separate camp, the grown men who are their mentors,
protectors and tormentors at the same time test the boys
with deprivation of sleep and rest, blows on the head, running

of the gantlet, forced bleeding, tearing out of the hair, knocking out or filing down of the teeth, and stabbings with lances. These tortures, intensified with threats of death, induce faintness, numbness, and fever in the boys. Only then are the means of revival introduced: ecstasy and trance. The circumcision itself usually takes place in a hut which is decked out to look like a voracious monster. In the belly, one undertakes this operation: it is the bite of the animal. As soon as the wound heals, sexual activity is not only permitted but ordained. Thus the puberty rites are usually finished off by wild orgies, sometimes also of a homosexual nature, especially where a subincision has created something like an artificial vulva.

At the return to the tribe or the village, the initiates are often painted with a white "death scar," their eyes are daubed with chalk, they stagger back and forth, and they know neither their parents nor their own names. They have to start learning all over again and conduct themselves as if their existence had just begun. It is difficult to determine whether this condition is the result of hyponosis or simply an organized form of obligatory deception.

In Australia, the whole ritual bears an additional imprint of misogyny. Threats of death keep the opposite sex away from the camp and its secrets, which is connected with an emphatic and distinct homosexuality. Matriarchal areas, on the other hand, have neither misogyny nor subincisions, though the rites lose nothing because of this. In all tests of courage among the American Indians, for example, the women are present; great value, in fact, is attributed to their admiration, as if the return of the boys-turned-men occurred only for their pleasure. Nor is the separation from the childhood environment intensified into a misogynist act; a possible addition of newly arisen homosexuality always fits in with a nonvirulent female rule, as demonstrated by the Spartans and Teutons. Only in a true gynocracy is homosexuality intolerable.

H. Schurtz in his well-known book *Altersklassen und Männerbünde* ("Age Brackets and Male Associations"), espoused the opinion that the boys' initiations belong to the category of male associations, which, in turn, stand in opposi-

tion to the family, because they are an independent, fundamental form of association. In his opinion, "only the sympathy
of the men, above all the sympathy of men of the same age,
make possible a closer social cohesion of larger groups." R.
Thurnwald goes still further and calls these male associations
with their club houses "the first concrete forms of political
organization." Probably Hans Blüher perceived the problem
more profoundly and more boldly when he substituted "the
role of erotics in human society" for vague sympathies and
gave this title to all of his dashing intuition, for "nothing exists
without Eros." The man-to-man element founds the state; the
man-to-woman element founds the family.

Theodor Reik ventured to psychoanalyze "the puberty rites
of the savages" in connection with the couvade, applying the
same premises to it, namely, the slaying and eating of the
father, that he presumed was the prologue of the original
horde. He did this so thoroughly that, no matter how one may
stand on the topic, a few sketchy remarks cannot do full justice
to his work. In this book, however, we are not concerned with
a comparison of diverse opinions on the circumcision of males
but rather with a comparison of the characteristics of boys'
initiations with those of girls' puberty rites. For the essential
problem here is girls' circumcision.

For Freudian psychoanalysis, male circumcision—and that
is the only form with which it is concerned—is an "equivalent
of castration, which most effectively supports the incest prohibition. . . . It was suggested by the unconscious fear of
vengeance on the part of the man who himself had become a
father. It contains residues of an unconscious remembrance
of incestuous and hostile feelings directed toward one's parents during childhood. The man fears the realization of these
wishes now directed against him by his own child . . . ."
Circumcision, then, would be a punishment for the boys'
incestuous wishes who, when their maturity approaches, are
forcibly separated from their unconsciously desired mothers.

According to psychoanalysis, the tortures, hypocritically
cloaked as tests of courage and fortitude, are a sadistic vengeance of the fathers for the evil wishes directed against them
by the youths. In the course of events, the men waver between the spiteful satisfaction of hostility and tender homo-

sexual trends, thus becoming tormentors and protectors simultaneously. The "rite of devouring" by the monster is a
death threat which is a phenomenon of psychic reaction to
the unconscious murder wishes of the youths. The devouring
monster is the totem, ancestor, and grandfather. The fathers
now identify with the monster: "They are the ones that har-
bor the evil intentions against the youths ascribed to the monster," and they project their wishes into the totem animal.
Its "bite" is the penalty of castration. "Why does the father-
monster consume its sons during puberty? If we subscribe
to the theory of the original horde, the answer must be: Because the sons once killed and ate it themselves."

Reik does not think of the revival rites as a direct continuation of the death drama, which perhaps was not play acting at all when it began but was its real conclusion. In his
opinion, revival rites belong to the opposite, affectionate
tendencies. The primitive fathers are ready "to accept the
youths benevolently into the circle of the men, but only
under the condition that henceforth they relinquish any incestuous or hostile sentiments. . . . The death threat demonstrates the fate that might otherwise await them." This also
explains the necessity of forgetting, the extinction of the
former existence during the awakening on the paternal side,
which the boys have now joined.

The identification of the father with the totem animal and
the ensuing initiation into the tribal rites of the adults, in addition, is sealed with new blood bonds and a solemn meal,
the swallowing of the totem. Through their new birth, which
this time does not occur of the mother, the boys are incorporated into their own sex, and their infantile wish of identify-
ing with the father is satisfied. Since the incestuous tie has
been abolished, the sex urge can be set at liberty thereafter.

C. Jung, the famous Swiss psychoanalyst, arrives at very
different results. He describes the rebirth as "going-through-
the-mother-again." He sees the mother in the devouring
monster and identifies her with the "whale-dragon" of early
myths from whose belly the sun—hero always arises victorious. In contrast to Freud, Jung thinks that the deepest foundation of incestuous desire is not a wish for cohabitation with
the mother "but the peculiar thought of becoming a child

again, to return to parental protection, to creep back into the mother in order to be born anew." "A hero, then, is someone who is given life by a woman that already was his mother once before . . . a man who can create himself anew through his mother."

That is why the myths give so many heroes two mothers and disguise this trend with the fable of exposure to the elements in order to give a second mother to the infant in this manner. Dionysos, the typical hero of death and resurrection, had the name *bimeter*, "of two mothers," because Zeus, after the death of Semele, planted the embryo in his body and finished bearing the child as if he were its mother. In Jung's rite of death and resurrection, there is neither fear of retaliation nor any of its consequences, because "the problem in reality is the sublimation of the infantile personality . . . a sacrifice and rebirth of the infantile hero." The "hero," however, is the projected libido, which is to be understood not only in the sexual sense but, going much further, as the concept of aspiring yearnings. The imagination speaks for Jung and against Reik. Devouring beast in the shape of a hut or a room can never mean "grandfather."

Perhaps one should recollect at this point that even in the misogynist rites of the Australians the bodily mother of the novice must during the whole period of his "rebirth" remain in close contact with him and those procedures in the monster's belly if he is to return safely. The "wound," however, the "bite" of the mother animal, interpreted as a severance of an umbilical cord, releases him into his new life.

R. Briffault, finally, without paying much attention to the details of the accompanying ritual, cites several reasons why male circumcision is only a copy of the older, female form. Circumcision, he says, is an analogue to defloration because of the shape and nature of the thing that is removed. But whereas defloration seems sensible and necessary, the male variety lacks all independent justification. Furthermore, this is the only case in which the blood taboo, otherwise restricted to the feminine sphere, is transferred to the male wound, which is thereby characterized as female. Finally, the incumbency of having sexual intercourse as soon as possible after the operation makes no sense whatsoever for the boys, whereas in the case of the girls who suffered radical circumcision, it offered a preventive means against the formation of scars and their disturbing effects.

Briffault's opinion probably does not pay attention to the purely male, fighting elements in the symbol of the boys' initiation. The idea there is not blindly to emulate a female example but, on the contrary, to become different and acquire identity.

Many interpretations have been attempted for the "central mystery" of the puberty rites, because such a large slice of cultural evolution still remains concealed in it. None of these theories are entirely satisfactory. Without wishing to establish a new one, I merely want to state what the male and female forms have in common and what separates them. Perhaps the bodily and psychical sense of girls' circumcision can be clarified in this manner. Much has been written on the topic, but too little thought was devoted to the writing, because the female form was always thought of as an emulation of the male. Briffault came to the opposite conclusion, but he obscured the male form in favor of the female. In the female form, he was probably right in considering artificial defloration a protection against the malevolent moon blood of the torn hymen. There is an original feud between things emanating from the moon and from the sun, and they must avoid one another.

The mere existence of puberty rites in the entire magical part of mankind proves that here an overwhelming original instinct deems the maturation and the manner of reaching puberty to be the most decisive thing in an individual's existence. Furthermore, this instinct seems definitely averse to leaving the form of the end of childhood to a more or less benevolent chance. The instinct interferes radically in order that nothing shall be carried over that does not belong to adulthood and so that nothing shall remain behind, "for a human being needs his entire libido in order to reach the limits of his personality; only then will he be able to do his best," as Jung explains.

Puberty rites enforce a radical detachment from the infantile state through shocks so strong and new that one's past history drowns in a sea of forgetfulness. They are experienced collectively in order that social ties and tribal feelings may be promoted. Whoever cannot sustain the initiation or has not participated cannot "belong," because there is no guarantee that his childish identity was replaced properly in the sense of the tribe. And whoever has successfully completed the rites does lead a different life, has a different heaven and hell, a different way of existing, and even a different death.

The difference between boys' and girls' rites enters into the picture only when it comes to methods. To be sure, both sexes must sacrifice something, for the sacrifice means power: every new step—and inner objections arise against each one —is achieved only through courage and pain, which is the reason why many people suffer a premature spiritual death. But whereas in the case of the boys, the "sacrifice," the "wound," the "bite," the "tear," or the pain lies at the center of Life itself, the girl child is merely cleansed of the remainders of bisexuality that it has retained. It sacrifices the clitoris, the rudiment of a penis with its male shudders: the knife ends a hermaphroditic state of being, leaving only pure femininity.

Where, however, this perverse collateral realm has not been removed, a number of nations attribute to it responsibility for every disturbance: If the Kehals, a caste at the upper Indus river, or the Brahuins in Beluchistan find that a young bride is not yet pregnant after six months of marriage, she has her clitoris circumcised, which supposedly will permit her to conceive. Modern medicine also sees the main cause of female frigidity in an overdevelopment of this sphere, resulting in a dislocation of sensitivities.

Since the "bite" in female puberty rites occupies a secondary place, there are no death-and-resurrection rites. No such profound replacement with an extinction and a resuscitation of consciousness seems indicated by instinct, for the girl novices, after their cleansing, remain on their inborn path to motherhood, whereas the boys must be forcefully severed from their childish dependency and thus enter the male road to the other pole of destiny.

The knocking out or filing down of the front teeth repeats the same idea. Teeth always have a phallic significance. Their stunting or removal in the case of the girls corresponds to the circumcision of the clitoris. In the case of the boys, it corresponds to the "wound," the "sacrifice," the removal of the old connection with maternal depths. Since their umbilical cord was cut before, this may be expressed only at a corresponding source of life, the penis. And when Frobenius learned from some patriarchal Ethiopian tribes that they considered the circumcision a sacrifice to mother earth, that the wounding of their bodies was an atonement for their future violation of the bush through the tearing of its ground with the plow, that was only a slightly different image, a slight variant of the same reason. The boy born again into a man tears up the female earth when he plants grain, but the precondition for tearing it up is his "pain," his "wound," his "bite," his own surgical removal from a mother-connected preadult existence or, according to Jung, from the "infantile hero."

Probably male and female circumcision arose contemporaneously, for they belong to the same mental attitude, which received and transmitted its knowledge in pictures. To be sure, the female rite itself is divided into two entirely independent segments of different significance: artificial defloration and circumcision. The removal of the clitoris frees the girl child of the dangerous rudiments of the other sex that survive within her own body, thus paring down its femininity. Artificial defloration, on the other hand, is not undertaken for the benefit of the girl but for the protection of the man from contact with the tabooed moon blood of the hymen wound, which is a source of fear even in patriarchal society and which only a specially consecrated person such as a priest might touch with impunity.

This special taboo, however, is only a variety of the great, universal shudder before the demoniacal correlatives, woman and moon. Demoniacal is anything subject to time and therefore any contact with woman. The moon governs the rise of one's lifespan itself and, with it, all further contacts and severances of life, for the female cells detach themselves from the ovary according to its rotation, though the spermatozoa are always available. The first "demoniacal meeting" of a flagellum cilium with the female egg, the beginning of a new life, depends on this rhythm. Menstruation and delivery are multiples of the lunar cycle. It governs the action of female hormones. Astrology, "that original thought of mankind," probably started with the moon. Like ebb and tide outside, the inner life waters are directed by the moon. But why only in woman?

Darwin thought that, since animal life spent the greater part of its evolution in the sea, its rhythm since time immemorial has been incorporated into everything living and its physiological functions, so that the tide phenomenon is still pulsating in the land species, and the restriction of the phenomenon to the female is due to the fact that the longest period of time was dominated by marine forms that have parthenogenesis. In the male principle, which arose later, the fixation of the lunar tide rhythm was not so profoundly anchored and therefore was lost on land.

VIII

TOTEMISM, EXOGAMY, AND MATRIARCHY

Since totemism and exogamy are psychologically among the most significant developments and also are pervaded largely by eerie riddles from unknown sources, they provoke extreme opinions. Frazer has voiced three different theories, two of which he had to recant, and it is to be hoped that he will also recant the third. But then, he is the author of the statement, "I have changed my views repeatedly and am resolved to change them again with every change of the evidence, for, like a chameleon the candid enquirer should shift his colors with the shifting colors of the ground he treads."

Frazer's third theory, in view of the fact that Australian bushmen and other primitives do not know the connection between conception and the sex act, has the totem originate with the "sick fancies" of the woman at the shock of the first movement of the embryo. Animal, birdcall, plant, breeze, stone, star—whatever takes up her attention at that devastating moment is supposed to be mistaken for the cause of the life that wants to have itself brought into the world through her. This would explain why the totem, which often is a male animal, is hereditary almost only in the female line and, as the mystical ancestor, may not be eaten by his progeny, except at important occasions for the purpose of solemnly renewing the identification.

In short, it would explain why every totem is taboo. Totemism, according to Frazer's third theory, then, would be a female creation. Male colleagues of his have collected contradictory arguments from far-flung sources, though this honor should belong to a woman. She would explain to these gentlemen that the "first" movements of the infant are not at all shocking, that a pregnant woman can only reconstruct long after the event when the "first" movements were felt and does so when the movements gradually become stronger. The "first" ones were something like the trembling of an anchovy tail in an extensive fluid, indescribably far away, where the ego borders on the center of things. There is, then, no shock that would cause a woman to connect external objects with an inner event.

Frazer's second theory was suggested by recently discovered ceremonies of the Australian Intichiumarites which, since they were highly degenerated, seemed to be the height of primitiveness. At that time, Frazer thought of totemism as nothing but a "magic consumers' cooperative." One group, according to this theory, was supposed not to eat its totem animal but to increase it by magic rites and use it as a barter object in trading with other clans. If it was a dangerous animal, such as a scorpion or a snake, they were supposed to render it impotent through magic and were paid for this service by the other clan.

Frazer, however, abandoned this theory very soon. He was suspicious of such rationalism because of his long experience, because magic peoples think differently, and he had never been entirely convinced. The pursuits of primitive peoples also were often too unrelated to their totems. "The Baganda have been elephant hunters since time immemorial, but their totem animal is a small water buffalo. Generations of blacksmiths had a tailless cow for a totem. The people of the Bechuana tribe with the iron totem are not ironmongers; they are not allowed to touch any metal."

A. C. Haddon, entirely reasonably, thinks the totem always became that plant or animal on which the tribe originally lived or which it used in trade. That opinion, however, is contradicted by the fundamental law of totemism that a totem animal may not be hunted, injured, or ridden, and that a totem plant may not be plucked or eaten, except at the rare, religious tribal ceremonies of reidentification. Even the most primitive peoples possess a detailed structure of totem usages. There is no chance of the totem's ever having been the source of nourishment.

We can similarly eliminate the theory of Eildermann that especially skilled hunters, specializing in hunting the kangaroo, the emu, or any other game, called themselves the kangaroo people, the emu people, or whatever. Their hunting monopoly had given them an economic superiority within their community. They had insisted on exogamy, since they liked to give their daughters to men of other clans in order to acquire some new varieties of meat. Unfortunately for this theory, primitives with old totems always are omnivorous and no specialized hunters. Moreover, the totem animal may not be hunted or injured. Thus they could not bring totem meat to their father-in-law's house or use it to achieve an economic ascendancy within the tribe. Finally, totems are often plants or animals, but they sometimes are rain, or a star, or a direction of the wind. Nor can we justify calling one kind of totem older than the others. The "economic interpretation" according to the theory of specialized hunters, then, does not answer the question.

Similarly irrefutable objections can be voiced against all the theories on the origins of the totem and especially the theories explaining exogamy with the totem rites. Frazer and most modern scholars believe that the two phenomena have totally different origins, because totemism is much older than exogamy. Sigmund Freud, on the other hand, needs both elements for substantiating his theory of the original horde arising at the eating of the father.

Only one thing has been fairly well agreed upon in recent years, and that is that exogamy has nothing whatever to do with racial hygiene; in other words, that the strict law of having to marry outside one's clan has nothing to do with the fear of incest in a sense of eugenics. Brother-sister marriages, after all, were not only preferred but also in common practice in Iran, among the Murung of Borneo, and among the Kalanga of Java, who believed that the coupling of mother and son would be especially blessed with good offspring. Moreover, it would be psychologically unrealistic to believe that primitive peoples would scientifically predict possible bad consequences for the heredity of future generations or enforce their prevention through threats of death against contemporaries, especially because the question of "bad consequences" has not really been decided.

Modern ethnology, on the contrary, shows that incestuous

races have been among the most harmonious, handsome, and vital. Degeneration phenomena observed in the Alps turned out to have been caused by other factors, such as cretinism caused by thyroid disorders or deaf-muteness by the altitude. Observations of animal breeders are not always very significant, because animals are bred *for* certain diseases, such as geese bred for enlargement of the liver, pigs bred for obesity, or cows for pathologically enlarged development of the lacteal glands. Wherever animals are bred for any purpose closely related to their natural function, as for instance, the speed and temperament of British Thoroughbreds, the results at the race track bear a direct ratio to the strictness and duration of inbreeding. Nowhere in Nature is there a fear of incest in the animal world; on the contrary, there is an aversion to crossbreeding. Herds never admit alien specimens. Where, then, do the most primitive races get their strict laws of exogamy?

MacLennan, the discoverer of totemism and exogamy believed the latter was the product of a lack of women. But this thesis would not explain why the tribe should forego also the enjoyment of the existing women. Westermarck was of the opinion that peoples practicing incest had simply died out of its consequences, while only those practicing exogamy survived. His opinion has been contradicted by the notorious longevity of incestuous races. Jeremy Bentham and Walter Heape saw the explanation in the attraction of a strange woman. That, however, would amount to a preference for non-related women rather than to a strict law of exogamy, and it is psychologically untrue because childhood friendships in primitive peoples often result in erotic relations when puberty sets in, as illustrated by the famous examples of Aucassin and Nicolette, Paul and Virginia, or Daphnis and Chloë. Havelock Ellis also seeks too facile an explanation when he states that fear of incest is merely a result of lacking sex appeal. Why would anyone place a death penalty on an action for which no one felt any inclination?

For Professor Emil Dürkheim, totemism and exogamy are connected insofar as a fear of shedding identical totem blood forces one into marriage into another clan, considering the realities of defloration. But in the great orgies and sometimes in so-called "moon marriages," sexual intercourse is precisely practiced by men and women of the same clan, to whom a union for life would be denied. In the Great Mother clans of Assam, the girl usually has premarital relations with a man whom she is not allowed to marry. There must, then, exist a reason for the exogamic rule that is unconnected with the blood taboo.

Darwin assumed that the reason was the jealousy of older males and said they drove the young ones out of the herd. If, in view of certain animal customs, we agree for the sake of argument, that would still not indicate why these males do not resist an intrusion by males of another clan, and why those males living in other hordes did not do the same. One could then assume that young males never mated except when they overcame an older one in battle; for that, however, opportunities would be as great in their own horde, and the incestuous, rather than the exogamic, union would be the rule.

In the social structure of known primitives, jealousy, or the domination of older males, is unimportant. The thesis of the jealous older male meant that certain analysts jumped in their conclusions from the jealousy of comparatively primitive Europeans to an assumed jealousy on the part of males in the original horde. The stealing of women was rarer than ordinarily assumed. Such customs as carrying the new bride across the threshold have nothing to do with the stealing of brides but, as Frobenius demonstrated, go back to a desire magically to detach her from her old clan in order to have her give birth to reincarnations of the husband's clan rather than her own.

Darwin judged the hypothetical conditions in the original horde by equally hypothetical conditions among anthropoid apes. In his times, one did not yet know that primates vary in their social organization. Modern science has dispelled the older visions of simian patriarchs with monopolies on women, gnashing their teeth at intruders. It seems that anthropoids do not live in strictly patriarchal families at all, but sometimes live alone and sometimes in small groups of males and females of different ages. With or without the gorilla, however, exogamy remains as puzzling as ever.

Freud said, "This darkness is illuminated only by the experience of psychoanalysis." His theory further develops Darwin's fundamental assumption of jealousy by connecting fear of taboo, the tabooing of objects, and the pronounced changes of feelings and tensions among the primitives with observations made on mentally disturbed cases. That is why Freud's world-famous four disquisitions on *Totem and Tabu* have the subtitle, "Some Coincidences in the Mental Life of Savages and Neurotics."

Psychoanalysts tend to regard primitives only as patients living in savage environments and to consider all of magic, the confidence in the "omnipotence of thought," a kind of "narcissistic hypertrophe." It is, however, a fact that primitive peoples live quite well with the aid of their magic methods, while neurotics live badly with their neuroses. The civilized person, were he to try to copy the methods of the primitives, would probably die a pitiful death. In times in which every day reveals new cosmic rays with astounding effects, hitherto unknown and discovered only through our new instruments, so that all living beings turn out to be senders and recipients of invisible forces, one cannot simply deny that more old-fashioned men, endowed with greater powers of instinctive feeling, might exercise some powers on each other and their surroundings with the aid of these rays, especially considering the abundance of evidence regarding their hunting spells and their telekinesis, just because we are unable to do the same.

It is highly deceptive to diagnose neurosis or dementia praecox in the case of primitives claiming to be in touch with such forces, even if they may have degenerated somewhat by now and are no longer in full possession of their magic. One cannot expect to find a savage after simply stripping a civilized man of his inhibitions. A modern neurotic is no longer in possession of the other mode of existence that preceded the scientific age. Magic formulas are not the same thing as the verbal garbage with which a demented patient greets his psychiatrist within the whitewashed, soulless cell.

Goethe said: "We all walk in secrets, are surrounded by an atmosphere of which we do not even know all that moves within it. This much is certain, that in certain conditions the antennae of our soul can reach out beyond their physical limits and that it has a premonition, even a real look into the future."

In *Totem and Tabu*, Freud assumes a single family patriarch, overwhelming in force and authority, envied and feared at the same time, who drives out the sons when they grow up, not a number of older males as did Darwin. In complete contrast to the Darwinian assumption, these brothers later return and kill the father by common effort, which any one of them would have failed at doing. "For the cannibal savages it was a matter of course that they also eat the carcass." Now, they had hated the father, who so vilely stood in the way of their claims to power and sexual fulfillment, but they also loved and admired him. "After they liquidated him and had satisfied their hatred and their wish for identification with him, they had to assert the tender emotions they had to overcome. It happened in the form of remorse. There arose a feeling of guilt. . . ." The sons now were "in the psychic situation of posthumous obedience, so familiar from psychoanalysis. They canceled their deed and forwent its fruits by denying themselves the women they had liberated."

These sons of the "original horde" most decidedly have read too much by Dostoyevsky and talked far too much about their "psychic situation" in the café. Furthermore, it is maintained, the incest taboo through which they all denied themselves the desired women was erected in order to rescue the new organization, for this organization had made them strong. In a possible fight of all against all to gain possession of the female—for each of them, at the bottom of his heart, wanted to have all of them, like their father—they would all have perished. The self-denial was made easier, Freud asserts, through homosexual activities that might have arisen during the times of their exile.

Psychoanalysis here overlooks the fact that the young brother organization would have broken up immediately because of exogamy. Sexual ties among primitives practicing exogamy have consistently been matrilocal in almost the whole, wide world. The man does not take the woman into his house but moves into her clan, living at the periphery as a guest. Therefore, the brothers must either scatter among all tribes, which would dissolve their association, or they must stay at home while abiding by the incest taboo and remaining homosexuals. But then, they would have no progeny to whom to pass on their traumatic experience, and there can be no totem animal replacing the father, remaining active for thousands of years, causing ritual slaughters by priests and solemn meals where the totem animal is consumed.

In other words, a later ethical and social application of the tradition would not be possible. It would be astonishing too, that the ambivalence between fathers and sons would always have remained latent at later stages. Finally, it is a fact that primitive nations hardly have a feeling of any sort for fathers, the feeling of close relationship connecting the children only with their mother. The author of *Totem and Tabu* himself frankly acknowledged that he did not know just where the actual arena of the drama he sketched could have been.

Freud in his old age wrote a beautiful sentence, full of reasoned modesty:

> . . . only that one is seldom objective where he is concerned with the great problems of science and Life. I think each person is, in those matters, governed by deeply-founded prejudices, which his speculations are unwittingly designed to strengthen. In the face of so many reasons for skepticism, there probably remains no more than a calm benevolence toward the results of one's own thinking.

In 1927, Robert Briffault published *The Mothers* in three large volumes. He compiled and also utilized huge amounts of material. Briffault here appears as something of a Copernicus of exogamy, because he shifts the center of gravity of the investigation. In this manner, he brings order into chaos. The prejudice of patriarchy is removed from exogamy altogether. For as long as the woman was supposed to join the husband, exogamic phenomena seemed confused and perverse. The father complex of the psychoanalysts was especially misplaced in this subject, for to them, the mother appeared only as an object of sexual desire. They naïvely forget that this *object* can also become the *subject*, that is, that she also has something to say about her sexual utilization.

Briffault shows the origins of exogamy in the very nature of the mother clan, as the backbone without which the clan could not have existed.

In contrast to the protagonists of the "original horde," Briffault asked: Where would exogamy be indispensable? How could such a thing as a mother clan ever come into being? Even Bachofen had failed to perceive the key problem of the great mother clans, for he only saw the dominance of original female matter over the man, and he visualized the woman in the matriarchal family she created. All other theories on exogamy, however, took their point of departure from the male sex drive.

Wherever the men were sex partners and brothers at the same time, their rivalry for authority, their restlessness, and their drive to power must necessarily lead to a patriarchate. The mothers as the basis for social order, for this reason, allowed the growing males to take no liberties with their clan sisters but protected their younger sisters against their brothers, while the older sisters were entrusted with the authority of mothers. Growing males were made to leave the community as soon as possible, and marriage outside the clan was arranged. They were then barely tolerated outsiders in their new clan, subject to the mother-in-law taboo.

The women, however, remained inseparable. No daughter was given up. Husbands were admitted only as guests, occasionally forming male associations on the periphery of the clan, roaming feely like flagella around the female egg. The blood bond between the women was much stronger than any sexual ties connecting them with their men, not only in the great mother clans of Sumatra, northern India, and among the Indians of North America, but also in the matriarchal parts of Africa. Even where the women moved into their husbands' villages, they often ran away and went home at the slightest provocation.

It was, then, the authority of the reigning mothers that enforced exogamy and defended the organization against male instincts that were welcomed only occasionally. Some sixty close-printed pages in Briffault's giant work are covered with the names of the peoples and tribes on our five continents among whom marriage has been matrilocal and exogamy is enforced against the males only, in the sense of the mother clan. It means very little merely to state that there was exogamy; the important thing is who had to leave home to move into the other's house. A female association would have lost its unity if the sons had brought in alien women and the daughters had moved away. It would then have become a male herd, where the female intuition is permitted to atrophy. For this reason, exogamy in so many primitive societies has proved essential for the preservation of their matriarchal character. The man, less conservative by nature, tends more easily to leave his clan. He is not a homemaker, but rather a roving adventurer. In societies where women and children sleep in huts, the men often still sleep outside under a tree.

Briffault arrives at a conclusion that is the exact opposite from Freud's: not the authority of older men but that of older women enforced exogamy, because it drove the sons away from the young daughters. It is reputed that this habit has had strange consequences, for the children born in matriarchal societies presumably look more like their mothers; in societies with equal rights, the environment supposedly has greater influence upon them; in societies with patriarchal conditions, the children presumably take after their fathers, so that the women never establish the apparent type.

Briffault went even further in his investigations. He asked a question that had not been asked by the other anthropologists: How were larger human groups formed? Social theory from Cicero to Westermarck replied that it was by a conglomeration of families. But though nothing seems easier than to bring several families together, the difficulty there would lie in keeping them apart and having them preserve their family character. In an unconsolidated mankind without firmly implanted social instincts—which are reshaped mother instincts, transmitted second hand to the males—the initiative of untamed male sex impulses would soon have transformed the whole family complex into a male herd or, at any rate, have changed the nature of the association. We know that this is actually what happened in many cases.

Wherever in the animal kingdom families meet in larger numbers, the unity of the family tends to be destroyed through promiscuity, the initiative lying with the males. This even happens with birds meeting at their nesting places for only a brief period. Group formation creates conditions opposed to the foundations of the family. The biological family is a manifestation of the maternal feelings of the female, tending to protect and preserve. The female separates from the others to give birth and retires into a cave, where the male may follow or not, but seldom stays longer than until the cessation of his reproductive urge.

The choice of the birthplace, the suckling and rearing of the young, the protection of the weak and helpless, are the instincts that found the family. If it is altered into a group of families where the males are always present, this formation is not an expression of the formative and regulative forces that create family organization, which are the maternal instincts. The type of organization is then changed, and the male instincts create the herd or the male horde. Female influence would thus be destroyed and, with it, those sentiments so essential in the initial creation of society.

Characteristics predicated on higher development, such as the use of language, are the results of larger associations. If the disciplining, constructive, orderly, eminently social mother instincts were to be firmly rooted in these associations, the growing sons had to be assigned a place outside of the central mother-organization. This was done by exogamy. It was a strange arrangement, but it was the one used by evolving mankind. Of course, it was not planned scientifically in order to arrive at our own "superior" plateau. Briffault rather assumes that the cause of it all was the jealousy of the mother of her daughters. The mother, then, drove the sons away from her daughters, thus exiling them from the clan, and to the females of another clan, where she did not have to witness their sexual intercourse with other females. According to Briffault, motherly love is always instinctively possessive. Darwin claims to have observed the jealousy of mothers in cases of incestuous relations among the great apes.

The female must form basis and bond of every animal or human society, because the man has no more to do after the sex act. But it is at this point that the biological career of the female begins, her transmutation into an entirely different creature and the tremendous physical and mental adaptation to motherhood. She is reborn at the same time that the child comes into the world and becomes the educator of mankind.

The burgeoning female family, however, was formed and dominated by two kinds of maternal instinct. First, there was the defense of the satiated female, which in the animal world will absolutely not allow a male to approach her any more and in the human world is profoundly opposed to male domination. This instinct creates a type which necessarily becomes superior to the male because it is not such an easy prey to sexuality. Second, there is the mother instinct jealously opposing any sexual activity of the son and driving him into exogamy.

Briffault's correct, even ingenious, explanation of exogamy demands a deeper explanation, quite apart from his slighting of other social groups, such as the horde formation of men based on camaraderie and homosexuality, which may have arisen independently from the great mother clans for different erotic reasons. I shall attempt that explanation here.

"With the first prohibition come the first neurosis, but from where did the first prohibition come?" Who may refuse permission to the Great Mother? Why must she become jealous? What can prevent the powerful, mystically revered mistress of the clan from reaccepting her son into her abdomen after his puberty, since he is so powerfully drawn to it, before he even gropes for his sisters as primary substitutes?

This question reaches back into a primordial area even deeper-rooted than the sexual instinct, the thing that first gave birth to the sex urge. In the beginning, there was woman. She parthenogenetically severed activity from herself and made it into flagellum cilium: the male. She not only severed this principle from herself but painfully drove it out. It is her creation, and the more thoroughly she can drive it out of herself, the more successful it is. First of all, there is the flagellum; then there came the phallic form; and later there was a whole little man connected with the phallus. A continuous original activity derived from him and, by using him, created the new, male world. She does, to be sure, also expel female births in the same manner, physiologically speaking. The urge to expel, however, ends with the birth when it comes to the daughters. The daughters, repetitions of herself to some degree, often remain close to her for a long time, strengthening the female substance with their youth. The son, however, is a successful birth only to the extent that he removes himself from her in every respect, exceeding that activity which she created in his image.

Here lies the original conflict of maternal emotions. Like every true tragedy, it is inextinguishable in its ambivalence, beyond love and hatred, a contradiction of sentiments, because she wants to possess and to lose her son at one and the same time. As the White Mother, she wants to protect him. As the Black Mother, she expels the helpless creature. The animal mother herself bites through the umbilical cord; the Australian aborigine mother, waking and fasting, hurries the novice through the puberty rites; the mistress of the female clan ordains the law of exogamy; Thetis herself brings the suit of gilded armor to Achilles so that he can go down to certain death. They are all deeds of the Black Mother with the white, tearful face.

But the births themselves may also feel a certain ambivalence toward their creatress. In the life of individuals as well as of races, there always recurs the moment when the sons as well as the daughters strive for a dissolution of the ties: daughters because they also have some original activity, for the female principle is variable and capable of, as well as eager for, new forms of expression. This inclination is the product of a heroic, self-willed phase, since it involves a dissociation from magic maternal powers, a sacred tie far exceeding physical reality. The severance of the magic umbilical cord is the fateful point for races as well as for individuals. At all stages of extraversion and introversion, there recurs the dual urge to go out and to go back in, to unfold and to garner in. The rhythm of these oscillating tendencies determines how far a person may go.

Where the umbilical cord has been torn, the realm of sons and daughters begins. Their growing old does not restore things to their former order. A new type has arisen. In the new layer of their soul, this fresh young two-ness, if they are of homogenous race, is often united in brother-sister realms, symbolized ideally by the dynastic incest of ancient Egypt, the "Two," the dual system of reigning heart siblings with a slight, magical superiority of the female partner. This is still a hermaphroditical stage. For the man, the uterine tie has been advanced by one generation, from the mother to the sister. For the woman, the human value of the man resides in the honor of descent from the same mother, resulting in a union of souls between brother and sister. In civilizations like those still existent in parts of Africa, where the magic umbilical cord has never been torn, there continue compromise solutions: the age-old power of the queen-mother, strong management of the royal son, and inheritance of the kingdom by or through the king's sisters.

It may also transpire, of course, that independent young realms of sons and daughters of very different descent may meet in deadly battle. A clash between male-dominated and female-dominated civilizations is a war indeed.

IX

THE COUVADE

Couvade (derived from couver, to hatch) means "male child-bed." In the case of a number of societies in transition, it has generally been considered one of the means by which the men take over the governing functions of the women. Roughly speaking, it means the following: When the woman gives birth, the man goes to bed sobbingly, writhes with ostensible pains, moans, has warm compresses applied to his body, has himself nursed attentively, and submits to dietary restrictions for days, weeks, or, in exceptional cases, even for months. Until his first bath afterward, he is considered unclean, just as though he had himself given birth to the child.

This custom, deviating widely according to the tribe in the time covered and other variables, was known very early, being mentioned by some of the famous travelers of antiquity. Herodotus lists its existence among certain African tribes. Nymphodorus attributes it to the Scythians at the Black Sea; Diodorus to the Corsicans; Strabo, to the Celto-Iberians of Spain, whose direct descendants, the Basques around the Pyrenees, practice it still. On the island of Cyprus, there used to be a couvade that was unconnected with any special birth: every year, at the festival of Aphrodite, a handsome youth had to lie down in an open tent and imitate by voice and emotions, a woman during her birth pangs. As for China, Marco Polo was the first European to report on couvades among the mountain tribe of the Miau-tse, and modern English explorers have confirmed his data.

The friendly zeal with which people are currently exploring, registering, and studying all exotic races photographically, phonographically, and photometrically in order to catch them before our indigestible civilization can ruin them and they disappear altogether has gradually uncovered the fact that the number of women writhing in childbed is not so much greater than that of men doing the same, that there has recently been, or still exists, a couvade in places from Siberia to South America, in the Malay Archipelago, in Africa, China, Brazil, and India, with cultured as well as uncultured races.

As obvious as the data seem, the meaning is obscure. There are as many opinions as there are scholars. Since customs are older than logic and have grown into our level as ancient hereditary property, the question about "reasons" is of little avail to those who ask it. Genuine customs exist and fade away within the zone of pure feeling, without brushing the area of reason. Primitive nations, apart from their possible inability, dislike giving information about their actions, sense any suggestion of what the questioner wants to hear, and respond according to the unspoken wishes of their interlocutor. Could anybody ascertain in Germany or Switzerland today why a man's shirt is hanged in front of the prospective mother's window in Thuringia; or why in the canton of Aargau the woman dons her husband's trousers the first time that she leaves the house after the confinement; whereas in the Lech Valley she puts on his hat? No one in those places remembers what these customs are good for; the ethnologist, with his comparative data from five continents, says these are remnants of genuine couvades with their characteristic swapping of roles by the two sexes.

When the wife of a Brahman becomes pregnant, the husband stops chewing betel, which is more difficult than going without tobacco is for a smoker, and he fasts until she gives birth. In the Philippines, the father must stop eating sour fruit a week before the delivery; otherwise, the child will have a stomach ache. In Borneo, he is not allowed to use a cork; otherwise, the child will suffer from constipation. In China, the man must guard against violent movements or the embryo will suffer in the mother's body. For the same reason, the Jambim man abstains from fishing: the sea (great fecund water) is not to be stirred up by the beating of oars. The Malayans of the archipelago touch no sharp implements, kill no animals, and avoid any action that injures anything.

Before the babe is born, both parents are almost everywhere subject to strict dietary rules. But whereas the woman is usually permitted to move freely after the birth and, some food taboos apart, may resume a normal life, the man's postnatal couvade often begins at this point, with sadistic annoyances far exceeding the prenatal one. The Caribs of Cayenne make him lie in a hammock and fast for six months. Afterward, when he rises from it to return to his house for the first time, a mere skin and bones, the guests assembled there inflict bloody wounds on him with an aguti tooth and rub pepper into his bleeding sores. Really sick this time, he returns to his hammock and until the end of the seventh month eats neither fish nor fowl. La Borde relates that many Indian tribes of South America slash the skin of a young father after he has fasted a long time, left his hammock only at night, and been subjected to many other privations. Having inflicted bleeding gashes upon him, they then rub pepper and tobacco juice into them. He is not allowed to utter one cry in pain. His noble blood is then rubbed into the baby's face, so that it shall become as brave as he.

One can imagine what it would mean to be a father to suffer all these tortures in a polygamous society! Much of this maltreatment obviously belongs to the realm of sympathetic and imitative magic and is not an integral part of the couvade. Lucien Levy-Bruhl, and the entire French school of thought with him, thinks that these proceedings are only part of the precautionary measures and taboos that both parents impose upon themselves. The European only noticed them, especially in the case of the male because it seemed so unusual, and for this reason the couvade was analyzed as something apart from other birth rites, which had been a mistake. The "common fate," "mystical participation," "blood bonds" are, in his theory, so strong that whatever one person does is noticed and experienced by the other. That is why the Brazilian Bororo drinks the medicine where he buys it—in the pharmacy—if his child is sick in bed at home; for it is just as effective that way.

Thurnwald supposes that the real couvade is not a kind of make-believe but that the man actually feels the birth pangs. Tyler also concludes that it is sympathetic magic, which had always been considered a means in Ireland for transferring the birth pangs to the man. This is the much-discussed "transference of pain" discussed by Frazer. It was kept a well-guarded secret by the Celts. No scientist has ever been successful in watching it; we only know for certain that, if it is to be successful, the man must give his consent. The English observer Pennant tells us: "I saw the progeny of such a child-bed come into this world gently, without causing his mother the slightest inconvenience, while her poor husband roared with pain in a strange, unnatural anguish."

In Esthonia, every bride at her wedding gives her husband beer and rosemary to drink. She then crawls between the legs of the intoxicated bridegroom, which is supposed to transfer some of the birth pangs to him later on, if he does not wake up during the ceremony. Here, there is no consent, whereas the Celts consider it essential. According to Frazer, the birth pangs are not necessarily transferred to the husband but may also be given to other men or to a wooden statue. Ploss and Bastian believed that the demons of puerperal fever were to be misled by the exchange of roles, confuse the man with the woman, and, after discovering their mistake, would be embarrassed and powerless. The Vaertings' theory is probably wrong: they thought the couvade was a survival of gynocracy, because the man, acting the part of the nurse, stayed in bed with the child to keep it warm, but this custom is practiced mostly below the equator.

Psychology, on the other hand, bases all the tortures and dietary restrictions on a father complex, with its traumas, commingled guilt complexes, fear of vengeance, tenderness and hatred. Its entire reasoning concerning the couvade hinges on the well-known Freudian hypothesis of the patricide in the original horde, the mutual relinquishment of the desired mother by all the sons, and the establishment of the totem meal as a reminder of the eating of the father, "that remarkable event in human history which led to the formation of religion, art, and social organization."

Bachofen, who compiled countless examples of the couvade, settles on the *birth-giving* gesture of the man as the essential thing. He also regards the couvade as the father's attempt to a right to the child, though in a different sense from that of psychoanalysis. He sees in it a typical symptom of the transition from matriarchy to patriarchy. Actually, the couvade is found almost exclusively in matriarchal societies. "The father's masculinity subordinates itself to the female potential and reveals itself in maternal characteristics." The act of giving birth, then, still outweighs the act of procreation. Fatherhood alone is insufficient; only when the man has undergone the natural state of motherhood can he be a father.

Bachofen was the first person to include an analysis of adoption ceremonies in his discussion of the couvade. For instance, Zeus could not legitimize his illegitimate son Hercules until a goddess had performed the act of giving birth to him. "Hera mounted her bed, took Hercules to her body, and then let him drop to the ground along with her clothes, with which she mimed his true birth." A similar ceremony still accompanies the adoption ceremony among the matriarchal Dyaks of Borneo: the adopted mother climbs on a high chair in the presence of many guests and has the adopted child crawl backward through her legs. Medieval Europe, Arabia, and Byzantium had similar practices. The Abbot Guibert describes how Baldwin of Flanders was adopted by the duke of Edessa "according to the popular customs," that is, according to matriarchal laws: "He had the naked man step inside of his linen undergarment, embraced him, and affirmed the whole with a solemn kiss. The same was done by his wife."

A touchingly unselfish couvade is exercised by women who help their sons with their own bodies in overcoming the pains of the puberty rites. These ceremonies are accounted the same as a rebirth. Through fasting, suffering, fainting, and trance the boy must re-create himself into a man. He endures the dangerous circumcision as well as a ritual of several months in the bush under the guidance of older men.

In Australia, where the women are badly suppressed, the acceptance of the son into male society means complete severance of relations with the mother. The mothers, therefore, are treated by the initiates "like persons in mourning and women in childbed at the same time. The women abstain from the same foods as their sons, who are enduring the circumcision far away in the bush; otherwise, he might be in danger. They rub down their bodies with oil or grease, which are considered medicinal in their effect. They live alone at

fires separate from the tribal camp; no one may approach
them or speak to them. Every morning before dawn, the
mothers sing the prescribed songs. They sing while standing
up, while waving burning logs in the direction where they
presume the camp of the initiates to be. If one of the boys is
freed from one of the dietary taboos, his mother seems also
freed from it." (Matthews) Never before was their mystical
tie as strong as in the very period when the mother uses it for
the last time as a last means of final separation. The paternal
couvade wants to acquire a right to the child; the maternal
couvade cedes it.

X

AMAZONS

Were there actually such things as the fabulous nations of maidens, the mounted demons, galloping from the edges of the world to make ice and golden sand splash to all sides? Was there ever a "man-hating army" with clanging tresses and awesome customs?

The average Greek faced with such questions would approximately have responded with the same look that would come to a German's face if he were asked whether there actually were such things as Frenchmen. They had been a hereditary enemy, apparently ordained by supernatural powers to oppose Greek civilization from the bottom on up. All of Attica festively commemorated the battle with the Amazons near Athens every year, just as Germany used to commemorate the Battle of the Nations at Leipzig of 1813, although the liberation of Germany from the Napoleonic yoke was far outshadowed by the liberation of the Acropolis after four months of siege by the Amazon army of Oreithyia.

The uncontroverted testimony of all of Greek antiquity regarding the Amazon expedition against Athens has met with a certain surly resistance on the part of scholars down to our own times. It is reminiscent of that curious verdict in a biography of Goethe, in which the poet's confession that, of all his women, he loved Lily most is "corrected" by his biographer with the words: "Goethe is mistaken here, for that was rather the case with Friederike." Were the Greeks mistaken when they asserted the reality of the Amazons, with whom they fought overseas as well as in their own country, and when they called this life-and-death struggle more fateful even than the Persian Wars?

It is objected that the defense of Athens is attributed to

Theseus and that the registers of kings listing Theseus are not complete or verified. This objection can best be met by the Ridgway[1] quotation cited above, relating to the vital force of proper names. Thus, Cecrops survived as the founder of the Acropolis, Erechtheus as the victor in the war with Eleusis, and Theseus as the unifier of Attica. His name, by the way, is connected as closely with the detailed legislation of the new state as is Lycurgus' name with that of Sparta.

It is objected also that the names of the Scythian Amazons reported are Greek and not Scythian, so that they must be phantoms of the Greek imagination. But that would also reduce Xenophon's *Anabasis* to fiction, for he also gives Greek names to the Persians. Furthermore, it would eliminate Rameses II, because the Greeks called him Senostris. But we are given the answer by Critias, who makes the following remarks relating to the traditional stories about the lost kingdom of Atlantis: "I must preface my report by one detail, so that you may not be astounded why non-Hellenes bear Hellenic names. You shall know the reason." It is reported that exact inquiries were made of the Egyptian priests as to the meaning of the foreign names, which had been translated into Egyptian. The Greek equivalent was then used for each name. This was the Greek practice.

Another objection is that Greek historians speak not only of Caucasian Amazons but also refer to others in North Africa with similar customs. This "suspicious redundancy" was presumably proof of the fact that legends had been taken over and the locale changed. But independent Chinese annals also speak of a "western women's kingdom" between the Black Sea and the Caspian Sea. Cherkessians, knowing less about Greek literature than the Chinese, confirm that there were nations of female warriors in those regions. Some knowledge about Amazon realms was retained throughout the Middle Ages among nations in the area.

A recent travel book by Essad Bey tells of two newly discovered tribes in the land of "eternal fire" between the Black Sea, the Caspian Sea, and the Caucasus, the same old heart-

---

[1] Ridgway, Sir William (1863–1926), *The Early Age of Greece, The Origin of Tragedy.*

land. According to him, there lived a "nation of maidens" and the "blue-eyed Ossetes" in that area, both of which had customs strongly suggestive of the old Amazons. Only their women bore arms, hunted, and rode. They took men according to their needs and then sent them packing. Briffault says, "The fact that there were so many Amazons is not a proof of their nonexistence."

In time and reality, the Amazon kingdoms not only comprise an extremist end of matriarchy but also are a beginning and a purpose in themselves. Roaming daughter realms, excluding everything male except some enslaved boy cripples, they markedly differ from the serenely tolerant mother clan as old as mankind, which pacifically exiled a young upstart manhood by exogamy. In the mother clan, there was a constant progression of great mothers begetting more great mothers. Amazons, however, reproduced the daughter type, which practically skips a generation and is something altogether different. They were conquerors, horse tamers, and huntresses who gave birth to children but did not nurse or rear them. They were an extreme, feminist wing of a young human race, whose other extreme wing consisted of the stringent patriarchies. The Greek tribes, those ordained by fate to become the Amazons' enemies, acted like newly grown "sons," not like future "fathers," for the emotion of fatherliness is a mimicry of motherhood. Nor do the two new types of human beings, the brother states and the sister states, unite against "matriarchy" in the sense of "mother power." The sons and daughters rather met head on in a sanguinary clash.

According to the ancient historians, there were two foci of the Amazon system: Northwest Africa and the Black Sea region around the Thermodon River. Although later in time than the African Amazon kingdom, the Black Sea kingdom was more renowned. Living in the steppes bounded by the Urals, where the Greeks thought the world ended, the Amazons of the Thermodon region were considered the enemies of the griffins. The griffin was the totem animal of the soil and represented the ancestral soil. In its twin nature, there loomed the eagle-beaked threat of winged fear hovering above the abyss, mixed with the snake and lion bodies of arid, golden sand. Whoever wanted to live there had to fight it.

THE THERMODONTINES

Several hundred years prior to the Homeric period, there was a brief interval of Amazon triumphs. Internecine feuds, revolutions, changes in dynasty, and massacres of one group of men by another unsettled a great number of women and brought together a good many of them who had been accustomed to fighting in the army and participating in all the pursuits of the men. Probably there were several female armies founded from remnants of diverse tribes, scattered over broad stretches. "Amazons" is a collective name for belligerent hordes of women with self-government, whose aversion to any kind of permanent, matrimonial ties varies in gradation.

The mildest form of this aversion caused them to engage in a quick assignation with their male neighbors, totally indiscriminate as a matter of principle, every spring. Female offspring was retained; the male was sent to its distant fathers. The more radical kind of administration did not send any babies away but crippled the newly born boys and rendered them innocuous for life through the twisting of one hand and one hip out of their sockets. Despised slave cripples, never touched erotically by the Amazons, they were used by them for the rearing of children, the spinning of wool, and domestic service. In the most extreme antimale society, the male offspring was always killed, and sometimes the fathers were, too.

All varieties of Amazon society share the characteristic that they reared only the girls into fullfledged specimens of mankind. The Scythians, to whose general category most of these hordes belonged, called them *Airorpatai*, "men killers," although some of their varieties hardly differed much from the old mother clans, where grown men existed only at the periphery of society most of the time and were tolerated in the house only as guests, while growing boys were removed by the law of exogamy.

When the ancient Greeks said "Amazons," they meant the

Thermodontines. Their glorious kingdom extended from the Sarmatian plains to the Aegean Sea. They found themselves forced into a series of preventive wars in order to preserve their kind. First of all, they subdued the Caucasian mountain peoples. Then came the decisive advance to the mild southeastern coast of the Black Sea, with its famous mines, woods filled with game, nut trees, vineyards, and verdant meadows. This region, their largest permanent site, was the later core of their realm, with the capital of Themiscyra near the rivers Thermodon and Iris. From the mouths of these rivers, water-borne commerce could be carried on directly with the cities of the Mediterranean. This connection with the Mediterranean world, however, brought the Amazons no good results. They were able to use rivers only for swimming themselves, since they lacked all talent for sailing, and the navigation of other peoples brought them nothing but ill fortune.

On land, the Thermodontines were irresistible. They annexed one piece after another of Asia Minor. Their curved double ax mowed down anything standing in their way, the star-like scar of their seared-off right breast contracting in the blow. Though bestial until victory, they later, like the Romans, became conciliatory. Gentleness and foresight earned them the adoration of the vanquished. Europe has certainly always suffered incursions from the East, but the Thermodontines' fame acquired a special luster because they demonstrated the creative strength resident in the temperament which, on the other side of the Don, had been no more than rashness, contraction of the pores, savagery, and racial substance in the midst of icy gales, clouds, steppes, and the eating of one's relatives. In the bright light, their boldness turned into wisdom.

The entire Ionian tradition refers to them as the founders of cities and sanctuaries. Their tradition was maintained uninterruptedly by temples, graves, cities, and whole countries. A large number of important cities boasted an Amazon as founder and godmother: Smyrna, Sinope, Cyme, Gryne, Pitania, Magnesia, Clete, Mytilene, and Amastris. The most illustrious cultic image of Asia Minor, Artemis of Ephesus, ringed with beads of rubies and chains of sacrificed Amazon breasts, goes back to them. Before that idol, they performed their clanging sword and shield dances. The Amazon statues of our museums are copies of those created by Phidias, Polycletus, Cresilas, and Phradmon in a contest for sacrificial presents for the Artemis of Ephesus.

The laws of the Thermodontines remained entirely uncomplicated even at the zenith of their power. The abysmal contempt of women for statutory law permits the recognition of only two crimes: theft and mendacity. Ethics demanded that they must always resist the temptation to marry or to rear a male child. For this reason, they must perform the sex act indiscriminately with any stranger chosen at random, without any emotional or sensual ties, and only for the sake of reproduction. They must work for their meals every day or hunt for them in perspiration and danger, and they must obey only the orders of those who have attained the throne through election or royal descent. Two queens administered the kingdom at the same time, one being the administratress proper and the other the leader of the armies guarding the frontiers. For people of their kind, emotions dictated a duality of leaders.

Naturally the horse is the totem animal of the Amazons. It was not a totem in the orthodox sense, for Iranians and Central Asiatics were never real totem races. It was, however, in a magic way something of a symbol of strong desires and a propellant of their urges, especially when its hoofs struck fire and thus symbolized fire, "the shiny tongue of the gods." For many peoples the horse also has always held some elements of madness. Iran, Aryan India, Central Asia, and especially the Amazons felt a profound magic connection for the horse. The transliteration of many of their Scythian names often contains the word *hippos,* which is Greek for horse: Alcippa, Melanippa, Hippothoë, Dioxippa, and many others. It also has a bearing on the myth that Pegasus sprang forth from the blood of the Libyan Amazon Medusa. Therefore, the Amazon presumably has magic horse blood in her veins.

Athenian comedy, true to its mental level, always adopted a snickering attitude when there was talk of Amazons and their horses, suggesting that stallions replaced the men in Amazon tribes. Once a year, the Amazons had an orgiastic feast of dedication. At first, it used to take place on a granite rock in the Caucasus; later, on the reedy Ares Isle in the Black Sea. In highly secret rites, a milky white stallion was sacrificed. One can hardly overlook the similarity to the Indo-Aryan sacrifice of horses, called Asvamedha. The "sacred marriage" between the divine animal and the queen supposedly served the magic renewal of the people.

Amazon babies never drank out of their mothers' breasts but suckled on the breasts of their totem mothers, the mares. Adult Amazons partook of a vitamin-enriched diet of mare's milk, honey, blood issuing forth from dying animals, raw meat of animals they had killed, and the marrow of reeds, gathered before the dew settled upon vegetation. They had no bread and ate no carbohydrates, even after agrarian nations began to pay tribute to them.

There is some doubt about the origin of their Greek designation. *A-Maza* would mean "no barley bread," that is, those who live without bread. The derivation *A-Mazo* was more popular; it was supposed to have come from *amastos,* "without breast," referring to the burning of the lacteal gland on all girls, through the application of hot irons, when they reached their eighth year. With some groups, the breast was merely limited in growth by being tied up with cloth, a custom surviving in such countries as Japan.

The particularly significant thing in the ceremony of the breasts is the assurance, recurring from writer to writer, that only the right breast was singed or made to wither away. It is a known fact that the effeminacy of the male always starts on the left side, whereas the increase of masculinity in the woman begins on the right. The whole idea of the Amazon is the cancellation of the first, parthenogenetic female action, the separation and formation of the active principle and its shaping into a male. Amazons deny the man, destroy the male progeny, concede no separate existence to the active principle, reabsorb it, and develop it themselves in androgynous fashion: female on the left, male on the right. Their dematernization begins with the shrinking or the removal of the right breast as a symbolic action of bold style. The Amazon does not mime the male principle but denies it in order to unite the two fundamental forms of life in paradisical harmony which had been divided by the Great Mother. Homer developed the right feeling for the Amazons, when he called them *antianeirai,* which may be interpreted as "man-hating" or as "mannish." He is reputed also to have written an Amazon epic.

Another derivation of the word Amazon was supposed to be *amazosas,* which means "opposed to man"; one also considered *azona,* "chastity belt." Etymology, of course, depends largely on the fashion of the day. It may well be that the word Amazon came from a Scythian word that was corrupted by the Greeks. Perhaps it was the Cherkessian *emetchi,* which means "those who count by the mother" and would indicate that they regarded the Amazons as a matriarchal tribe. In the Kalmuck language, a healthy, strong, heroic woman is called *Aemetzaine.*

Amazon dress and appearance in the early traditions were always represented as typically Scythian: long, narrow trouser; long coat; soft, long boots; a Phrygian cap on their heads. Later representations have the Amazons wear a fur coat, buttoned over the left shoulder, while the right shoulder is left bare; their wavy hair is tied in a bun on their backs, and they wear soft, long boots. The type of the statue of the "dying Amazon" comes still later, with the Doric *chiton* and sandals, varied by Pithias, Polycletus, and others. The last, almost baroque dress is the Macedonian armor, a purple sash between naked thighs, with ostrich plumes on the helmet. The weapons, however, remained the same. There were the famous *sagaris* or double ax—an androgynous symbol of all gynocratic nations; the tiny *pelta* or shield, shaped like a five-day-old moon; bow and arrows; and a short sword. They added a lance only after they had seen it used by the Greeks.

A role of dual importance was played by the belt. As a golden and crystal sword belt, it was one of the Scythian royal insignia inherited from their ancestors. In more intimate form, it was a symbol of virginity and of their belonging to themselves alone. "Virginity" during antiquity never meant "without a mate, untouched" but rather "unmarried." When Greek adventurers in the thirteenth century B.C. first sailed their war fleet into the mouth of the Thermodon to the capital of Themiscyra for the avowed purpose of taking the Amazon queen's belt, this meant her deposition and her ravishment.

There were a number of stories about the stealing of the queen's belt, though no pretense was made about the nature of the theft. In one version, Hercules and Theseus together fell upon the undefended city and its queen, Hippolyte, while Oreithyia, the other queen, was defending the borders with her army. The small garrison was overcome and slain, Hercules took Hippolyte's belt, while Theseus used trickery, love, or violence to get Antiope, the third sister, in his ship. A different version had all these events transpire on three different expeditions: the stealing of the belt, the taking of the city, and the elopement with Antiope. At any rate, the next event was the vengeance of the Amazons.

Oreithyia, once she was informed of the *coupe de main,* came rushing back with her army. The enemy had already departed when she arrived. A penal expedition then marched across the frozen Bosporus and moved on Athens. The city was invaded, the Areopagus occupied, and the Acropolis besieged. There is no doubt that she actually was inside of Athens, for historians named the places she occupied and the graves of the slain, and there was a tradition of festivals and cultic rituals in the city connected with this event.

Both sides hesitated before engaging in the decisive battle. Theseus finally began it after a favorable oracle. According to Plutarch, the battle took place in the month of Boedromion, which was the reason for continued sacrifices made during that month in Athens. According to one version the Athenians were pushed back to the ravine named after the Eumenides, but another version had the besiegers losing heavily. Finally, a compromise was concluded, which was commemorated with a sacrifice to the memory of Theseus in later days; it was the custom to eulogize the fallen heroes of the Amazon war. The Amazon army rode away without achieving its aim—the avenging destruction of Athens.

A gamut of graves indicates the route taken by the retreating "children of the gods," beginning with the Itonic Gate at the temple of the moon, where the abducted Amazon (Hippolyte or Antiope) was killed by one of her people, fighting at Theseus' side. The road runs through Thrace, where Oreithyia died of grief and shame over the disastrous outcome of the campaign. Luck now left the Amazons. No more than remnants of the old group ever reached their home. The prestige of victory was lost. New inner turmoils and waves of nomad invaders destroyed the female realm little by little. The only thing surviving was a mortal hatred of everything Greek. It was so strong that, several generations later, Penthesilea took an elite corps to the defense of Troy against the army headed by Agamemnon of Athens even though King Priam had himself fought against the Amazons in his younger years.

After that, there is ever less information on the Amazons of the Thermodon, although isolated groups of them flash like lightning through historical reports. Soldiers of Pompeius claimed to have found some Amazons among the allies of Mithridates, and there continued to be some traces around the Black Sea. We read in Archbishop Lamberti's *Recueil de Thèvenot* that Dadian, prince of Mingrelia in the Caucasus, received the news that three groups of tribes had come out to fight the Muscovites in the vicinity, and after the aggressors had been defeated, there were some women among the dead. The messenger brought weapons and clothes of these female warriors: helmet and cuirass of steel plates, supple and fitting the body, a short skirt to be worn beneath the armor, and soft, high boots, embroidered with stars, while their arrows were gilded and had a steel point, broad as a pair of scissors. Such Amazons were often encountered in the fight with Tartars and Kalmucks. Dadian promised a rich reward for anyone who would bring him such a woman alive.

The Chevalier Chardin's *Voyage en Perse* reports some tales told there about Amazons: The prince of Georgistan told the Chevalier that five days' journey to the north, a great people was engaged in perennial war with Tartars and Kalmucks. It was a people of nomad Scythians, ruled by mounted women warriors. And that is where the track ends. The last tangible survival are those soft, high boots, ornamented with stars, in the hands of a prince.

In Attica, however, there began something not otherwise customary after a victory: the idolizing of the vanquished. Temples were built and sacrifices made in their memory, families of priests were appointed and festivals were founded.

Every spot where they had lived and died became a sacred precinct with pillar and monument, inserted into Greek ancestor worship by a deeper Eros. To the Greco-Pelasgian world, they had seemed miraculous, surpassing mortal measure, more dangerous than all other nations put together and also more exacting. At the celebrations in honor of the dead, Demosthenes, Lysias, Himerios, Isocrates, and Aristeides praise the victory over the Amazons as more important than that over the Persians or any other deed in history; for Thracians, Persians, and other enemies had merely been driven from the country, but the Amazons had been driven from human nature. The wars between Greeks and Persians were wars between two male-dominated societies. In the Amazon war, the issue was which of the two forms of life was to shape European civilization in its image. The cleavage into sons and daughters had been unsettling even for the male victor, who sensed the polarity of human nature for the first time and with it the riddle of ultimate values.

No mother, no wife, no hetaera remained as inseparably attached to Greek imaginations as these hostile sisters of the opposite pole, called daughters of Mars and Harmonia. Hardly were they banished from Nature when they returned victoriously into the realm of the spirit, where an odd, magical change of gender occurred. All of Hellas permitted itself to be impregnated by the spiritual image of the mannish Amazons. Every art was suddenly big with their nature. Their expulsion began their omnipresence.

THE LIBYANS AND OTHER AMAZONS

Young "daughter realms" of an uncompromising Amazon structure need at least three components: a temporal, a racial, and a spatial one. They seem to be connected with certain developmental stages, with certain races, predisposed for such a social form, and they culminate in certain areas from which they suddenly emerge into their greatness and destiny. Long after the stars of their splendor have paled, however, something of their indestructible nature simmers on and, from time to time, breaks out of its obscurity, if it has remained in the people's blood.

The spatio-cultural phenomenon of the Amazons, as far as we know, reached two culminations, one at the Caucasus near glaciers on primeval rocks, golden sand and metal, northern steppes and storms, in tight-fitting clothes, Phrygian cap, and long, soft leather boots; the other, long before that, at the feet of the Atlas mountains, also in an environment of extraordinary proportions, below craggy craters and blistering suns, in desert and pasture, but somehow touched by the wide expanse of the Atlantic, from which the silky green breakers roll on the shore.

At first, they rode to the west. Clad in red leather armor, snakeskin shoes, and with python-leather shields, they galloped to the area of Lake Triton to a rich oasis inhabited by the Ichthyophags, a fish-eating Ethiopian tribe. According to one version, that whole area was swallowed up by an earthquake and the land was torn up all the way to the Atlantic ocean. The Amazons founded a city at the lake, practiced animal husbandry but no agriculture, as everywhere else, lived on meat and milk, soon felt the urge to try greater enterprises, and soon after that ruled a good part of Libya and Numidia. One fine day, they reputedly encountered a surviving colony of Atlanteans, who were extraordinarily civilized, refined, and decadent people.

Herodotus also speaks of Atlantis and its people, but locates them nearer Mount Atlas and attributes their name to that of the mountains. It would hardly be possible to draw a more delicate image of such an exhausted culture than did the ancient tradition: "They are the most civilized people on earth, eat no living creatures, and have no more dreams." In other words, they had no more to sublimate, lived without fear or desire, and were not agitated by emotional experiences. Plato said of Atlantis, their idyllic country surrounded by brazen walls: "For many generations, the inhabitants obeyed the laws and were receptive for everything divine. But in time, they proved unable to tolerate their good fortune and degenerated." The catastrophe by which Atlantis was engulfed presumably manifested itself in the direction of Europe as the Great Deluge and the opening of many ravines, including the famous one in Athens.

The Libyan Amazons, themselves engaged in creation of a

political structure, met a mainland colony of Atlantis in the Northwest, by which they were mightily impressed and from which they learned a good deal. After some initial savagery and destruction, the women's army shamefacedly rebuilt the capital and concluded an alliance with the vanquished. All of North Africa seems at that time to have abounded with Amazon tribes. Strabo tells us: "There have been several generations of belligerent women in Libya. The Gorgons, against whom Perseus waged war, were described as a people of great courage." These tribes were in rebellion against the Atlantean colony. The Amazons, under the stipulations of the new alliance, were asked for help. Thus there came a battle of Amazons against Amazons. Thirty thousand Libyan horsewomen under Myrine delivered a pitched battle to the Gorgons, won the day, and took so many prisoners that it proved to be their undoing.

The victors, exuberant about their great success, neglected to take proper precautions. At night, there was an uprising of the prisoners. Many Libyans died before the rebels were surrounded and killed. The queen had the bodies of her warriors piled on three huge funeral pyres, and monuments were built over the ashes. The hills with the monuments were still in existence at the time of Diodorus and were pointed out as the graves of the Amazons. The tribe of the Gorgons later recuperated, grew in power, and was raided by an expedition under Perseus, much like the expedition of Theseus against the Thermodontines, which occurred many generations later. Perseus killed the Gorgon queen Medusa. It is hardly necessary to mention that names like Medusa and Myrine were Greek translations from the old Libyan.

After the Gorgon war, the Libyan Amazons started their tremendous campaign. They rode through Egypt peacefully but went through Arabia fighting all the way. Myrine conquered Syria, Phrygia, and all the lands along the seacoast to the Caicus River. Wherever possible, she began the building of cities in the newly conquered vastness. Since the Thermodontines conquered the same lands some centuries later, it became difficult to keep the various foundations of cities apart, as the cities themselves, although they maintained traditions of their foundation by Amazons, never informed one precisely which Amazons had performed the act. The islands, such as Samos, Lesbos, Pathmos, and Samothrace, seem to have been conquered by Myrine.

The Amazons, being horsewomen, were always unlucky at sea, and so, the Libyans were surprised by a storm at sea and were shipwrecked on a deserted isle. Myrine, obeying an apparition in a dream, named the isle of rescue Samothrace and dedicated it to the mother of the gods, founded mysteries in her honor, built altars, and began sacrifices. Later, the united forces of the Thracians and Scythians invaded the Libyan colonial area. Myrine was killed in battle, and the remaining army of Amazons gave up their world empire and returned to their North African home.

Of all the African Amazons, only the Gorgons seem to have maintained a pure Amazon state; the others, though keeping the army purely feminine, maintained some men in their camps. The Libyan Amazons, who removed their right breasts, had compulsory military service for all girls for a number of years, during which they had to refrain from marriage. After that, they became a part of the reserves and were allowed to take a mate and reproduce their kind. The women monopolized government and other influential positions. In contrast to the later Thermodontines, however, they lived in a permanent relationship with their sex partners, even though the men led a retiring life, could not hold public office, and had no right to interfere in the government of the state or society. Children, who were brought up on mare's milk, were given to the men to rear, just as among the Egyptians, Kamchatkans, and some of the North American Indians.

Herodotus in the sixth century B.C. still found conditions at Lake Triton amazingly like those of an earlier day.

"Next to the Machlyans, there are the Ausans, who share the lake with them. Every year they celebrate a festival in honor of Athena, the virginal goddess. The girls are divided in two groups and fight with one another . . . proving, as they say, which ones were born in their nations . . . a traditional honor since the days of old. Maidens who die of their wounds are considered impure. Before ending the fight, they observe the following customs. The girls who

conducted themselves with the greatest bravery are decorated with a Corinthian helmet, put on a chariot, and led
all the way around the lake. I cannot say what weapons
the Amazons used before the Greeks came to live near
them. I believe, however, that they wore Egyptian arms,
for I am of the opinion that shield and helmet were originated by the Egyptians and copied from them by the
Greeks. . . . Their clothes and their shields with the image of Athena were copied by the Greeks from the Libyans, though the Libyan images wear clothes of leather.
. . . All the other things are the same. The name *aegis*
also indicates that the armor of Pallas Athena comes from
Libya, for the Libyan women wear red goatskins with rib-
bons over their clothes. After the goatskin, *aigeon*, the
Greeks named the shields of Pallas statues *aigides*."

Army service, as reported by the old historical sources,
then, had been converted into a game by the sixth century,
even though at times the game had a fatal end. Virginity was
still required of the girls on active service, and the single,
great goddess was still worshiped. The red leather armor
was still worn by the Amazons. The armor of Pallas Proma-
chos, the Vanguard Goddess, is traceable to this Libyan Amazon dress. Morocco, which is the Libya of antiquity, is still
known for its wonderful, red leather.

Strabo, traveling in North Africa six hundred years after
Herodotus, no longer found its women in the army but found
that they ruled the country politically, while the men were
still without significance in the state, occupying themselves
largely with body care and hair-do, greedy for golden
jewelry with which to bedeck themselves. The Berbers of
our times correspond to the old Libyans, though they do have
some Arab admixture in them. Near the Atlas Mountains,
where they have preserved the greatest purity, they also
have preserved a strong gynocracy. In some Tuareg tribes,
the women perpetuate the old culture and know Old Libyan
writing and literature. Their men wear veils and remain il-
literates.

Apart from the ancient Amazons of Northwest Africa, there
were the Gagans. They reared no male progeny at all
but destroyed all baby boys in true, classical Amazon fash-

ion, until their conversion by Christian missionaries. They were ruled by queens, had received their constitution from queens, and made great conquests under queens. The Arabian writer Magrizi described the Bedja, a Hamitic Amazon tribe between the Nile and the Red Sea. Their women made wonderful lances according to a secret process carefully guarded. They also killed all male progeny. A middle ground was occupied by female praetorian guards like those of Monopotera. They lived in their own province and decided the election of kings. Various gradations of Amazon influence are manifold in Africa, just as in the Caucasus area.

Herodotus tells us of the Sauromatians on the far side of the Don, a mixture of Amazons and Scythian youths who would not desist from attempting the beautiful warrior maidens and kept following them. Their offspring, the Sarmatians, retained some Amazon customs. No woman was allowed to marry before she had killed three male enemies. The same custom prevailed among the Iranian people of the Sigyns, who had their home on the Danube. Of the Sarmatian women, we are told by Pliny, "Some die old, without having ever married, because they were unable to fulfill the law." Changing culture, however, also altered the customs, even though a certain fundamental attitude remained the same. The Scythians, even the most "genuine" ones, had long ago deserted their diet of vile-tasting fathers, boiled with beef. They became globetrotters and cultivated sophistication. Such a Scythian gentleman, for instance, visiting classical Athens, dropped the remark, that "the wise Athenians talk, while the simple ones make the decisions."

Still, some northeast European peoples who did not have purely female armies sometimes chose women for leaders of mixed or purely male troops. The Scythian Zarina was famous for winning a number of decisive battles. Lithuania had female cavalry. In the old graves of the Terek region of the Caucasus, one found female carcasses in full armor. At a much later time, a Hispano-Arabic Jew tells us of an exclusively female realm in the East of the land Rus, where all male babies were destroyed. Thus there simmered on a tradition of Amazon warriors in eastern Europe.

Recently, the expedition of the Amazon queen Eurypyle

against Babylon has been confirmed by historical evidence, as has her capture of the Amorite capital in the year 1760 B.C. This proves the existence of Amazon kingdoms even before the foundation of the Thermodontine realm in the East as well as in Africa. The only genuine women's state of Central Europe, the kingdom of Libussa and Valeska and their Bohemian girls' war, was treated in the *Historia Bohemica* by Aeneas Piccolomini, later Pope Pius II. In view of so many gynocratic features of so many Slavic legends and historical scraps in Scandinavia and Ireland, this kingdom, though unproved, must at least be deemed a possibility.

The Amazon kingdoms, most extreme of all known ancient daughter states, were considered nothing but annoying claptrap until a globe-spanning ethnology was able to fill the gap in understanding and all the gradations leading into and from it. And more: In order fully to unfold the fan of Life, we cannot omit those "legendary" maiden-nations as the natural extreme Left. If that seam did not exist, one would have to piece it together with the aid of the imagination. Until the beginning of our century, the phenomenon of the Amazons seemed so out of the ordinary as to be an imposition upon human credulity. At the time, it was believed that a well-ordered cosmos could function regularly—and pay an annual dividend of three percent. The geological theory, based on violent upheavals, was considered as unacceptable as any eccentricities in cultural development. Fate was permitted to weave her threads of destiny only into doilies. Only the probable was allowed to be true.

Today, Amazon kingdoms like that of the Thermodontines may be understood as the necessary creation of fiery asceticism, a heroic method for the formation of passionate individuality of a new order.

XI

GREECE

It is well-known that the Spartans missed the Battle of Marathon because the moon was not in the right quarter for starting a campaign.

Seldom have any people lived such a classical example of matriarchy and its derivatives as the Spartans. The Dorians were named after the moon goddess, Doris. Dorians and Ionians both claimed descent from Helena-Selene, the moon woman. Spartus, or Spurius, means "mothers' sons," "swamp plants, procreated fatherlessly by an unknown planter." Spartan girls prior to marriage enjoyed free disposal over their bodies, and Spartan marriage was one of the most primitive, purely sexual kinds. There was no difference between legitimate and illegitimate children. There was some polyandry. One could continue this enumeration indefinitely.

A patriarchal world surrounding Sparta naturally handed down the usual verdict: "Therefore, they are reputed to have been very insolent and especially mannish and domineering toward their men, for they not only ruled their homes autocratically but also were permitted a free expression of their opinion in the most important matters of state." Euripides irately informed his audience:

> The daughters of Sparta never are at home,
> They mingle with the young men in wrestling matches,
> Their clothes cast off, their hips all naked,
> Truly, I find such manners shameful. . . .

From a biological point of view, such a state of affairs would seem an advance, not a degeneration, and it was far more shameful for the patriarchal Athenians to lock up their ladies, while they made love to hetaerae and talked philosophy to them but never engaged in healthy sports with their well-shaped young women as did the Spartans—which might have proved instructive for them. Plato, in contrast to Euripides, blames the Spartan women less than the perverse government, under which decent conduct had become an impossibility. Aristotle, on the other hand, heaps reproaches on the ninth-century Spartan constitution drawn up by Lycurgus, because no attempt was made in it to do something about the matriarchy.

Fundamentally, the Athenians were less exercised about matriarchy itself than they were about something that made the Spartans the most hated group in all of ancient Greece. The Lacedaemonians never "belonged" with the remaining Greeks, for their state, because of Lycurgus' constitution, remained an enclave of purity in the midst of a general degeneration. All other Hellenic tribes felt closer to the racially different Pelasgians, the autochthones of the peninsula and islands, than they felt to the Spartans.

Never before—or since—have absolute masters and absolute slaves lived side by side in the same manner as did the Spartans and their subjects for a period of some eight hundred years. The Spartans were as unmaterialistic as they were realistic.

> "Lycurgus prohibited all trades for Spartans and thus placed them into the hands of the subject peoples, or of strangers living in Lacedaemonia but not enjoying Spartan citizenship. Freemen remained free in every respect, because they were not allowed to engage in trades. The acquisition of money was permissible only for helots and perioeci. Freemen had the task of creating and maintaining ethical values."

The lower class was allowed to become rich, while their masters remained poor voluntarily as a strictly guarded privilege. The entire Peloponnesus belonged to these warlike conquerors, yet they lived on a ludicrously small rent that was paid by the helots for the land, living more modestly than Athenian day laborers. Meals were not taken or festivals celebrated at home. Blood soup and barley bread were the Spartans' nourishment. An old cloak was their dress, whether they were men or women. The women had to wear their hair in a simple bun and keep their limbs nude under their flimsy garments. Jewelry was not permitted. Young people received the scantiest rations,

> ". . . for when the spirits of life are unencumbered by food and, because of their lightness, rise to the heights, the body can grow freely and unhindered and thus takes on a slender figure. That is precisely what seems to add to the beauty of men and women. A spare, slender body is better able to benefit from training than a fat and well-nourished one. Women who take purging medicines during pregnancy will give birth to tender but well-shaped, pretty children, because substance can be better formed by Nature if it is light."

Nowhere in civilization was the standard of living as low, the philosophy of life as profound, and the inner attitude as elevated. The puberty rites and the public whippings of the boys were supposed to accomplish this attitude. These were ceremonies that were rehearsals for Life, related to American Indian practice. It was considered as dishonorable to speak of money and business or think of money and business as to place emphasis on things that could cost money. Representative arts including architecture therefore were not as cultivated as in the rest of Greece. On the other hand, everybody was interested in music, poetry, and song, went hunting, and practiced calisthenics in the gymnasia. Life was meaningful and free of purpose, with an unprecedented consistency of discipline as well as a certain narrowness, which is the unfortunate reverse side of these virtues.

Athens, on the other hand, had a constant glorification of activity. Idleness, which grants outer and inner liberty, was punished. Even Plato, in addition to his philosophy, carried on a profitable trade in oil and thus earned the money for his far-flung travels. During Imperial Roman times, Athenian diligence went so far that rivaling lecturers sailed out to meet arriving ships in order to garner in the students as they came.

Being a Dorian apparently was something incredibly strong, stronger than the original antipodes man—woman, so that the common Doric heritage drowned out the play and counterplay of sex. The Spartans, being a pure ruling caste, exercised their erotic instinct without restriction, indulging even in relationships between men and young boys, older women and young girls, free of jealousy or snobbishness, naïvely, and in rapturous awe. Loving the same boy or girl, in turn, formed a common bond between their lovers, who competed in their ability to educate and promote their youthful friend. Honor and shame of the love object were shared by the lover: he was punished if his protégé failed in public games or in the ordeals. The children, who shared their quarters, meals, and instruction from the sixth year on, elected their elder, a twenty-year-old leader, who possessed punitive authority over them, somewhat like the fagging system in the English college. (In sport and education, England seems like a Sparta turned maritime and globe-minded.)

In order to take full advantage of this homosexuality, young Spartan men were not allowed to marry until they were thirty years old. The women were in full accord with this rule, although matriarchy otherwise advances early marriage. Bachelors, however, were despised, which follows the usual rule of matriarchies. Just as marriage was prohibited before the thirtieth year, homosexuality was illegal after the thirty-fifth year. The wedding ceremony was preceded by a public wrestling match of the utterly naked couple, for whoever has been engaged in a sportsmanlike contest with the other for half an hour knows more about him than he could after years of more usual cohabitation.

> "After the wrestling match, a servant-girl received the bride, shaved her head as a gesture toward the ancient sacrifice to Aphrodite, dressed her in male garments and shoes, placed her on the straw, and left her alone in the dark room. The bridegroom, after taking a frugal meal with his comrades, then secretly sneaked into the room. Soon after the consummation of the wedding, he left for his usual bed."

The groom's life did not greatly change after this ceremony, for he only visited his wife from time to time in her house, without sharing "bed and board." She also was completely at liberty to have herself fertilized also by other youths outside of wedlock. Even aliens were considered acceptable partners, provided that their physique was without fault. The queen of Sparta was especially proud and became the object of general envy because Alcibiades, during his visit to Sparta, procreated a son with her. That was a genuine matriarchy, independent even of eugenics, because in matri- archies only the mother's blood is decisive. The handsome male animal may add his own splendor, but what the Dorian woman then does with it is recognized as Doric, while Doric law strictly forbade their kings any sexual intercourse with foreign women.

In Athens, Aristophanes once poked fun at the mad goings-on and said that the only thing the city had not yet experienced was the rule of women. But here he was wrong, for it had existed a few centuries before him. Its reflections, because of the brevity of Athenian memory, were preserved only very scantily in myth, tradition, vocabulary, a few cus- toms, and the register of kings. Tradition had it that Athens once practiced complete promiscuity like Sparta. Patriarchal marriage, it was claimed, was introduced by Cecrops, the founder of the Acropolis, shortly before the Deucalian deluge. Justin, Klearch, Charax, and John of Antioch report that he was the first Athenian ruler to unite men and women in mar- riage; prior to that, the Athenians had cohabited with their own sexes.

The best-known point of rupture between matriarchy and patriarchy is contained in the legend of Orestes with its heretical admission that matricide was atonable. Another, purely political rupture is the myth of the fight between Athena and Poseidon for possession of Athens.

In the council of Athens, the women had the same vote as the men. The women, it is reported, decided in favor of Athena by majority of one. Thereupon, Poseidon inundated Attica. In order to appease him, the women were punished as follows: they were to lose their citizenship and, with it, their vote in the state, and the children were no longer to be named after their mothers. The overthrow of spiritual female power is reported in the legends about the oracle of Dodona and the replacement of priestesses by priests.

The royal family of Athens was female. According to Pausanias, the old Cyclopic walls were built by the Pelas- gians, the autochthonous inhabitants of Greece. Hard pressed by foreign invaders, the Pelasgians called on the Achaeans for help. An Achean married the daughter of the old Pelasgian royal house. Cecrops, too, was enabled to rule by marrying a princess. Cranaeus, a later king, had three daughters, one of whom was Attis, the godmother of Attica. Erechtheus and Aegeus, Theseus' father, belonged to later dynasties.

Despite nineteenth-century doubts, it seems that these legendary figures really existed. In Athens, certain sacerdotal families, themselves of royal blood, had charge of the Erechtheum and the shrine of Cecrops. The Erechtheum is mentioned in the Odyssey, so that we have Homer's testimony for the fact that there was a real king named Erechtheus in the fourteenth century B.C. A proper name is something living; its persistence through the centuries shows this vital force. The myth-creating process merely endows the strongest personality with the most forceful traits. Genealogies tended to be maintained scrupulously, especially where ancestor worship prevailed, even where the people did not know how to write.

History will know ever less about the human past if it restricts itself to written testimony. The most important events will always transpire outside the records and must be ascertained through other means. A prevailing tradition, passed on from generation to generation and through sacrificial rites, has more continuity and force than daily newspapers, regardless of the fact that the press can spread its tendentious lies in millions of copies.

> "Whoever would doubt the existence of a human king named Cecrops because his person was symbolically represented in the form of a snake must doubt the real existence of half of mankind, above all of the totem races. American Indians with rain totems were represented as rainbows, other tribes as directions of the wind or animal masks."

Just as the Athenian royal line was female and Attica was named after a princess, so the male members of the Athenian clans were called *homogalactes,* "men nursed with the same milk." Half-brothers and half-sisters with only the same father were not considered related and were allowed to marry, although those that had the same mother would have been deemed incestuous had they tried to do so. The uncles also were differentiated, giving the maternal brother greater importance than the paternal one. According to Plutarch, Athenian women participated in great public trials until 300 B.C., with the right to cast their ballots.

In the older, Pelasgian-descended tribes, the Arcadians, Aeolians, and Boeotians, as well as their colonies, matriarchy was much better preserved. Mantinea in Arcadia throughout classical antiquity celebrated purely feminine mysteries. Diotima, the erotically experienced woman at Plato's banquet, was a Mantinean. At Elis, on the Peloponnesus, sixteen matrons, according to Pausanias, served as supreme court justices. In Thrace, tattooing was a token of maternal nobility. Locri actually means "motherland," and the Locrians considered Aphrodite in person their ancestress. She was surnamed Zephyritis and by that name became the godmother of the Locrian colony in Lower Italy, which was called Epizephyrion.

The Epizephyrian Locrians came to Italy on a kind of "Mayflower." Polybius said of them: "First of all, they mention the circumstance that glory and fame of descent with them derive from the women, not the men, and that only those are nobles who are descended from their hundred families." Some of the girls of this female nobility were on that "Mayflower" and took over the sacerdotal office in the Italian colony. The office of *pontifex*, that is, the performer of the sacrifice, always was bestowed on women in matriarchies. In addition to the beautiful, Aphrodisian name of *Epizephyroi*, the Locrian men had still another designation: they were called "stinking Locrians" because of their continuous occupation with goats and the dirty work that their womenfolk piled on them. They were a counter piece to the Lydians, whose domesticity and vanity the Vaertings considered a necessary accompaniment of female rule. The matriarchy, it may easily be seen, had many and diverse effects upon the men.

XII

INDIA

For many thousands of years, the tropical plains of India have received a stream of persecutors and their victims, pursuers and pursued. Their dense matting of vegetation has been fertilized by all kinds of blood—noble, brutal, and adventurous, of all shadings. Perfected cultures penetrated from the northwest, flourished to a point of excess, and withered away. But while the center resounded with the trampling of war elephants or vibrated with the hoofs of half a million Tartar horses, and finally spread out under the British-built railways, certain peripheral zones remained almost untouched: the extreme eastern frontier with the hills of Assam and a strip of the Malabar coast in the extreme south.

What has survived as a vital society in Assam is so surprising that it is almost miraculous. Its peculiarity lies not only in the unification of spiritual and temporal powers over the most important confederation of the region in the hands of a woman, or in the participation of priestesses in all important sacrifices, while the men act only as their assistants. We could find as much in Africa. The really surprising thing about Assam is the stubbornness with which every family has preserved laws that have existed in other places only during the brief period of complete matriarchy, laws which usually are changed by force of innate developments in the culture.

These mountains tribes—completely autochthonous, as far as anyone knows—still subordinate their households to a grandmother or a great-grandmother, the older the better, who is called "young ancestress" by way of contrast to The Ancestress, the family goddess. Grandchildren and great-grandchildren are grouped around her, though not the sons-in-law. These males are only utilized for perpetuating the family and are called *U-shongka,* "seeder." They are allowed

to visit their wives only at night. Marital ties are so loose that
hitherto no outsider has been able to decide whether there
is contemporaneous or successive polyandry. If the man is allowed to move into the woman's house—a mark of degeneration in such a society—as he is permitted to do in certain
tribes, everything he earns after the wedding belongs to his
wife, whereas his former possessions without exception belong to his mother.

Within these limitations, private property is a well-
developed concept, and there prevails comparative prosperity. All property is inherited by the daughters from and
through their mother; the chief heir always is the youngest
daughter. In Assam clans, we find at last the condition of matriarchal rule in which the youngest child inherits the most—
a condition that was predicted but never located by Bachofen,
who discovered it in legend and tradition as a characteristic
of the chthonial-material urge to heap all possible goods
on that person through whom death will be delayed longest
and the life of his generation is protracted most. Sir Charles
Lyall called this epitome of matriarchy one of the most perfect surviving illustrations of that system, "realized in a logical and thorough manner which might cause some second
thoughts in those who are accustomed to consider the father's
authority the essence of family and society."

In Assam, the father, naturally enough, is not considered
related to his children. He holds no claims on inheritance
from anybody, and whatever he earns is bequeathed to his
sisters and their descendants. The large, flat tombstones bear
the name of the clan mother; behind them, upright stones
name the male, uterine relatives. The living social units,
called *maharis*, or "motherhoods," have only a few variations
in custom: the Synteg, the Khasi, the Garos, and the Lalung.
The Synteg are the strictest conservatives; the Lalung, closest to disintegration. Males are not permitted to court females
and are not allowed any games of coyness customary among
even the most primitive peoples with matrilocal institutions.

In the long run, it makes no difference which sex does the
courting, if only the initial delay creates imaginative antici-
pation, if the tension of love preserves the precious potential.
The mother clans of Assam, however, seem to lack any ten-

sion, emotional upset, triumph, or other spiritual exploitation of sexuality. Neither the woman nor the man is conquered. There is no more than the tepid tolerance of the man as a "seeder." In this respect, Assam society resembles the old Amazon states, where an ethical standard required the women to engage in the sex act with any male chosen at random to the exclusion of the man's personality. The existence of the maharis remains without drama as a superficial morass pond with chromosomes, where there is no gradation.

The task and significance of strictly matriarchal clans, according to Briffault's perspicacious statement, lay in the codification of certain altruistic commandments for all of society which are necessary for its survival. In the opinion of many other anthropologists, the maternal instincts of protecting the young, weak, and helpless signify a weakening of the male's original instincts; such commandments are nothing original. In Assam, the pattern of aboriginal matriarchy became rigid because of a premature cessation in its evolution; apparently the inner rhythm only functions feebly; dependents were protected too long and thus always remained dependent; the ingrained customs failed to change when their time came. Life, to the extent that it is vital, however, consists of incessant successions achieved in triumph over the inner inhibitions of stubborn fears, and its last, crowning achievement is rewarded as a talented death, the required proof of a perfect personality.

Of the women of Central Asia, it was said, at a time when those regions were still rich and enjoyed a high standard of living:

> "They have more servants and pages at their disposal than the men, ride their horses in great state and adorn their houses with gold and jewels, but they are not chaste and unreservedly indulge in intercourse with strangers; their husbands find no fault with them for this reason, for their husbands are subject to their rule."

Today, this area is inhabited by Turkoman tribes, but wherever their original home may have been, it was from this region that the Aryans at one time invaded northern India. In all descriptions of their physiques and their customs, we get about the same picture, regardless of whether we are presented with portraits of Indo-Scythians, or *saka;* the *get-ti* of Chinese reports; or the *jat* in the Punjab; the same picture they presented in Vedic times: long-legged, slender, with dense, dark-blond hair, light, sharp, deep eyes, and, since all of them considered themselves of noble origin, without slaves. Their most important holiday was the sacrifice of the horse. They had an extraordinary respect for their women, who participated in all phases of the men's lives, and they had polyandry as well as matriarchy.

The "five nations" of Vedic Aryans, descended from the "five Jayati sons," traced themselves back to Ita, their creatress and the source of their name, as did the first Indo-Aryan dynasts, the moon or *parava* rulers. The demigods of the epics, the Pandavas of the Mahabharata, were called after their tribal mother Pandaia. All five Pandava brothers were married to the princess Draupadi. Since the five brothers lived in separate palaces with gardens, she rotated by living with each one for two days.

A later princess of the house of the Pandava undertook the expedition to Lanka (Ceylon) and founded her kingdom there; her seven brothers were sent after her by her mother, and each one, as regent, then received a part of the country from his sister. The Maura dynasty, founder of the first Greater Indian realm, with the illustrious kings Chandragupta and Asoka, the promoter of Buddhism, was also derived from a woman, Maura, and received its right to the kingship through her. King Gautamiputra named himself exclusively after his mother Gautami, without concerning himself about his real name, Satakarni.

Polyandry, seen by itself, is not a certain indication of matriarchy, but it belongs to the other symptoms. In the Vedic epics it is rather the rule. Draupadi was married to five brothers; another princess was married to ten. In a Vedic hymn, the Aswins, the divine charioteers and Indian Dioscures, were greeted by a woman after their triumph in the races, hailed and recognized by her as her two husbands. And in the Rig-Veda it says: "In the distance, the resplendent Maruts admire their young wife, who belongs to them all in common." Polyandry of brothers seems to have been a common usage among the Aryans and is commonly found; in the Scandinavian myths, Frigga is the wife of Odin and his brothers, We and Wili.

The greatest and most powerful enemy of the women's free participation in the affairs of the world was the Brahman priesthood after its victory over the warrior caste of the *Kshatriyahs*. In the earliest parts of the Vedas, generally believed to have been composed after the Aryan invasion of India, or in the twelfth century B.C., those two castes were still almost the same; in those days, we read about "the noble woman, accompanied by men, supervising the sacrifice," though the Brahmans later excluded women from all religious and official actions, and the women were no longer allowed even to read the sacred writings, which they had helped write.

The great national epics, a collection of ballads about heroes and knights, edited by Brahmans, still showed both tendencies side by side, but also give a clue of the suddenness with which the change must have come. In the Mahabharata, Pandy says to Kunty, his young wife:

"Now I will tell thee of the old customs as they were indicated by the illustrious Rishis, well acquainted with every rule of ethics. Hear, then, O woman of the beautiful face with the sweet smile, that formerly the women were not locked in the houses, dependent on husbands and relatives. They were accustomed freely to walk where they pleased, amusing themselves as best they could. In no way, thou woman of wonderful character, were they faithful to their men, and they were not adjudged guilty for that reason, for this was the accepted custom of the times . . . Truly that custom, so indulgent with the women, has the blessings of venerability. The present custom, on the other hand, that they are bound to one man for life, was established a short time ago."

After the rise of a sacerdotal estate among the Aryans in India, this estate busied itself primarily with the elimination of the woman from its sphere. She had played the major role in the *asvamedha*, the sacrifice of the horse; its ritual of fertility magic was acted out as a kind of sacred marriage exclusively between the queen and the slaughtered horse, originally perhaps with the stallion still alive, while the male only assisted. This had to be changed altogether. In the Mahabharata, there is a very significant passage: "The law has been established that the woman has nothing to do with sacred ceremonies, for there is a revelation about this. . . ." "The wife achieves heaven only through obedience toward her husband."

In the book of Manu, finally—the work of Brahmans, not of warrior princes—Hindu patriarchy achieves an absoluteness surpassing even that of Rome. According to it, the woman may never indulge in her own will but must remain subject to her father while a girl, to her husband as a wife, and to her son when a widow. "No matter how wicked, degenerate, or devoid of all good qualities a man may be, a good wife must also revere him like a god." On the other hand, a Vedic hymn proclaimed: "May she be absolute mistress over her fathers-in-law, absolute mistress over her mother-in-law, let her rule over her husband's sisters, rule over her husband's brothers." Even among the Brahmans, there still are remnants of matriarchy: the Brahmans of the Bengal, for instance, recognize as family priest only the son of a sister.

Independently from the Aryans, who had matriarchy but gave it up, the Dravidian races had always had it and retained it under independent rulers and in the south, where the Brahman influence did not penetrate. In the area of Malabar and Travancor, travelers found several female-ruled states, "where apparently only queens could rule." Shuddering at such "degeneracy," Meiners at the end of the eighteenth century wrote about a kingdom of Attinga, whose sole woman ruler, obligated to remain single, kept lovers as her whim might dictate: "For this reason, the most handsome youths of her court comprise her seraglio."

The same custom, as well as a succession to the throne in an exclusively female line, has been proved to be too typical by dozens of African examples for any doubts to arise regarding the reluctantly given data of older travelers about similar conditions in India. They only confirm a tradition that has been temporarily eclipsed. Strabo tells us of the ladies of Indian courts, who knew how to handle weapons of war and accompanied the warriors to battle. Only as residues of such an ancient instinct can one understand such phenomena as whole armies being led enthusiastically and unhesitatingly by women as their hereditary leaders, as for example during the Indian uprising of the famous Rani of Ghansi.

A guest at the house of a Portuguese family with traditions of foreign trade may hear the lady or the daughter of the house addressed by a hereditary first name which delights his ear as different from the other. Romance sounds. Nair. What might it be? A jewel? A tropical frankincense? Or a new variety of fine pride.

Nair, or Nayar, is the name of the aristocratic caste of the Tamiles on the Malabar coast, the southernmost strip of India, apart from the present lanes of world trade. The noble tradition of the Nair, their highest stratum, is ancient. According to their testimony, there never has been a single marriage for as long as that tradition reaches back that was not based on love and was not borne by pure feeling, unadulterated by economic or socially ambitious influences. For this reason, they have always been subjected to adverse ethical judgment. Other people said that sort of thing was no real marriage and did not even count.

Bothered with questions by governmental representatives and commissions, the Nair explained that their weddings were the "talikettu"-ceremony, the tying of the tali in the ninth or the eleventh year. But it was proved by outsiders that this was only a puberty ritual, not a wedding ceremony. The female initiate is not given to a designated partner in this rite; rather, she is declared available for sexual intercourse—and that with anybody. In token of this freedom she was given a pierced gold leaf to wear on a thread around her neck, which is customary also with other Dravidian peoples. It indicates symbolically that there would be no obstacle to a love affair with the young tali wearer. The obstacle itself is removed by a stranger, who represents their god, a Brahman priest, or some other initiate of sacred things, whom the evil magic of the hymen's bleeding cannot harm. But whoever that may be, he receives no rights to the girl; rather, he loses whatever rights he ever possessed as a possible husband. His service is singular, and further approaches are forbidden. The fiancé or the husband will hardly ever be chosen to perform this operation, which is considered entirely mechanical: it is unavoidable but unemotional.

After the tying of the tali, the little Nair lady is free for the rest of her life to choose whom she would and for as long as she wants. One word severs the relationship at the discretion of either partner. A young woman may also have several simultaneous husbands, if she wants, as long as they are her social equals. Relations with a man of lower caste is the only thing that is considered adulterous or denigrating, just as it would be dishonorable for a Nair male to sleep with nonnoble women.

On the other hand, there are no economic obstacles. Neither the man nor the woman can gain money or prestige through love. The woman remains in her family home, at any rate, giving birth to her children, who are not believed related to their father and are reared at her private expense or that of her clan. The man in the strictest sense of the word is the guest of the house, husband but never a father, takes none of his meals there, and has no duties to support anybody. It is customary for him to bring small presents, but it is not compulsory. A Nair can derive no advantage from, or be humiliated by, his wife's or wives' greater wealth. And if he happens to be the wealthier partner his wife and children gain no advantage from this fact, for his possessions never cease belonging to his own uterine clan and are inherited after his death by or through his sisters. K. Kennan Nayar (the word means "lord") relates of the customs of his caste:

> "Matrimony among the Nair remains truly pure and simple. It is matrimony only for the sake of matrimony, not intended for the perpetuation of the family but rather a social institution for the peaceful satisfaction of the blindest human instinct. Such an institution is, then, demonstrably possible without the slightest disturbance of the civil law regulating the inheritance of family properties."

Thus love was allowed to live here unencumbered as nowhere else according to its own laws, embroiled only in those intensifying conflicts arising from the demonism of erotics itself. The result were people who were as straight as could be, living in the pure agitation of their blood, ignorant of the fact that there could be such a thing as a woman living on the bread of her man, free of the defilement of dependence, secure all their lives. They lived without crudeness and without injury in the tellurian yet divine matrix of an unalienable family home. The women lived in their own houses which were more than mere homes and were beings of sophisticated discretion, filled in every pore with that charm called *shakti,* "the indescribable emanation of Woman," as Tagore calls it.

When the Portuguese in their great period landed as bold adventurers on that blissful stretch of the Malabar coast, impressed by the inhabitants' standard of living and initially uncertain as to how to proceed, they were actually begged by these exclusive nobles—could they believe their ears?—to take from their brides or young daughters that flower which stood in the way of their marriage. Such a foreigner was then magnaminously entertained, honored, and laden with gifts. Instead of tears, horror, stammered laments for something irreplaceable, he received only the friendly thanks of his hosts. Was it possible to have done everything with a girl child and not to mean a thing to her? For that was one thing about which the hosts never let the guest remain in doubt: a second night, anything like an attempt to repeat the adventure, would mean his certain death. Therefore, he had really been little different from a servant on the carriage or, to express it more charitably, one who generously opens the door for others and wishes them Godspeed.

Having returned home from successful voyages full of adventures and profit, the Portuguese trader during his pleasant reminiscences probably did not exactly emphasize this aspect of his scurrilous exploit, for it was associated with melancholy and relinquishment. Why should such a merchant–adventurer be especially touched by this episode, once he returned with a good cargo of ivory and copra? But when, perhaps several years afterward, he became a father and was told he had a little girl, the whole Christian calendar with all its good saints had no name like Nair to strike a familiar or sentimental cord in the merchant's soul. Finally, perhaps contrary to the protestations of his wife and his priest, that is what he called the girl child.

XIII

CHINA, JAPAN, AND FORMOSA

When the Tartars of Genghis Khan came to China, they found the streets full of lightly clad, free, and natural women without the "lotus feet." So did the hordes of Tamerlane. The Jesuits, a century after him, found chaste, domesticated cripples so shy that they deemed baptism an indecent act. The pretty pictures of Catholic saints with bare feet and loose garments, with the sleeves leaving the lower arm free, were studied by the Chinese but only as pornography, which certainly was far from the intentions of the missionaries. Even the manners of the courtesan insisted on keeping one's distance except for the actual assignation—a refined kind of sexuality.

The style dictated by an unlimited patriarchy in the Chinese upper classes imposed a kind of schism upon the woman, who became the bearer of children as well as the *hoa-niu* ("daughter of flowers"), an exquisite enjoyment for the male viewer. But the social position of the woman, despite the courteous manners, was very bad during the period of the greatest culture in China, and that even irrespective of the killing of female babies, which was designed to save the great expenses of a wedding, while male babies were heartily welcomed because of the exigencies of ancestor worship. An upper-class girl hardly left her house after her seventh year and remained entirely ignorant. Marriage was an economic and social matter arranged by the two families, an institution designed for producing progeny without any human attachments and calculated to secure legitimate paternity. The first wife, representing obedient loyalty, dignity, purity of the blood, self-discipline, was often joined later by subsidiary wives. Outside the house, there was an inspired sensuality with the aid of "free women," the finest selection of charm and erotic talents. From the patriarchal standpoint, this was a logical and complete fulfillment of all demands which could hardly be satisfied by a single female type.

By comparison with Chinese hetaerism, the much over-estimated Greek variety was a mere barbarian dilettantism. "There certainly were several gradations of *hoa-niu*," A. P. L. Bazin reports.

Before a young girl could gain admission to the highest caste of "red and green districts," where the prostitutes lived together like sisters, she had to be outstanding in beauty, charm, and intelligence, had to master singing, flute and guitar playing, history, and philosophy. In addition, it was incumbent upon her to know how to make all ideographs contained in the teachings of Lao-tse, the so-called Tao Te Ching. After spending several months in the "pavilion of a hundred flowers" and learning the last refinements of song and dance, she was entitled to be addressed "free woman." Now she was rid of the onerous burdens of her sex, giving birth and breast feeding, and might well feel superior to a young girl under her father's strict control, to a legal concubine under the thumb of her master, and to the legitimate wife, watched over by her husband, or the widow, controlled by her son.

The singular political influence exerted by "the daughters of flowers" in China is really a part of the male—and not the female—cultural history, for "female" characteristics could come to the fore only indirectly in it.

Professor R. Wilhelm, a sinologist of renown, traced matriarchal institutions in China through the third dynasty. Then the Chou family completed the formation of the father clan with the exogamy of the woman.

But in older times, it is said, people knew their mothers and not their fathers. Early clan names were compounds of the noun for "woman," and the very word which means "family name" today uses the ideograph for "woman" in memory of those times. These hundred clans, counted by their mothers, made up the "people liable for military service." All of this would indicate an original matriarchal society, which probably was not abolished without a fight.

Professor Wilhelm also deduces from sacrificial ceremonies for the ancestral spirits of the household, in which the first wife always had to take part, that women occupied a preeminent position in former times. Down to the twentieth century, uterine relatives occupied such a position in marriage negotiations. The Chinese word for wedding is *hunyin,* "to take a husband."

At a time when women could no longer hold public office in China, there still were powerful empresses, who did not rule for minor sons but because they themselves held power. In the first two centuries of the Christian era, there were three great and quite despotic empresses. Every empress dowager, moreover, selected the first wife of the emperor and usually placed her own brothers in his ministries—a sign of an avunculate.

In Japan, on the other hand, it was the common people who preserved matriarchal characteristics for a long time after the samurai caste slavishly emulated Chinese patriarchy. The lower social levels continued to have divorce and remarriage equally easy and customary for both partners. The woman was treated with respect and at the slightest provocation exercises her right of dismissing her husband. Old Japanese family law was entirely uterine until the fourteenth century and marriage was matrilocal: the woman remained in her own home and received her husband only for visits.

On politically disputed Formosa, Janet MacGovern found entirely gynocratic conditions. The Paiwans had a woman chief, and the dignity was always bequeathed by the mother to the daughter. The Taiyals, another Formosan tribe, elected a priestess–queen to make rain magic and for successful head hunts; her verdict decided legal disputes, and everyone had to obey. Land, hunting rights, and all possessions belonged exclusively to the female clans. The men were not allowed in storage chambers or agricultural workrooms. Before Formosa became Japanese in 1895, no youth was allowed to marry before he had killed at least one Chinese.

Of the Lit-si on the island of Hainan (near southern China), Wolter reports: "Women in all things have the last word with them and the men submit unconditionally. The women are occupied with agriculture, while the men hunt."

An American expedition under F. R. Wulsin encountered a pre-Chinese tribe near the sources of the Hoang-ho with the "old woman" form of matriarchy, which gave the old women all offices and dignity. There was an easily dissoluble form of polyandry, and the children considered as their father whomever their mothers designated as such, while calling all other men "uncle." These designations, however, had no significance, for name and property were inherited in the female line. Only women had the right to carry on trade, for all goods that could be traded belonged to them.

There were two other areas governed by princesses in southern China. "The Man-Tseu, a tribe of three and a half million people," according to W. Gill, "are governed by a queen of the sacred clan, in which the royal power has been hereditary, though it can only be exercised by a woman." J. Gray reports of the other female kingdom: "It is worth mentioning that one of the native tribes is always governed by a woman, a sovereign whom her subjects give the title *Noi-Tak*. They give her the deepest respects; the whole tribe is known as *Nue-kun*, "the ones governed by women." The privilege of governing the tribes is resident in the female members of a single family, so that there is little prospect of a dispute for the succession at the death of a ruler. Since the Chinese generally find it odd that Great Britain and other countries not subject to Salic Law are independently ruled by women from time to time, they are somewhat inclined to call the natives of such countries, especially the British, little superior, if at all, to the *Nue-kun* tribe.

XIV

TIBETAN MATRIARCHY

Chomo-Lungma, "God-Mother of the Country," or *Chomo-Uri*, "Mother of the Turquoise Peak," is the name of Tibet's—and the world's—highest mountain. Tibetans find it as natural to call the cornerstone of the earth "Mother" as the English call it by the name of a gentleman, Mount Everest.

Tibet's blessing of having fewer inhabitants than it could comfortably feed is probably due to its ancient practice of polyandry, which has been vigorously defended by its women. Perhaps they achieved the change of an original group marriage into the current polyandry of brothers. Probably it was customary in the beginning for all brothers of one clan to marry all the sisters in the other, not only the one who now commands all the working and erotic energies of a family by herself.

Tibetan women like to inveigh indignantly against the unholy barbarism which permits Western women only one husband. They do not understand how a woman in such circumstances can be well supplied with the necessities of life. They think the more the better. A Tibetan male with one brother or only a few can hardly manage to persuade a woman to become his wife. "Don't you think, too, that we Tibetan women are much better off?" inquired one Tibetan lady, when she learned of the strange, monogamous habits abroad. "In our society, the housewife is the real owner of the combined incomes and inheritance of all the brothers, all of them descended from one mother, all one flesh and blood, for brothers are a unit, even if they have separate souls." And since all the brothers she has married count only for one, the wife has the recognized right to complete her connubial bliss with other, strange men, whom she may pick at random.

While she couples with these outside mates, the brother–husbands are not at all at liberty to add new private wives to their association, although each brother is allowed to marry outside his home for a limited period of time, be it months, weeks, or years, without losing his rights to his home.

Two entirely different family systems coexist here: easily dissoluble individual marriages and the almost irrevocable group marriage as a result of a contract entered into between two clans. When the oldest brother, who concluded the marriage through the purchase of the bride, dies, the widow is passed on to the oldest surviving brother, his legal successor. Gynocratic Tibet, then, is patriarchal in its group marriage, for the bride is acquired through money purchase, remains a possession of the strange clan, and, if she is not a rich heiress herself, moves into the clan she enters, although there is neither an individual father nor a paternal family in the true sense of the word. Children bear the mother's name and remain the property of the family.

Group sentiments count for everything. So much does the woman feel responsible for her acquired clan and its welfare that she, if her mother-in-law should die and leave a male infant, would nurse him and rear him till manhood as well as add him to her husbands after he reaches puberty as if it were the most natural thing in the world. If the woman herself dies, her sister enters into succession with the widowed brothers, even though she might have become a nun—as is often the case. There is no obstacle to her sexual reactivation.

Here in Tibet, the well-known female power is not derived from priesthood or magic, but from naïve confidence in the natural ability of the female sex. It is the Central Asiatic aspect of matriarchy, predominantly secular and often culminating in military leadership. Savage Landor observes: "The Tibetan woman is far superior to the man, never shy; while the men ran away or hid from the foreigners, the women always received them with dignity, speaking fluently and unreservedly. . . . They have more heart and more character than the men. . . ." The entire, very significant trade in metals, wool and woolen cloth, furs, musk, and borax was conducted from the days of old by a supreme council of women. "The women buy and sell," says Messer Marco

Polo, and a Chinese report calls the reader's attention to the fact that no business deal might be concluded without the consent of a group of women.

Defloration of virgins was the only use this xenophobic nation had for foreigners. Once the blood taboo, the danger, the blood gushing out with the torn hymen has been removed from the girl, the young females are entirely free to do as they please. The value and reputation of a woman rises according to the number of her premarital lovers, whose number is made visible to all through pendants to be worn around the neck. It was for this reason that the governor of Leh did not understand what the Marquis of Cortanze was after when he asked which one of the brothers would be the first allowed to cohabit with the bride after the wedding. He replied it probably would usually be the oldest, but this was inconsequential.

An annual festival of general commingling called "choice of hats" gives any man who is able to steal this emblem of power from his dancing partner the right to own her that day. On the other hand, the great value of a married woman lies in the fact that she has been acquired as the administratress of all the brothers' property for life. "In that country, the women are the mistresses of the house. The men live in dependency upon them, show them great respect, and treat them with such affection and submissiveness that nothing is undertaken without their consent."

This description, however, only applies to the genuine, inner Tibet, with animal husbandry and venerable polyandry. In the luscious dales of agriculture, toward India, conservatism has been crowded out by unregulated polygamy, the prostitution of children, a system of brothels, and corruption of domestic life. By comparison, the polyandry of brothers is much cleaner in its effects, at least in that form in which it has been practiced since the heroic age in its old strongholds, starting at the Chinese borders and going through Tibet, Kashmir, Afghanistan, practiced even by people of pure Aryan blood, the Radjputani, and still existent among many millions of people.

The cause to which this institution has been most frequently attributed is poverty, but it is prevalent precisely in well-situated circles. Another cause was supposed to be a lack of women. But why should there be such a lack? Any possible surplus of males is swallowed by the monasteries, for one out of every four Tibetans is a lama, while the number of nuns is much smaller. Nor is it likely that female babies are being destroyed to create an artificial shortage. According to most eye-witness reports, there is a surplus of women in Tibet, who have to migrate to the valleys. Other causes often given include the conditions of life occasioned by animal husbandry. Certainly the pasturing of animals takes the herdsman far away from his wife, but there are many patriarchal animal herders who do not for that reason institute polyandry. These other herdsmen take no pleasure in the certitude that, thanks to their providence, their wives are being kept warm by other men.

One has searched for the cause of polyandry everywhere except where it might really be found, which is with the woman. At any rate, the most capable types of women insist on being secular leaders of a whole clan of men. Perhaps these women inherited this trend from the not-so-distant times when the men, and even a whole nation, received their orders from a queen in the center of a palace and gladly carried out their ruler's will. Now, after the fall of that great female kingdom, it seems that the great system is being perpetuated by a large number of small and similar cells. Those who no longer fit into the old tribe and its ways of doing things migrate into the valleys, which have adapted themselves more to Indian ways.

XV

THE MERRY WIVES
OF KAMCHATKA

G. W. Steller, the first Central European to tour the peninsula of drift-ice, seals, and flying salmon, reported in the eighteenth century: "They love their women so much that they are their veritable slaves. The wife always has the final say and keeps anything of value. The man is her cook and worker." He was taken aback by the phenomenon of the matrilocal service marriage and strongly disapproved. It was, according to him, at the root of these unnatural conditions: "This kind of marriage was the first step in the regime of the women and the subordination of the men, who must constantly flatter their brides, please them, and lie at their feet."

Furthermore, he took issue with the women for "always aspiring to freedom in all things, looking for strange lovers, being insatiable, and making this a matter of pride, so that she who can count the greatest number of lovers is considered the luckiest one." Although both sexes went fishing together and cleaned and dried the fish, the women still kept "all stores at their disposal."

The result, in turn, was especially irksome for Steller's contemporary Meiners:

> "If the men offend against their wives, the latter deny them not only the connubial embrace but also their tobacco, which is more indispensable than alcohol for the Kamchatkans. The men secure the satisfaction of this need and the favors of their women not by force but by the most humble pleadings and caresses."

But, if the women did not persist in primness, he thought that was still worse than the denial of sexual satisfaction:

"The Kamchatkan women are no less brazen than their men and not only give vent to the most unnatural lusts publicly and before the very eyes of their children, but they also give birth to their infants in public and surrender to the embraces of their husbands and lemans without reluctance, like the dumb animals."

The Vaertings, on the other hand, were delighted with the Kamchatkans because they provide support for the theory of the reverse division of labor in female-dominated society and the higher female intelligence as a result of this condition. The men do not like to leave home and children, even for a few hours, and never want to be without their womenfolk, since, according to Steller, "the women do so much work that one must suppose them to have more intelligence than the men, which is, indeed, in conformity with the facts." Another traveler reports: "In Kamchatka, the men are under the iron thumb of the women."

One is reminded of Tibetan conditions by Meiners' remark: "The greatest recommendation of an unmarried girl is an unusual number of lovers to whom she has given her caresses; such a girl can hope for so much the more love on the part of her future husband if she can show concrete proofs of her experience in love." If a bridegroom finds that his bride is a virgin, he is accustomed to engage in recriminations with his mother-in-law because of her insufficient attention to the girl's education. Of course, the women were completely at liberty to interrupt pregnancies. The numerical decline of the population, however, is not to be attributed to this habit—otherwise, all matriarchal societies must die out—even though there were only four thousand of them left in 1910. Rather, it is due to Russian alcohol and infection with diseases by unscrupulous Cossacks.

The Lapp and Eskimo women are not as gynocratically organized as the Kamchatkans, although independent and superior to the men in some ways. They often spurn any permanent attachment to a man, build their own huts, make their own nets, weapons, and gear with which they go hunting and fishing alone. The Great Mother of the Eskimos is called "She who wants to take no spouse."

XVI

THE MALAYS

The Malays do not look as if they would ever fight for anything but material possessions, and yet, during the last century they waged the Pandrie War in western Sumatra to defend their ancient matriarchy and still defend it against aggressive Islam in a weaponless, though tough and successful, battle, even though a certain decay cannot be overlooked. The Malays probably brought matriarchy with them from Central Asia, from where they migrated by way of India to the region named after them. The autochthonous population, related to the Australians, soon had to give way to the superior abilities of the Malays. All through the Malayan area—and that is a substantial piece of the tropics—there is matriarchy, even though it occurs in various gradations. The conservative form still exists in the large, rich clans of Sumatra, whose members are called *sabuah parui* ("of one belly") or *samandai* ("having one mother"). Tender consideration for women is usually greater in Sumatra than in Europe, a fact noted in old travelogues.

"Adult and married men may live only in the prayer-house, not in the clan house of the women. Children are born into the mother's family, which supports and rears them. The man, even though rich and respected, does not move into the wife's house but only spends a night with her from time to time. Inside her maternal house, she receives her own apartment and utensils as she needs them. Children inherit from the mother, not the father. His possessions are inherited by his sister's children, as are his titles and honors." (Nieuwenhuis)

The man has no influence whatever upon the life and education of his progeny, with whom he is not considered related.

The mother's oldest brother may attain dignity and leadership; the avunculate is noticeable here, always an indication that the period of change-over into patriarchy has arrived. The strength of the clans lies in their excellent administration and resulting prosperity. Wherever they fail in these respects, the men succeed in buying the women out of the female clan and to detaching them in every other sense from the economy of their families in order to incorporate them into their own. The sexes apparently enjoy an undramatic, concrete relationship, with the woman keeping the upper hand, because she keeps the lead in sensual matters.

The Malayan race also includes the Dyaks of North Borneo, notorious for their head-hunting and their ingenious manner of preparing the captured heads. This sport would have died out a great deal earlier if the women had not required these marks of courage before they consented to bestow their favors on a man. Dyak women equal the men in size, strength, and endurance. Reared like Amazons, they go to battle alongside their men or defend their villages alone against the enemy if their men are absent. Every one of them carries a spear and goes hunting with dogs.

Female physicians in Borneo are paid better than their male colleagues. Priestesses exercise the most important religious functions, using a language unknown to the men; they conduct the sacrifices and dance the sword dance, that highest warlike ceremony for the incantation of victory. All Nature and tribal ghosts who are believed to be the power resources from which one can obtain favors by special rituals are called "grandmothers."

Charles Brooke, the successor of his uncle, Sir James Brooke, the founder of the sultanate of Sarawak on North Borneo, demonstrated the greatest delight with Dyak women and considered them far more adept at political matters than the men. According to his statements, the Lingga tribes of Northeast Borneo were for many years ruled by two noble old women. The large island is something of an index of possible forms of matrimony, but premarital sexual freedom has been a well-used tradition throughout, even though the annual festival of promiscuous commingling—a fertility magic—

lasts for only a quarter of an hour, after which complete law and order are restored.

The customs of sea and mountain Dyaks are different. For instance, the tests of male courage demanded by the mountain women are as stringent as those of the American Indians. If a girl puts flaming objects into her admirer's arms, he must let these things burn out there without moving a muscle. The deep, white scars of this torture are considered erotically very attractive. Opinions vary as to whether the fantastic forms of circumcision, including the placement of odd objects into the wound to prevent it from closing, are a consequence of female domination.

At any rate, such rites are found wherever matriarchal Malays live or wherever—as in Burma—their influence is strong. J. H. van Linschotten saw men there whose glans penis was encumbered in front by bells the size of hazelnuts or even walnuts. Some ethnologists, cultural philosophers, and physicians believe this practice to be a counter piece of that painful operation ordained by tyrannical patriarchy which demands the maiming of the women. For instance, the Nubian women were sewn up, and the Chinese women used to have their feet crippled, for no reason other than increasing the pleasure of the dominant sex. Ploss, agreeing with this opinion, reports:

> "In order to increase the woman's enjoyment of the love act, many Dyaks pierce their glans penis with a silver needle from the top to the bottom; they leave the needle in there until the pierced portion has healed up as an inner passage. Before the assignation, a firmly implanted apparatus is then placed into this passage which brings about a strong friction and thus materially increases the sexual pleasure of the woman. The objects inserted into the passage vary: small staffs of brass, ivory, or silver, or even of bamboo."

Sometimes a ribbon made of the lid hair of a he goat, with the whole border of the lid, is tied around the male organ, looking like a dog collar. Another apparatus, carrying bristles in the staffs, is called *ampallang*. The woman symbolically indicates to the man that she would like such a stimulant: he finds in his rice bowl a *siri* leaf with a cigarette inserted whose length indicates the measurement of the desired *ampallang*. The variables of this practice are countless. On Sumatra, the prepuce merely has an incision performed on it; triangular gold or silver pieces or rocks are inserted under it to grow into the skin. In Borneo, one uses brass wire with cloven ends protruding like tassels. We know for certain that Malay women prefer men with such provisions and reject others who have not made them.

The extent of this painful and dangerous operation, no doubt, is due to female rule; whether its origin is attributable to men or women is something we do not know. The question is complicated by the wide popularity of similar incisions for the insertion of objects near other apertures, such as ears, nose, and mouth, where they have no influence upon erotic enjoyments and serve instead as protection against the evil eye. We should also consider the world-wide custom of holding one's hand in front of one's mouth while yawning, for it originated as a defensive measure and much later received an aesthetic motivation. Body apertures as such are considered in constant danger of invasion by black magic and believed in need of gold plates, bristles, boar teeth, rocks, and other proven amulets. The precious sex organs, so exposed in the case of the man, must be protected by counter magic, which may well use shiny objects such as gold, silver, or metal bells.

Symbolic, instinctive, and magic actions, however, are closely enough related to vary quite a bit and have one function overlap another. The Romans wore silver crescents, *lunulae*, on their shoes, to indicate their maternal descent and, at the same time, to acquire the protection of the metal against the evil eye. The evil element deprived of its more important booty, then sank down to the end of the body where it could barely menace the toes. It is possible that the bell, though a widely recognized symbol of the libido, serves as a talisman when used on a Malay's male organ.

In all matters connected with puberty rites, that is, with circumcision, it is especially difficult to decide what is primary and what is secondary and where there are overlapping motives. A certain kind of scar may sometimes be a tribal membership certificate or a passport into the tribal heaven, ensuring that one does not enter the hereafter assigned to one's enemies.

It would never do, of course, to deny the influence of female sexual tastes upon the kind of incisions made at Malayan puberty rites or the amulets placed inside, as some anthropologists have done; there is too much evidence to the contrary. On the Aru Islands and neighboring Serong, near New Guinea, the circumcision of the boys is carried out according to the detailed wishes of the girls and in a certain manner "designed to heighten the woman's sexual pleasure in the love act." (Riedel) Perhaps an originally unintended, coincidental side effect has become the main purpose, as so often happens. There have been other, even more definitely matriarchal societies which did not demand anything like this from the man, but they may simply have had a less erotic temperament. Any carnal sensation intensified by freedom and self-determination naturally seeks to fit the partner's body into its own wishful fantasies.

XVII

NORTH AMERICA

The North American Indian face of matriarchy has always been self-possessed and rough-boned but, with the single exception of the Natchez, who turned from lunar to solar worship with great violence, it never was domineeringly harsh. It remained the experienced face of the old woman who never dies, from coast to coast and from Alaska down to Mexico. To be sure, there were some patriarchal Indian tribes, but, by and large, North America was an overwhelmingly matriarchal and democratic continent, so much so that the tide of immigrants gradually absorbed this ancestral soul. This appears to be a physical process, too, for according to a well-known experiment, a thousand faces of third-generation immigrants, superimposed on the same photograph, yield the picture of an Indian. Because of this tradition, this matriarchal-democratic soil never spawned a real monarchy. There only were chiefs with designated duties, local predecessors of the elective President, who temporarily acted upon certain dangers.

Typical Indian society approximately corresponded to Father Lafiteau's observations on the five great tribes of the Iroquois in the east:

> "All real authority rests in the women of the country. The fields and all harvests belong to them. They are the soul of the councils, the arbiters of war and peace, and the guardians of the public fisc. It is to them that the prisoners are delivered. They arrange for the weddings, govern the children, and determine the laws of inheritance according to their blood."

Some of these Iroquois dealt especially severely with their young men in sexual matters: they were excluded entirely

from the girls of their own clan and married off by their
mothers into another, according to the exogamous rule, usually to much older women. This typically matriarchal symptom was not necessarily based on unilateral egotism, since
the youths of this type of society retain a long-lived fixation
on their mother image. Indians marry many times, and they
could later choose other wives entirely untrammeled. The
exclusion from the huts of their own clan is the exogamous
rule, which has entirely different origins.

So strongly does the significance of the female inheritance
predominate in the Indian mind that, when the Cayugas had
lost most of their manpower in the constant wars of the sixteenth century, they asked the Mohawks to send them some
men for their women, so that their tribe should not die out.
Had the Cayugas observed patriarchal laws, they would have
sent for wives for their remaining men in order not to die out,
but with them it was the female bloodstream that counted.

The most typical image of matriarchal Indian communal
life is presented by the Seneca, the main tribe of the Iroquois.
Prior to the arrival of the Europeans, the Seneca inhabited
long houses built by the women; separate bedchambers lay
to the right and the left, while the dining-hall with the fireplace was in the middle. This mother house, or *hodensote*,
some sixty to a hundred feet long, was ruled by the women.
Men of alien clans were accepted as husbands, but the
women watched and parceled out the food stores, and woe
to the hapless husband or lover who had neglected to con-
tribute his share! No matter how many children he had procreated or how much private property he had in the *hodensote*, he had to be ready at any moment to pick up his blanket
and leave. Disobedience was neither advisable nor salutary:
if no old aunt or grandmother intervened in his behalf in the
last moment, he had to start looking for a different woman in
another clan. The divorce proceedings consisted entirely in
the woman's placing the man's bedding outside the door.

Yet the man, too, was free to leave any time and often did.
Delaware and Iroquois braves almost always left their
women when they were pregnant. Many braves also left during the long breast-feeding period and then proceeded to
repeat the same pattern of behavior with the next squaw.

Half-brothers and half-sisters therefore abounded in most friendly tribes, though they often did not know one another. Sometimes they married each other, since they were not related according to matriarchal law.

The Indians also practiced polygamy and polyandry, the remnants of ancient group marriages of brothers and sisters, which permitted sexual intercourse between a man and all of his wife's sisters or between a wife and all of her husband's brothers. Such was the case with the Seneca and other Iroquois, the Dene in Alaska, the Kiowa, Mandans, and Omahas, as well as the Sauks and Fox, along the Mississippi. It was the custom, though not compulsory. In Vancouver, a husband acquired hunting rights only through his wife; "after the divorce, the right reverted back to her and comprised her dowry for her next marriage." Except for exogamy, there hardly were any limitations on people's sex life, as much lamented by Father Theodat:

> "The young men are at liberty to pursue evil as soon as they become able, and the same applies to the girls. Father and mother often arrange assignations for their daughters. At night, girls and women run from one sleeping chamber to the next; the young men do the same and take pleasure where they find it, though without application of force: they can trust entirely that they will meet with the good will of the women. Husbands do the same with regard to the neighbor's wife and wives regarding the neighboring husband. Of jealousy, one can see none with them, and they consider their behavior neither shameful nor a disgrace."

This specific description pertains to the Wyandotte Hurons, whose political organization also was entirely matriarchal.

The inclination of the Indian braves to leave their squaws when they became pregnant naturally caused the women to undertake frequent interruptions of pregnancy. The young girls of the happy Plains tribes, such as the Creeks and the Cherokees, performed skillful and effective abortions and did so normally, since their erotic valuation rose with the number of their lovers. This premarital career with excellent chances of marriage was not intended to be sacrificed to accident.

Primitive nations have always viewed chastity or maidenhood as a form of insanity much to be pitied.

In matriarchal society, the free disposition over one's body leads to a good knowledge of its laws. African women are especially well-famed for their natural methods of preventing pregnancy through a muscular contraction practiced from an early age, whereas in extremely patriarchal nations, where sometimes the first two children are killed, the sexually ignorant and stunted women have to endure all the pains of pregnancy and birth for nothing. On the Solomon Islands, all new-born babies used to have to be buried alive at the orders of the men, and in order to save oneself the trouble connected with such babies, somewhat older children were imported from outside.

The Creeks had some female chiefs, as did some other tribes, such as the Narraganset of Rhode Island, the Potawatami, and the Winnebago. Viewed as part of the whole, they form a small minority—a frequent objection to the importance of matriarchy. But where emphasis is placed upon magic abilities, a female sacerdotal clan commands the spiritually dependent hunters and warriors, who may physically be ever so bold; where the women do not exercise sacerdotal functions, as for instance in the case of the Central Asiatic nomads, they sometimes lead the army. In democratic America, the chief usually was only *primus inter pares* and did not anywhere attain a power that could not easily have been withdrawn from him in case of need. The significance of female Indian priests, prophetesses, and magic medicine women, especially with the very primitive tribes, is confirmed by epics, ritual customs, and many reports of conversions: "These old witches are held in great awe. Though they talk nothing but nonsense, the men abide by their intuition, and these women are their rulers." Or again; "How many of them the good padres of the mission of St. Francis —present-day San Francisco—had to burn, before these heathens had matured into acceptance of the religion of love!"

The longing for sexual variety was apparently rooted in the forceful Indian temperament and was encouraged by the insignificance of the father under matriarchal laws stipulating constancy only for the mother clans. If the marriage endured, the man sometimes even lost his name. This was the case with the Creeks, who named the fathers after their children rather than the other way around—a custom prevailing also among matriarchal tribes in Patagonia, pre-Islamic Arabia, and the old Cantabrians. The Aleutians of Alaska during the era of Russian rule gave husbands the names of their wives. (Holmberg)

In many tribal societies, the man is not allowed to see his mother-in-law. The Tlinkit of Alaska, the Navajos, Ojibways, Cherokees, Arapahos, and the Dakota tribes used to warn a son-in-law of his mother-in-law's approach by loud noises, both screams and rattling of wooden noisemakers. In the Navajo language, mother-in-law is "doyishini," or "she whom I must not see." Any offense against this law was presumably followed by blindness, death, sterility, or other, unspecified misery. An Australian bushman almost died of fear because the shadow of his mother-in-law had traveled over his feet while he was asleep. In Melanesia, the man avoids the beach until his mother-in-law's tracks have been obliterated by the water. While in a missionary conducted school on New Guinea, a six-year-old boy suddenly fell under the table like a log, because his big brother's mother-in-law was passing the building.

Travelers in Australia, Africa, Melanesia, and America have found this taboo a source of never-ending hilarity. "Perhaps the most amusing view of my life," Captain Bourke tells us, "was a desperate Chiricahua Apache named Ka-e-tenny, renowned as the boldest and bravest man of his people, when he tried to avoid meeting his mother-in-law. Clutching some rocks, his face hidden, he was suspended from an exposed point and would have been crushed to bits, if the rocks had given way."

The origin of this taboo is a riddle. Its sense has never been satisfactorily explained. The layman may wonder why one doesn't simply ask those who believe in it, but genuine customs are much too deeply implanted in people's blood to reach up to the level of rational explanation. That is what makes anthropology difficult. "These people are incapable of just describing their customs, much less to explain them, that is, to clothe their attitudes in words." (Frobenius) Lord Avebury connected the mother-in-law taboo with the theft of women, which used to be a favorite explanation of many different things: the mother-in-law, he said, had to be avoided because one had abducted the daughter. But would not such an origin suggest a taboo against seeing the father and brothers of the abducted woman? I. B. Tylor demonstrated that this taboo occurred most frequently in matrilocal societies, where the daughter never leaves the house, while nations practicing the theft of women had the taboo only in a weaker form, if at all. Other explanations would have it that the danger of "dishonorable advances" is to be excluded—a wonderful subject for psychoanalysis!

The Navajos evaded the entire menacing taboo in a simple manner: they married first the mother-in-law and then the daughter. The same ingenious solution was also found by the Cherokees and the Caribs of South America. The Wagogo and the Wahehe of East Africa have the custom of making the man practice intercourse first with the mother before he may marry her daughter. The theory of an application of the incest taboo, therefore, can hardly apply here. Where the taboo is milder, the mother-in-law may also be placated by presents: the Dakotas used an enemy's scalp.

According to Briffault, the mother-in-law taboo has its origins in the matriarchal view that the exogamous male possesses no right to the female clan and becomes subject to its chief, so that he becomes the subject of an alien, "insulted" mother. The intruder may not let himself be seen or caught by her without having to anticipate dreadful consequences, unless he can placate her through a present or by becoming a member of the clan through sexual intercourse with her. Thus the taboo preserved, according to Briffault, something of that reverent awe due to the primitive tribal mother and her natural domination of the family that was her creation.

Feelings so general and so profound that no custom, no family law among the uncivilized races of five continents seems more long-lived, no family law more binding than . . . these absurd inhibitions and traditional rules attached everywhere to the wife's mother—such feelings never are mere tomfoolery, but their original meaning is as significant as it is vital.

In cultivated society, the taboo of the "evil mother-in-law," with its spiteful and banal irony provides a mere faint echo of the taboo.

Under the influence of a European immigration, a number of Indian tribes gradually change over from a matriarchal into a patriarchal society, while they are dying out in their conflict with the settlers or moving away to reservations. How rigidly matriarchal laws persisted among the Indians, however, was best demonstrated by that Choctaw who during the 1840's confided in Dr. Byington, a missionary, that he wished to become an American citizen only so that he could bequeath his property to his children, for otherwise it reverted to his maternal family without fail.

Much of the original Indian nature has been preserved by the most advanced and the most primitive tribes, the Pueblos and the Seri, both of which were entirely matriarchal.

The Seri Indians of the Gulf of California, because of their flint arrows and their general xenophobia, remained almost unknown until recently.[1] They excused themselves from answering any questions by killing the interlocutor. Their poverty made it unrewarding to wipe them out, and, at any rate, their internecine feuds gradually performed this function. Dr. MacGee succeeded in at least observing those living in the province of Sonora, Mexico, and learning the most important facts about the life of the others through an interpreter. Their social units are mother clans, headed in each case by an old woman. Their tribal pride attaches largely to the hierarchy of daughters and granddaughters and is connected with the purity of their blood. The Seri call themselves "kunkak," or women's association. Their totem is the pelican. "It would be giving them too much credit to state that they lived in the Old Stone Age." They use nothing prepared by themselves except for flint arrowheads. For grinding a bone,

[1] Reader should bear in mind that the work was written in 1930–31.

they simply take a rock. If one gives them a knife, they have
no idea what to do with it, nor do they want to learn.

The women rule autocratically. The husband is hard to
identify, because he is incomparably younger than the wife
and has no authority. His relationship to the household remains unclear, for regardless of how miserable and provisional
the hut may be, he may never enter it, while only the brothers are allowed to share in its occupancy. It remains uncertain
whether fatherhood is recognized at all. There is no word
meaning "fatherhood." In order to marry into this lowly state,
every prospective bridegroom is first subjected to ordeals by a
college of matrons, which decides whether he may join the
clan. The men hunt, fish, and fight. In any dispute, the clan
mother has the power of decision, which is accepted piously.
Jurisprudence is exercised only by the women, who send out
their brothers to execute the sentence. Only for warfare
against outsiders do they ever elect a male chief, and that
largely with respect to the magic powers exercised by his
wife, since in his unemployed hours he must be available also
for making rain, which is the original purpose of feminine
magic and therefore impossible for a man to accomplish by
himself. At any rate, he remains a "homeless dignitary," moving with the seasons according to the whims of the women,
who decide all movements of the tribe in their own councils
and in addition hold a seat and a voice in the war council of
the men.

While the Seri never got beyond a sloppy weed shelter,
the Pueblos could have shown New York how to construct
a skyscraper. They began by building their houses of twenty
and more stories against the steep canyon walls of New
Mexico and Arizona, constructing them in terraces with flat
roofs, accessible from outside by "fire-escape" ladders and,
for this reason, resembling the skyscraper. These construc-
tions may still be seen in ruined states of preservation all over
the Southwest and belong to the sights of America. Later
the Pueblos adopted this style in the plains, too, for their
fortress-like villages of solid brick construction. All of this was
invented by women and built by them, from the foundations
up. Until the arrival of the Spaniards, no male in those parts
had ever occupied himself with problems of architecture:

when the first man was supposed to build a wall at the orders of the missionaries, he stood there, steeped in shame, jeered by women and children. The Spanish missionaries relate with pride of the beautiful churches and monasteries constructed for them by the natives. It was the women, the girls, and the little boys who built them, for with these peoples it is the custom that women build the houses. That is how it had always been, and that is how the Zuñi still do it.

The Pueblo Indians also built large steambaths and temples in single buildings, for bathing, cleansing through heat, and tattooing were intimately connected with religious ceremonies consecrating the hunter.

"Every village has from one to six of these round edifices. A large, subterranean room is, at one and the same time, bathroom, council house, club room, and church. It consists of a wide hole, for the roof is almost level with the ground, only sometimes a little higher . . . All around the walls, there are benches, and in the middle of the floor, there is a square, stone container, in which aromatic plants are constantly being burned. One enters the house with the aid of a ladder through a hole in the roof, which is located above the fireplace and thus at the same time serves as ventilator and chimney."

Previous opinions that these round halls were exclusively male clubs are refuted not only by the indubitable matriarchy prevalent among the Pueblos and the fact that they were built exclusively by women but also by their shape: round, burrowed into the earth, with only one, narrow entrance, opposite the fireplace. Could there be a "men's club" in this uterus? If anywhere, the male would give expression to his masculinity in a men's club, for "nothing is real that is not apparent." The typical emblem of the male club also is missing: the skull, hard-shelled counter uterus, spiritual egg, the use of which as an object of veneration and an ornament makes the club rooms of male associations in primitive nations veritable houses of skeletons.

The lone Pueblo round houses are easily explained from the matrilocal customs, much more stringent in former times, which admitted the men to the houses only as visitors. Therefore, these domiciles, called *estufas* by the Spaniards, were

erected for them to sleep in. Now, everything has become
laxer. To be sure, the matriarchal organization still exists, but
the transition has already set in, and that always means the
end is approaching.

According to Kroeber, the Pueblos are always getting
divorces, so that both men and women have had many marriage partners by the time they reach the middle years, and
even old age is no protection against divorce. Establishment
as well as dissolution of marital ties proceeds voluntarily and
without compulsion. Whenever the woman is tired of a man,
she makes a bundle of his things and puts it out in front of
the door, without scenes or quarrels. Both before and during
marriage, everybody does fairly much as he pleases. Young
girls sleep with married men without shame. The matriarchy
is always generous in sexual matters; what does it care about
virginity? The stern caliber of the race was preserved, not by
sexual hardships, but by ordeals that were part of the puberty
rites customary among most primitive nations, most stringent
among pure nations of warriors, regardless of how matriarchally they may organize their society. The necessary discipline here is centered on a different area, not on the erotic
realm, which thus remains free of neuroses.

Pueblo mythology seems more entwined than that of other
tribes with rites and minor legends, like baroque Christianity.
At its roots, there is a Demeter cult connected with fertility
magic, whose mysteries degenerated into a flour-and-snake
dance. It was a mimed mystery of the seed-mother Muyen-
mut and her son-lover, a snake-demigod, moon-god, and
ruler of the realm of the shadows. The immortal mother's
mortal son, eternally shedding his skin, descends to her as an
impregnator. What the phallus in the Cista was in Eleusis is
replaced by the snakes wriggling in the flour here; for it has
long been recognized that only the missionaries, who wanted
to spread the cult of the Christian God, invented a mono-
theistic cult of Manitou and claimed that the true Indian cult
had been this and not a pantheon of gods. The Indians
had their great world spirit Manitou *in addition to* that Pantheon, a world spirit as dualistic as the black-and-white egg-
mothers or the Greek Dioscures.

As a pure life principle, Manitou is equal to breath, spirit, or soul. Whomever he sneezes on becomes young again, and wherever this spirit delimits itself rhythmically and scans a name, he creates the individual soul by pronouncing its name. The essence of puberty rituals is the search for communion with Manitou; regardless of what else they may mean, their innermost intent is *rebirth,* in which the boy must re-create himself out of the great world soul to become a full-fledged member of the tribe. Only then are the markings of the tribes tattooed on him. No one who has not undergone these puberty rites can marry, regardless of how virile he might be otherwise; he could barely dance the "dance of the unworthy dogs" and similar children's hops, and no girl would touch him. His mother, far from keeping her son back, urges him to undergo that second birth. After fasts lasting weeks or even months, tortures, and similar practices designed to test his spirit, the "entranced" boy is isolated from the tribe and left in some sort of a trance to seek the "dream of life" that is to reveal to him his private Manitou, his individual totem, his new name, and his new soul.

Unlike the Australians, Africans, Semites, and Malays, the Indians had no circumcision in their puberty rituals, but their ordeals were so much the more cruel. Both initiation ceremonies could be equally dangerous, but our perspective on dangers is different from theirs: numerous peoples relentlessly executed members of their society for bodily deficiencies or even mere failures that seem unimportant to us, because we have shed the mystical background of life. The African Ewes immediately kill any child that has difficulties in teething; the front teeth, apparently so important in many countries, are important to them, not only for biting but also for being knocked out during their puberty rites. Indian secret associations punished any stumbling during a ritual dance by death.

The mythical is represented by pictures; the demoniacal is incarnate in the dance. Its rhythm propels the dancer out of his own level and into an alien one. Every kind of dance occupies a different demoniacal area with fluttering feelings. Every step, every gesture keeps a world of spirits in suspense; he who stumbles loosens a chaos of unruly demons upon his fellow dancers and breaks the collective ecstasy. With every ritual test, one acquires the right to a new dance. Other dancing rights are hereditary; some can be acquired by marriage; another still remained the exclusive property of the women. In order to judge the predominance of one sex over the other, it is insufficient to ascertain who owns house and children and whose name is preserved: rather, one must also know who may dance and under what circumstances. The argument that medicine, under natural conditions, must be a female dominion because the mothers are gifted with magic words by Nature with which to alleviate pains is contradicted by many ethnologists with the fact of the male medicinal association among the Algonquins, the Midiwiwin. But the Midiwiwin had four steps, into each of which one was initiated with a dance representing the death and resurrection of the initiate. Each higher grade of healing magic was shot into the body of the unconscious initiate in the guise of a seashell, that is, projected into him in the shape of the female genitalia. Only this rite gave the person his full membership in the association of magic practitioners. It is another instance of the significance of the Kauri shell.

Buffalo dances and similar hunting magic, on the other hand, remained the preserve of the men. Totem dances of both sexes were not held in honor of the totem like a ballet for an illustrious guest but rather were mystical communions. When a clan danced "the rain," "the prairie wolf," "the translucent rocks," it did not portray in its masks what it danced, but rather itself became the thing, reverting to the essence of "rain," "prairie wolf," and "translucent rocks." Having the same totem meant much more than being of the same blood; it meant partaking of the same Platonic idea. Whoever stumbled in such a dance had a false soul, which had to be transported back by radical means.

The Indian woman at her first menstruation usually had to spend one or two months in solitude and fasting.

> "When a Mohawk girl-child notices the first indications of her maturity, she flees and obliterates her tracks. When her disappearance is finally noticed, her mother and other relatives begin looking for her. Often three or four days pass until the lost child is found. Only then can she take some nourishment that is brought to her. After twenty days, she returns to her wigwam."

The worldwide custom of not walking under an open ladder is supposed to be connected with the fear that a menstruating woman might sit on top. (Briffault)

This taboo, which exists also in such highly civilized societies as those of the Chinese, the Aryan Indians, and the Persians, cannot be explained from a general fear of blood. Blood, on the contrary, usually is something highly desirable. The taboo is directed at the specific origin of the blood. This consideration also explains the widespread practice of artificial defloration before marriage. Caucasian parents in China often were taken aback upon discovering to what extent their Chinese nurses had fulfilled their "nursing duties" in this respect. Where artificial means are not customary, the priests usually have the obligation of performing this act, as do, for example, the Brahmans of India, whose sacred estate makes them immune. Some American Indian tribes sew the young girls up in sacks when their puberty begins, as otherwise they do only with corpses, leave them only a small aperture for breathing purposes, and loosen sacred steams upon them for such a long time that some of them have been asphyxiated in the process. Thus, the women finally become the victims of an exaggerated dread—probably originated by them, which seized not only themselves but also the man—of the lunar being which irresponsibly circulates inside of them on the critical days with an independent demonism.

The further a social structure removes itself from the matriarchy, the more is the sancity removed from this taboo of femininity. The Church Fathers regarded it more as a taboo of the satanic element than anything holy; this is so much the more true of Puritanism, which considered that its duty before God was to keep down the women in an iron vise of innocuousness, since every one of them bore within herself a miniature replica of the satanic pit.

It is extremely interesting to note how the original force of American matriarchy has overcome the patriarchal-Puritan tide of immigration which interrupted it. Its victory was almost uncontested and of an amusing completeness, with only the difference that the present-day male has to work for the matriarchal clan much harder as a dollar hunter than the buffalo hunter did formerly. The man's situation in the United

States is approximately the same as in the matrons' long house of the Seneca: if, in case of a lapse in manners or obedience, some old aunt does not put in a good word for him at the last minute, he is ostracized and has a fate as mournful to look forward to as did his predecessor, the red warrior. The new—or rather, the old—matriarchy has achieved all of this, not through constant noise, force, and law, but rather through the natural course of events, which always is the most mysterious and most secure manner of acquiring authority.

The Indians themselves, of course, have been changing over to patriarchy under the influence of the same Puritan immigrants whose immediate descendants are regressing into matriarchy under the imperceptible countereffects of an inexhausted base of culture. Perhaps that soil will change them partially into something like the aborigines, whose premature destruction made it impossible for them to live out their civilizational life. The case of North America in all respects is without precedent. One of the most immense, mechanical civilizations, coming out of a late European hereditary accumulation, is there placed upon the naked soul of an alien giant continent. Otherwise there always was a buffer of natives in the colonies who absorbed and continued the aboriginal culture, or the conquerors, for reasons of self-preservation, isolated themselves strictly from any inner relationship to their country, resulting in the well-known dual structure of many "settled" countries.

There was only one sun clan in North America, the Natchez. Nowhere in this world have there been sun matrons, only sun virgins. The center of the stage here is not occupied by the old woman chief; she has rather been relegated to the background and directs the actors from there, while the center and front of the stage are occupied by the daughters and one son. This daughter clan, incubated by the Caesarian sun to become autonomous, aristocratic, young priestesses, leads a privileged existence, free of responsibility except for agricultural rites and medical magic. One brother or son from this strictly female-descended line always was endowed with the trappings of power and the title "great sun" by the Great Mother in the background. He remained responsible to her and was not allowed to engage in the dynastic incest with his sisters otherwise customary in such arrangements.

The priestess-princess, on the other hand, could choose whomever she wanted from the people to be her slave consort or lover, since male heredity did not count. These sexual servants remained without rank, were exchanged or tomahawked at will, were called "curs," and had to wait in humiliating positions in the presence of their mistress. When their mistress or one of the children procreated by them died, they were executed, much as are the consorts of Africa, who are executed by the dozens.

XVIII

CENTRAL AND SOUTH AMERICA

On the Peruvian plateau, where jeweled dusks cast ingots of light across one's path so compact in appearance that one seems to feel their impact upon crossing them, there stood a nunnery made of pure gold, with golden furniture, a golden hearth, and golden pots, pans, mugs, and other objects of utility. Golden doors opened into a golden garden with golden paths and golden trees, where golden birds dwelled in golden nests. Golden maize stood tall with golden leaves and ears, and golden herdsmen with golden staffs guarded a golden herd on a golden pasture. Violent sons of the sun had surrounded their fire vestals with this gilded world: the Incas. The vestals there guarded the flame night and day which was lit again once a year, at the summer solstice, with a concave mirror directly from the divine rays. There they wove the white woolen garments of princes and priests, prepared wine and bread for the religious rites, and shaped and glazed the ritual vessels for their magic service in a procedure known only to themselves.

They were called *mama-cuna*, Peruvian "mothers," but, despite the solar flame and their betrothal to the fire and all the gold with which they were surrounded, they had remained moon women just as in times immemorial, and once a year they carried the image of their own goddess *mama-quilla* to the solar temple on their shoulders. The shrine of their goddess in the capital of Cuzco, a dangerous institution, had been destroyed by the first Incas upon their arrival. They left the other local services alone but started a new cult for their father, the sun, which had a male clergy and became the official religion of the realm. The independent mountain tribes paid lip service at the most to the new religious decrees and continued to adore their local deities, headed by the moon and the "maize mother," whose service was still attended to by domestic priestesses with sacred dances, rituals, and agricultural magic. Even in the sovereign light of that great sun land Peru, it took a late monarchy to introduce the sun cult by force. Peruvians and Chileans believed, as did Mexicans, that their life and fertility were gifts of the moon. The "great goddess" Bachue arises from their waters with her son. After he grows up to become her lover, the two of them procreate the human race, after which Bachue returns into the self-created, fecund waters in the shape of a snake.

The sun cult of Cuzco remained a matter of the court and dynasty. Separated from their country, the Incas performed their strong and yet unreal existence for themselves on a separate plateau with the sacrifice of boys and girls on an unprecedented scale. The evaluation of the heavenly bodies always corresponds to a state of mind. Merely viewing the sun is inconsequential until the sun receives a special value from another source.

Both Peruvians and Mexicans paid more attention originally to the rhythms of the moon than to the fairly continuous sunshine in their countries. This adoration of the moon is closely connected on one hand with the obvious relationship of the female cycle to the lunar one, and on the other hand to the reverence in which the art of pottery, a strictly feminine art, is held among the Indians. According to popular opinion, every object manufactured by women absorbs their secret connections with Nature. This opinion also explains the care with which Indians avoid impinging on female property rights. Even now, no Indian male from New Mexico would dare sell eggs or chickens in the absence of his wife—at least not without asking his daughters, who may still be quite young. (Bandelier) Herrera says of the Nicaraguan natives that the women carry on the trade of the marketplace alone, while the men are allowed only to sweep the house:

"So strongly are they under the domination of their women that, when they make them angry, they are simply shown the door. The beaten men then go to their neigh-

bors and ask them to put in a good word for them in order
to bring about their reacceptance. The women use their
men as servants and treat them as such."

In western Peru, the women are the only ones that can
tame their unruly, pugnacious men: "The women are extremely powerful. They conciliate the parties to disagree-
ments and order the restoration of peace, for these highly
barbarian men grant anything to those who suckled them."
(N. del Techo) Among the Guaranís of Paraguay, "the men
see their greatest satisfaction in seeing their old women
happy. They obey them and do anything they require." The
ruling ladies compensate by an easy relationship of *noblesse
oblige* in erotics. One of them, of high social rank, is reputed
to have stated that ordinary women without a good upbring-
ing might sometimes behave rudely, but no well-bred
woman with a natural tact would ever be so ill-mannered as
to refuse her favors to an admirer. (Briffault)

The Incas were upstart chieftains. According to their tradition, the foundation of their dynasty in the first four generations was connected with native women. It has often been
the primary concern of usurpers in history to seek legitimacy
through connections with the female lines of the conquered
country that determine the succession to the throne. According to Briffault, those four women must have been the leading priestesses. At any rate, the native female priesthood became the model for the "holy women" of the Incas, who were
now redirected toward the sun cult. Later, the royal daughters and sisters, to the extent that they were not used for dynastic incest, entered the vestalic service. The fact that the
Vestals belonged to the royal family may be gleaned from the
manner of their execution in cases when they lapsed from the
rule of virginity: they were buried alive, as were the Roman
vestals, whose royal blood was not allowed to be shed either.

The Mexican dynasty also incorporated vestals into its sanguinary sun cult, though in a less rigorous form. They could
take their orders for life or for a limited period in order to
marry later, just like the other priestesses of their country.
Their task was to guard the eternal flames on the two large
pyramids, to burn frankincense for the idols, to weave the

priests' garments. They themselves went clad in white wool and without jewelry.

The Mayan towns have been rotting away for a long time in the forests of Yucatan, and the sun cult of the Incas is as dead as the mummies in their crypts, but Peruvian men and girls, fresh coca leaves between their teeth, still flit about in "the new air of the young moon" and pray "mama-quilla, do not die," for their lives depend on the moon from month to month.

South America is the Land of Promise of mediums. No continent, not even Africa, is therefore so rich in secret societies founded upon spiritualism, telepathy, prophecies, and trances, naturally conducted by priestesses. The practices common from Central America all the way down to the southern tip chiefly consist of "Nugualism," using the "nugua" or soul of the bush, incarnate in an animal. The higher orders of the societies learn to detach the human soul from its body, to take up residence in an animal as they please, roaming about at two different places simultaneously, invulnerable, clairvoyant, endowed with all the secrets of jungle craft. The Indian tribes supposedly were first introduced to this art of detachment by a mighty sorceress. Others of her ilk among the Aztecs founded their own cities as headquarters of magic, as, for example, Malinalko, or ruled as fairy godmother queens, as did Coamizagul in Honduras, who "went to heaven while alive." There is hardly an Indian national hero who, according to his legend, was not guided by prophetesses.

Dr. Brinton, the expert on nugualism, emphasizes that the women of the priestly caste not only take the highest, most esoteric orders but also frequently are the chiefs and maintain the mysterious succession in the organization indestructibly from generation to generation. These female adepts became the soul of the revolution against the Spaniards and were persecuted by the Spanish colonial masters with fear and hatred. Almost a century after the forcible conversion of the country to Christianity, a twenty-year-old girl, Maria Candelaria, the prophetess and Jeanne d'Arc of Central America, started a general insurrection for the old gods, intending to drive out the foreigners. She organized an army and for a while was a real menace to Spanish power. Even after suppression of the revolt, she never fell into Spanish hands. The Spaniards caught two of her adjutants and rewarded their loyalty to her with death by torture.

Young Indian girls are accustomed to enduring pain with stoic complacence from childhood on: they are circumcised by the severance of their labia and clitoris. The tortures of the Spaniards did not crush their spirits. The Indian women of South America enjoyed a superior standing through their mediumistic and visionary instincts throughout the continent, even all the way down south in the miserable extremes of Patagonia. According to tradition, these Patagonian women exercised such a sacerdotal tyranny that a kind of male revolution occurred, with a massacre of women and the introduction of male rule. Opinions, however, vary on whether such a male rule really exists in the twentieth century. The natives, driven ever farther toward "the edge of the world" by their enemies, live in the most miserable condition, polygamous as well as polyandric, but the women do the wooing; they are also larger, more regularly featured, and more intelligent than the men.

In former days, the women also went hunting, though now they have only the fisheries as a source of income. These women sit naked in their canoes and steer them out to sea. Their fishing is done in the most primitive fashion but successful; missionaries and foreign sailors with their more advanced methods can never keep up with them. Their ropes are made of fibers; their bait attached without hooks. When the fish bites, it is caught with the bare hands. Any part of the catch that they do not need is then exchanged at the mission house "for theology and bisquits." Only the women can swim and are famous for their mastery of the art. The men box and wrestle instead in public games, spurred by the women, who admire nothing so much as brutality.

Whether the Patagonians are degenerated Indians or aboriginal natives is not quite certain. The mass of the real Indians is supposed to have migrated to South America across the isthmus of Panama, although the South American languages have nothing in common with those of North America. No one any longer knows which races were the bearers of that ten-thousand-year-old culture which, on the other hand, has left us the titanic ruins of Bolivia.

The entire, gigantic triangle of tropical plains between the Andes, the Orinoco, and the tributaries of the Amazon River, rich in cotton, tobacco, and sugar cane, is inhabited by matriarchal tribes; the Tupi, Caribs, and Aruacs. The Tupi have a matrilocal service marriage: several contestants have to work gratis in the woman's or her parents' house for two or three years, and the one who has performed best is accepted as husband. The ancestor of the Tupi is supposed to be the moon. Their medicine women are famous. The Aruacs as well as the Caribs have inheritance through the mother. The Caribs have the mother-in-law taboo, which can be circumvented by marriage to the tabooed mother. The masculine puberty ritual includes the sewing of the boys into a sack full of starved ants. Whoever survives this test without making a sound is permitted to marry right away if he wishes. The female endurance trials also are characterized by calculated cruelty. All these tribes, however, are experiencing their transition to patriarchal laws. This becomes clear from two phenomena noticed by Bachofen; the couvade and the pre-eminence of the maternal brother instead of the mother herself in the clan.

Many of the Gran Chaco tribes still practice polyandry. The woman chooses the man, but the existence of the couvade testifies as to a transition from maternal to paternal predominance. With the aid of runaway European horses, the Gran Chaco people have become equestrians; they have social classes and the beginnings of chivalry and hereditary nobility. One of their tribes, the Chamacoco, sends its young men before marriage to marriage schools conducted by experienced widows. Such characteristics hitherto always were those of matriarchy and its transition into patriarchy. But there is another transition: that of control by the old into control by the young. It would make possible the rule by brother and sister without interference of matrons or elders, with a division of labor into a sacerdotal and a war chieftainship.

The papers of a deceased German explorer and engineer contained the following description of a ritual incest dance between the chief brother and the priestess sister in an Indian tribe at the boundary between Brazil and Venezuela near the sources of the Rio Taquado, witnessed by the engineer-explorer himself:

In the sexagonal temple-hut, the ruling siblings danced, chief Luluac and his sister, the priestess Zaona. They danced the ritual incest dance before their lord, the pig-god Mocki, the blood-idol, the demon dancing into the air, with two sculls, a large eye in the shape of a blackberry on each forehead. The divine abdomen consists of a thick shaft as tall as a man, a barkless tree, which bore the neckless head like an immense collar. Out of the shaft, there grew six pairs of pommel-like claws, arranged like two rows of goat udders.

Mighty hunters sat around in a semicircle, the door in their backs, the chief's best people. Their muscles swelled up in their intoxication, came to life in the fluttering of the flames, a rotundity of solidified chaos. The flesh of these knotted bodies billowed and entwined in odd knots and convolutions, an oddly swelling, mystic mass. In fist-sized growths and formations, frightening powers were stored. A discipline of limbs coagulated the chests of these savage men, and they uttered rhythmic, woeful, burning shrieks or hummed with closed teeth like a swarm of mad mosquitoes. The tuned clappers of the wood instruments banged melodically on one another. The gathering was inscrutably supported by the idol's bloodthirsty mien, which could be grasped only humbly in its effects. Glances shot out from its green eyes. It, the ogre, was able to elicit an ephemeral beauty.

Zaona began to dance. The god bore her. She balanced herself on one leg. Her torso, thrown backward, formed a sophisticatedly thin arc, a tickling curve that seemed wicked. Her straight, shoulder-length hair brushed the floor. Then she cowered, jumped like a panther, carried a stick away from the fire and waved it furiously with her teeth, describing a fiery circle that lit up her slender figure in all its hollows and undulations. Her savage little face glowed in the grip of ecstasy and greed like seething bronze. The chorus of the hard men in the shadows, sitting on their haunches, answered her muffled gum-cries with a kind of animal echo, a strong motif of physical yearning with a bestial melancholy that made one tremble and hope. Zaona looked like a fiery warrior and yet was all gentleness, all woman, the priestess, the dancing-girl, the courtesan in the aboriginal state. The sparsely built, naked girl, a sling made of muscles, nerves, swirls, and tame bones, whirled through the room, soared from corner to corner like the crack of a whip, lay before Mocki on the ground like a narrow thread. And the voluptuous god stood still and was potent. His silence gave birth to rhythm, was the fundamental tone which motion lifted itself away from. She had danced the bloodthirstiness of her soul, the puma dance, the mosquito dance, the grasshopper dance. And now, something decisive happened on this memorable evening: Zaona danced a fourth time.

When she rose again from the floor, Luluac stood there, her princely brother. She only went up to his hips. He was tall, and his upper torso was planted like a wedge in his hips. . . . On his small, vaulted skull sat the crown of all Indian feather crowns. The wildest and most brightly colored wings of the jungle had contributed to this chief's ornament. The slightest inclination of his head in this manner received a specterlike significance on the head of this young chief.

This model of a feather bush made long Luluac superhuman, when he started the dance with his sister Zaona. The grotesque superiority of the man was an enjoyment for all who watched. Zaona seemed touched into her last fibers. She pleasingly wound herself under him. While they danced, their bodies received the significant symbols of a maddening sexual excitement. They looked upon each other out of the slits of their lids with a bestial concupiscence.

The instinct of incest rising in primitive or sophisticated races that are still healthy made itself felt in their feelings. Although Zaona was small, her body showed striking resemblances to that of her brother. They were both long. The expressions on their faces were almost identical. They were in love with their own kind. Their dance expressed their joy in the absoluteness and racial uniformity of their nature. Was not the double-budded, Narcissistic mood, the principle of the continuation of one's own kind, the same as the tendency of beauty to improve and maintain itself? Resemblance in differentiated mammals seems repulsive to the imagination. But in well-developed races, it attracts a balanced and mature taste. Inside of noble races, the sharp sexual difference suffices for the satisfaction of the craving for variation by differentiating into hard-male and soft-female types.

Zaona danced profoundly and with dedication. She yearned for the feathery arrow Luluac. Luluac moved in manly, calculated curves with visible technical mastery. He remained hard, rhythmical, formal, with fire being emitted only by his eyes. One understood that he wanted Zaona, but he remained reserved in the face of her blandishments. One could not know how dangerous the little female might be, whether it might be permissible to touch her: a priestess, a princess—catastrophe might threaten whoever touched her.

Zaona's ankles were shackled: the bracelets had caught in each other. She jumped short, bouncy steps that were like balls. She circled around Luluac, sank down to her knees, and crossed her arms behind the nape of her neck. Luluac let her approach. He grabbed her with a posture that drastically exposed his nudity, but shrank back. He defended himself against the reality of such a superhumanly desirable woman. She was a deception of the senses signifying one's destruction. Perhaps she was a pantherwoman and would tear the male lover who permitted himself to be ensnared. He swung out his arms, flashed his spear and shield, for he was about to keep a puma away from his body. Suddenly he lapsed into the well-known war dance, lifted his legs with his thighs horizontal, and ran in place.

Zaona fawned on him with perfect lines. Her manacled ankles followed him with small, submissive steps. It was sad how the cartilage of her tensed knees touched. Now, even Luluac could no longer resist her. A suggestively danced embrace symbolized his taking possession of her. He did not touch her; the gesture remained aesthetic. Everyone understood the implication of their entwining arms. Luluac accepted the wooing of the pantheress. The two bodies' sexual tension rose: they were both happy and both close to ecstasy. Zaona was as febrile as a young mare. A gentle music swelled her muscles and nerves and awakened the top and the innocence of his masculine sensations. The cyclical rapture of his nature caused him a slight dizziness. Their temples pounded, and their eyes joined their brains in a single, yearning mass. Luluac uttered a frantic yell, and the men joined in triumphantly and satisfied. The savage, beautiful warrior prince now led Zaona, his priestess sister, to his hut, which at the same time was the temple of her god.

XIX

EGYPT

The longest and most harmonious reign of the ruling brother-and-sister pair was in Egypt. According to Egyptian mythology, the tradition goes back to the twins Isis and Osiris, who loved each other in the belly of the earth goddess. For a period of twenty-four thousand years, there were supposed to be the predynastic ruling families, descendants of Isis' son Horus. Queen Neith-Hetep of Lower Egypt and King Namar of Upper Egypt were the ones to unite the red and the white crowns of the two realms. Thus they founded the first historic dynasty of the double diadem with the wise regulation of the Nile that was to provide for Egyptian harvests down to our own time. Their people numbered only about a hundred thousand: one needed no more than that for civilization.

The first dynasty contained the queen-mother Shesh, known to us as the originator of the first pomade designed to make the hair grow. It was mixed for her by her son Teta of one pulverized donkey's hoof, one pulverized dog's paw, and a brew of dates and oil, blended with them. Thousands of years later, in the days of Diodorus, the preparation of hair pomades and body salves belonged to the sphere of male responsibility, in addition to washing the laundry and making the beds.

That old Egyptian legend about the love of the divine twins proves how correctly psychoanalysis has traced erotic attractions as grown near the roots of being, and how incorrectly it has speculated that myths reflect forbidden wish dreams. For the marriage of brother and sister was never outlawed. On the contrary, it was considered "the thing to do" in accepted circles of society.

Whereas every princess of the blood was born with royal

titles and dignity, a prince did not attain these until his coronation day, and he could be crowned only as the husband of his royal sister. Only she carried the dynastic totem, the golden Horus, in her crown, because the divine right of kings rested on her. She reigned, he ruled; she inspired, he carried out. The difference between reigning and ruling is well formulated in inscriptions. One of the Isis pillars says, "What I have made law can be dissolved by no man." On the Osiris pillar, it merely says, "There is no place in the world where I have not come to bestow my beneficence." The name Osiris, *hes iri,* means "Isis' eye." He is, then, a part of her, the watching, governing part. Every queen was Isis' representative, even (foreign-descended) Cleopatra: "She shows herself to the people in Isis' garment. Antonius follows her throne on foot. The Roman soldiers' shields bear Cleopatra's name. She towers above her Osiris-husband (Antonius)." Above the Rameses statue, one may read: "See what the goddess-wife says, the royal mother, the mistress of the world." She herself was goddess and mistress of the world, while he appeared among the retainers.

In the eighteenth dynasty, Thutmose I had to abdicate after the death of his wife and surrender the throne to a teenager, his daughter Hatshepsut, although he had two sons, was of pure blood through his mother Ahmes, and was a great-grandson of Nefertari. Nefertari was worshipped for eight hundred years after her death, because under her and her brother-husband's rule, the Hyksos were driven out of Egypt, but this family fame did not help Thutmose I, the male descendant. It benefited Hatshepsut, who was titled "Queen of North and South, son of the sun, golden Horus, giver of years, goddess of dawns, mistress of the world, lady of both realms, stimulator of the hearts, main wife of Amon, the powerful woman."

Every princess also was the wife of a god, of the local totem. She was *ex officio* the god's priestess and obligated to carry on sacred prostitution until the advent of her first menstruation, for any foreigner who visited her in the holy premises was considered a representative of the revealing god, her celestial bridegroom. Her brother, the pharaoh, also was her husband only as a temporary incarnation of her god.

Egypt had world gods and local gods. The local ones usually were age-old animal totems, some male, others female. The local god of the residence of each dynasty became especially powerful. In Heliopolis, it was the sun-god Ra, who is the parthenogenetic offspring of the world goddess Neith: "No one uncovered me. The fruit to which I gave birth was the sun." During the great dynasties of Thebes (Luxor), to which Hatshepsut also belonged, the Theban totem Amon became so important that it absorbed the sun-god Ra and was called Ra-Amon. When Hatshepsut called herself main wife of Amon, this signified the sacred union with the local god of Thebes. As a symbol of the sacred union of the princesses with the moon bull Apis, they were accompanied into their graves by an embalmed bovine phallus.

Hatshepsut was one of those princesses who not only reigned but also exercised their powers. After the death of her husband, Thutmose II, she allowed her son, the later Thutmose III, as little influence over the government as she had accorded to her husband. Thus the prince—later famous as "the Egyptian Napoleon"—became an enemy and, after her death, had her name removed by chisel from the temple at Deir-el-Bahari in the Theban mountains, from the Sphinx Avenues, and from the obelisks at Karnak, in order to have his own name inserted in its place. This local infamy, however, did not really serve the purpose, for her deeds were proclaimed by papyruses and statuary from the Delta to Aswan and from the Libyan Mountains to the Sinai Peninsula.

Diodorus reports on Egyptian matriarchy: "Among the citizens, the husband by the marriage contract becomes his wife's property, and it is stipulated by them that the husband must obey his wife in all things." Despite many doubts of nineteenth-century critics, contemporary scholarship has confirmed this statement. One such marriage contract states:

I bow before thy rights as wife. From this day on, I shall never oppose thy claims with a single word. I recognize thee before all others as my wife, though I do not have the right to say thou must be my wife. Only I am thy husband and mate. Thou alone hast the right of departure. From this day on that I have become thy husband, I cannot oppose thy wish, wherever thou desirest to go. I give thee . . . [There follows an index of his possessions.] I have no power to interfere in any of thy transactions. I hereby cede to thee any rights deeded to me in any document that has been made out in my favor. Thou keepest me obligated to recognize all these cessions. Should anyone hand me any moneys which now belong to thee, I must give them to thee without delay or resistance and pay thee another twenty measures of silver, one hundred shekels, and another twenty measures of silver.

The terms relative to the man's obedience to his wife was a regular clause incorporated into every marriage contract.

The reason why any man entered into such an obligation was that he wanted to escape certain provisions of the matriarchy. It was, as Briffault demonstrated, precisely the wish to establish a patriarchal line of inheritance that led to an intensification of the matriarchy. If the man wanted his children to inherit his property, he had to give all of it to his wife while he was still alive and comply with any conditions she might set; otherwise, anything he acquired would be inherited by the children of his sisters.

It obviously was most advantageous for the Egyptian to marry his sister. Then the sister's children who would be inheriting his property some day were at least his own. This patriarchal motivation for the Egyptian brother-sister marriage was effective in all classes. It determined conditions for thousands of years, until the second century of the Christian era, for brother-sister marriages until then made up a majority of Egyptian couples. Obviously, the close connection of the "two" had much to do with this. It was not necessarily monotonous, because both partners could enjoy relations with slaves of the opposite sex as much as they pleased. If the wife tired of her husband, she could always divorce him, since it was her exclusive right and at the same time very easy. For all practical purposes, then, the Egyptians had polygamy and polyandry along with their incestuous marriages.

In Egypt, as always under matriarchy, the woman did the wooing. In sixteen out of twenty erotic poems transmitted to us by the Egyptians, it was she who took the initiative. She climbs through windows and reports triumphantly: "I

found my brother in his bed. My heart is inordinately happy."
Nor do the women lack for succinct language when the lyrics
have to do with financial facts of Life. The authoress of a
courting song of the times of Rameses II frankly confesses to
her friend: "Oh, my handsome darling! I am longing to become your wife and the mistress of all your property." If anything came of the courtship, the property transfer was auto-
matic. If the man built or bought a house, its ownership
immediately was vested in his wife.

By comparison to their ancient Egyptian colleagues, even
the best-situated women of our time, the Americans in the
women's paradise of the U.S.A., are rather ill-treated. While
nowadays such a girl can barely take a healthy slice of her
husband's possessions when she divorces him, the Egyptian
male had to transfer everything he owned when they were
merely engaged. Since the bride then retained the sole right
to divorce in the marriage contract, she could easily send
the husband away from "her" home, where even during the
marriage he was only considered a privileged guest. She did
not have to give any reasons. To be sure, this fatal arrangement was usually preceded by a trial marriage, and if it had
no consequences, the man only had to pay a slight compensation to get out of marriage.

Since the Egyptian woman could always interrupt her
pregnancy, there was little chance that children might result
before the marriage contract was concluded in the desired
form, inclusive of the clause pledging the husband's allegiance
to her. Even then, the children took on the mother's social
class and usually bore only her name.

The men seem to have been especially fond of children
in Egypt, while "matriarchy" is not nearly as domesticated
as it sounds. Infants were immediately given to the men for
care and artificial feeding, and the men were excellent dry
nurses. The office of nursemaid at the royal court was an exclusively male one. One of the greatest male offices was the
rearing of the royal princes and princesses. The prince of El
Kab under Amenhotep I, for instance, was called the nursemaid of Prince Uadmes. The gigolo of Queen Khnemtomun
was entitled the nursemaid of Princess Ranofre. The men

also took care of the laundry, the preparation of the bed for love, and the rubdowns for the care of hair and body.

Because of matrilocal marriage and of the manifold professional life open to women, they often decided the place of residence. That is why Rameses III said, "The foot of an Egyptian woman may walk where it pleases her, and no one may deny her." The Egyptian woman had a choice of careers which, at least until the twelfth dynasty, included everything. Before, as well as after, her marriage, she could become a priestess, which does not mean that she became a nun, the position rather corresponded in rank to that of an archbishop or a cardinal. We know of careers of girls who started in the businesses of their fathers and changed into the government service. Some became provincial governors or even commanders of substantial parts of the army.

Throughout Egyptian social history, however, there was a tendency to abolish the matriarchal order. It began with a decline in magical functions. During the first several dynasties, there often were female names listed among the lists of priests; they disappeared after the twelfth dynasty (that is, after 1785 B.C.) with the exception of the royal princesses who held sacerdotal offices by virtue of their birth. There were a number of female religious associations with large endowments and well-paid jobs at Thebes, but their aims and purposes are puzzling to us.

Egypt, however, never entirely quit the matriarchal system. When a Nubian dynasty managed to be accepted in the eighth century B.C. because of its descent from a princess of the blood, female dominance once more was intensified, this time to barbarian extremes. Two great queens were associated with each pharaoh for governing the realm, one to have her headquarters at Napata and the other at Thebes. It is from this period that the name Kandake was used for the queen dowager, which was to play such an important role in the later romances of Alexander. Nubia itself maintained a matriarchy into the Middle Ages. When the Ptolemaeans tried to introduce Greek (patriarchal Athenian) laws into Egypt, they remained dead letter. Matriarchal laws overcame Hellenism almost entirely and endured until the advent of Islam. The favorable economic position of women in African Moslem states is a carry-over from Egypt.

Hereditary wealth, to be sure, also meant hereditary obligations. Old relatives had to be taken care of and honorary offices, such as many duties in religious rituals, had to be discharged by the women or at their expense. Greece, where patriarchal laws largely prevailed even during classical times, ridiculed the "women's slaves on the Nile." Herodotus speaks of the "world turned upside down": According to him, who saw everything, the two sexes even discharged their bodily functions the wrong way, the women standing up, the men sitting down. Whereas he was amused by the strangeness of the pattern, his compatriot Sophocles was outraged: "Oh, how they imitate the customs of the Egyptians in their ways of living and thinking! There, the men stay at home and work at the distaff, and their wives run about and supply the necessities of life."

Diodorus especially occupied himself with Egypt. He correctly estimated the matriarchal character of the royal family and whose assertions about the matrimonial contracts were validated so thoroughly that no historian could ask for more. He exaggerated, however, when he said that public offices were generally held by women, while the men stayed at home. Lists of dignitaries, papyruses, and sculptures contradict him there. Men were at least as common in public offices as women, which does not exclude the possibility that, as Diodorus reports, "they lived according to the will of their wives."

We learn something about this in a small papyrus from the times of the Ramessides, that is, at the beginning of the New Kingdom. In this interesting document a Theban widower begs his deceased wife to stop haunting him. Flatteringly he calls her "Exalted Spirit," reminds her of the consideration he showed all through her lifetime, how he never had neglected her after obtaining the excellent position at the pharaonic court, but rather had conformed to every wish of hers and had consented to no audiences without her consent. "Whatever they gave me, I brought to thee," he assures her. "Never did I hide anything or keep it back for my use."

Even though a female ghost may have been guilty of misconduct, the living women seem not to have misused their power too badly. "If I should dismiss thee as husband," such a young lady generously declares in her marriage contract, "because I might come to hate thee or learn to love another better than thee, I shall return half thy dowry to thee, in addition to a part of everything that I shall acquire with thee while thou art married to me." Only the Thebans were mad for money. Not only did they take possession of all the man's money and all his possible inheritances in the future when they got married, but they also stipulated annual attachments to everything he might earn in the future, so that many a man, in order not to starve after the divorce, stipulated that he wanted to be supported by his wife until he died and buried decently afterward. He was, of course, given his allowance by her. The earliest meaning of the Egyptian word for "wife" is "she who clothes her husband."

One last word about the wisdom of the Egyptians. In the *Maxims of Ptah Hotep,* perhaps the oldest book of the world, dating back some five thousand years, that delightful philosopher said:

> If thou art wise, keep thy home, love thy wife, and do not dispute with her. Feed her, adorn her, massage her. Caress her and fulfill all her wishes as long as thou livest, for she is thy property that brings great gain. Attend to that which is her desire and to that which occupies her mind. For in such manner thou persuadest her to remain with thee. If thou opposest her, it will be thy ruin.

XX

AFRICAN QUEENS

The business of government originally was magically sanctioned. Even warlike conquerors later placed great store by a magic calling. Before there were any gods, there was magic. By comparison to a ruler inheriting a magic title, even a king "by the grace of God" was a johnny-come-lately, a ruler by the grace of the people, a mere opportunist, a ruler by virtue of his own achievements, a turbulent corporal; an "enlightened" potentate, however, is almost a contradiction in terms, for his power ("potestas") is precisely lodged in him because of occult talents, not enlightened or enlightenable gifts.

The priest-kingship, demonstrated by Frazer to have been the original government everywhere, was formed out of a sacred clan whose heredity guaranteed such gifts and remained associated with that clan where the monarchy was to endure. Son after son of this aristocratic family was entrusted with the highest office. In the beginning, it was not a much-craved office, for it was inconvenient and full of responsibilities and, even if the administration was without blemish, ended prematurely with ritual slaughter. In primitive nations, the future ruler often had to be chased out of the bush where he was hiding, captured, and crowned by force, after which he led an arduous life, hemmed in by incredible taboos night and day.

A priest-king's daily routine included: Making or stopping rain, keeping the seasons in proper order in general, averting epidemics and plagues from his people, regulating births (indirectly), keeping animals and fields fertile. By comparison, wars against external enemies seemed a form of recreation. And if his people suffered any sort of disaster, he had no opportunity of taking his royal treasure and absconding in some sort of fast vehicle to a neutral tribe and there to write his memoirs on why he failed.

But even if rich harvests, peace, prosperity, and fertility accompanied his reign, the ritual murder of the king awaited him. After a specified number of lunar or solar years, he either was beheaded or the royal wives choked him to death at the first signs of declining powers, which could be known only to them. He was no more than a tool delegated by the priests' clan which almost everywhere traced itself back to a great ancestress, even in the sun realms of Peru, Chile, and Mexico, with the Natchez, in pre-Aryan India, in Tibet, with the Celtic tribes, with the pre-Chinese as well as the Chinese tribes, in the early kingdoms of the Arabs and in Asia Minor, in the mountains of Assam, and even in the otherwise patriarchal Samoan archipelago. The giant, Dark Continent of Africa is even now witnessing the death of this priest-kingship, where it existed in all its phases with tremendous pomp; and where it has already passed away, the tradition still feels as warm as blood. What has to be carefully gleaned from the debris of many civilizations in the rest of the earth is to be seen contemporaneously in Africa, raised into the same layer of time. It will not be there for long. Our generation is the last one that can study these phenomena at first hand.

As late as the sixteenth and seventeenth centuries, there were thriving realms spreading far over the continent, as, for example, the Congo empire under the Mani-Congo. Through European exploitation and the abduction of whole tribes into slavery, these states were first depopulated and impoverished and then melted away. The massive lands with the ancient urban and chivalrous cultures bore many different races and different kinds of government. But wherever the kingship existed in the original heartland of matriarchy, including West Africa, or was introduced by the matriarchal Hamitic conquerors from the North into the East, it received its strength and legitimacy from a magic-sacerdotal female clan. Even a common shaman in Africa, in order to be accepted, had to have a rainmaker for a mother. In some instances, he also was dependent upon his wife: if she became pregnant, the Zulu rainmaker lost his powers, because gravidity temporarily paralyzed her magic powers and he could not deal with Nature by himself.

In most African kingdoms, power then originally emanated from priestly princesses. Whether there was one queen or two, such as the Dioscures; whether there was a queen dowager as a fixed reference with a son and a sister-wife for satellites; whether a brother-sister pair had the reins in their hands—all these were mere variations of the fundamental scheme founded on ritual knowledge of female dignitaries. Queens, however, have never anywhere been subject to ritual murder; they only order the ritual murder of the men constantly changing within the female field of gravity, once more abiding by the ancient law of mortal son–immortal mother, who is the Black Death-Mother and *mater dolorosa* at the same time. The "son," the spring man, as Tammuz, Attis, and Adonis, is the selected victim, the scapegoat who bears the world's burden and must atone for its sins with his death.

> In the oldest times [Rehse says], there were no reigning princes in Africa, but the Negroes had great kingdoms, ruled by goddesses. These goddesses had priests and priestesses who took care of all government business in the name of their sacred mistresses.

Since nobility remained female without being susceptible to change through male interference the priestess-princess could take for a lover or temporary husband whomever she pleased. A king, even if born within the inner core of the female clan, held a legitimate claim to the throne only through his marriage to a princely sister; *he* seemed to govern and had the responsibility, but *she* actually ruled. With the Banyoro, as in many other monarchies, the queen-sister was not allowed to have children by her husband and performed an abortion if she became pregnant by him. For pregnancy would have separated her too long from the king, whose occult capabilities were believed to be thoroughly dependent upon her, comparable to the Zulu rainmaker's powers, which depended on his wife. Today, the kingdom of the Banyoro has been Christianized, and the queen-sister is only nominally the king's wife.

The Bantu kingdoms knew only queens without prince consorts, selecting commoners or slaves for lovers. Seven queens in succession ruled over Angola; the last one, Singa N'Gola, heroically defended her kingdom against superior Portuguese arms. When finally she was offered retention of title and crown under the condition that she recognize Portuguese sovereignty, she was too proud to accept and relinquished the title in favor of a shadow king. Two mighty queens of Mpororo in East-Central Africa are the heroines of an entire collection of legends. They were high priestesses, somewhat like popes, and jointly governed the realm out of their spiritual power. So great was their sanctity that they were not allowed to touch the earth: all through their lives, for this reason, they were carried around in baskets by their ministers. In Latuka, the northernmost part of Uganda, an old queen occupied the throne by herself for many years because, as she declared, no one was worthy of being called her husband.

Independent queens ruled the Fanti on the Gold Coast [Ghana], which was a center of matriarchy. A queen also was the ruler of the Ubemba in Northern Rhodesia. The number of female chieftains in smaller tribes is legion, for women were often chosen because they were less cruel. Livingstone, Stanley, and Von Wissmann, in their African travels, met a number of female potentates. There were female rulers in the whole Zambesi area, in the northern Congo basin, and in the central Sudan, as well as lower Kasai.

Women often were the real rulers even where a man exercised the nominal power. Not always was she the real mother; sometimes she was the oldest woman of the clan, as the "Earth and Fire Mother" of Loango. H. Baumann tells us: "Often she enjoys great freedom of a sexual nature and has several lovers, but she may neither conclude a formal marriage nor have children by her lover."

In Togoland, the queens were given chieftains to help them rule, but they could make decisions only with the consent of the female council. And where profane female power was abolished by rising patriarchal law, religious female power survived. With the Laduma, the king was crowned by a priestess called the Simo. The ruler of the large Lunda kingdom of Central Africa was crowned by his mother, and the female hierarchy administrating the kingdom withstood all attempts on the part of the men to overthrow it. The Lukokesha, the chief priestess of the Lunda realm, was a royal princess, appointed by the female clan to exercise joint rule with the king, and she was always unmarried and childless, though she was allowed as many slave lovers as she pleased. Two other princesses were the king's legitimate wives, one of whose sons always became the crown prince, a direct, male succession, which would have been impossible in other women's kingdoms.

The royal dignity notwithstanding, however, the female clan, represented by the Lukokesha, or "sacred clan mother," retained its power. The Lukokesha was inviolable, had her own court, and had a veto over any edicts or laws. She could even depose the king and name a new one, a power which she is known to have exercised at least once—in 1873. When going to receptions or councils, she rode on a man's back, like the Aphrodite of Plutarch's legend, who rode on the back of a he goat.

Representative rides on the back of a man were customary also for other African princesses, as, for instance, for the royal sister of Uganda. This Ugandan potentate, though the wife of her brother the king, was also allowed to have slave lovers, but was not allowed to have children, so that she would not lose her magic powers. She and the queen dowager were not only associated with the Ugandan king in his power but also had themselves the title of "king." Whenever the queen dowager died, the people—the most intelligent and cultured nation of the African interior—were seized by great unrest, and a new queen dowager must immediately be found from the clan of the deceased. The death of the king was held to be less important. The thirty-eight other African monarchies still in existence at the turn of the last century very closely resembled the Ugandan pattern.

The Baganda and Bakitara queens also were sisters of their husbands and remained childless for the same reasons. Almost everywhere that sisters were associated with the rulers in joint rule, they enjoyed a complete sexual freedom subject only to the limitation that they must perform abortions in case of pregnancy in order not to interrupt the magic double life they led with their brother-kings, while the other princesses of the blood had the obligation of ensuring that the royal house did not die out. For this purpose, they kept slave lovers who, at the queen's whim and fancy, could be beheaded, changed, or humiliated, or kept behind lock and key, like Mohammedan harem wives. At the slightest suspicion of infidelity, of course, they were tortured and executed. If they were permitted the special dispensation of being allowed to leave the palace, a bell drove the population out of their path, so that no woman's eye should strike them.

We know these conditions best in the case of the Ashanti of the Gold Coast. Central power was exercised prior to the British seizure of power in 1896 by the old woman chief of the clan, called queen dowager. The king was selected from among the sons of the princesses, subject to the queen dowager's consent; she also could depose him, which she often did. The last queen dowager, according to British reports, had several dozen husbands executed, for she was accustomed to liquidate all of her royal harem from time to time and then to start all over again. All princesses were at liberty to marry whom they pleased, as long as their husband was handsome; otherwise, he was a subject of complete indifference to everyone. If a princess died before her husband, he had to commit suicide on her grave. If a child was born, the father had to bow before it and swear fealty. But if the child died, the father died, too.

Even disregarding the fate of the slave husbands, the female clan originally decided the life-and-death rhythm of the king born and selected by it. With the Shilluk of the White Nile, the royal sister-wives alone determined the exact time of the execution; formerly they actually choked the king with their own hands. A weakening of this function, which was considered sacred, and the first step toward patriarchy, is to be seen in the replacement of the sister-queen by her brother: with the Mundang, the rules called for him to behead the king in the ninth year of his reign. A long time ago, these periods, determined by lunar measurements, probably were much shorter, as was evidenced by the custom of the Banyoro of East Africa of announcing the new moon to the king by messenger, who always said, "Lord, thou hast outlived the moon."

The events transpiring with the Shilluk, the Mundang, and similar nations always showed the dynastic matriarchy of Africa in the shape of a "sacred clan," which permits the male element to pass over it like a chain of youths whose power is due to the clan and wilts with it. These youths were mere bearers of the spring, without a true personality in the eyes of the women, and therefore without a claim to get as old as they; the repetition of their sacrificial deaths guaranteed the eternal youth of the world.

According to Frobenius, the sacrificial slaughter of the king always took place at the time of the boys' initiation, "so that he might become the merciful spirit of the bush." "In order to win the favors of the bush spirit, one makes the blood sacrifice of circumcision for him. With it, all those who are going to clear the bush in order to found farms have already wounded themselves so as to put the bush spirit into a good mood."

A strange condition evolved in Dahomey. One king there succeeded in breaking the power of the women to such an extent that he had only to tolerate the joint rule of the queen dowager. He put an end to the promiscuous activities of his sister-wives by converting them into cloistered vestals and outlawing any male harem for them. He thus removed them from the administrative and political sphere and limited them to their supposed control of the cosmos, which they did by scooping up water in home-made jars out of the sacred springs for the rites of the rain god. Like their ancient Roman colleagues, they were called "mothers."

The Amazons of Dahomey were made assistants to the vestals; they were given sacerdotal functions like those of the princesses and also became the official wives of the king in his capacity of representation of the moon-god, the lord of the female world. One of these priest-kings refused to place his name under an official document destined for French President Carnot: in a touchingly naïve estimation of European statesmen's abilities, he feared that Carnot might engage in black magic with that signature.

The king's Amazons would stand fast and die for him in

case of need. Without their heroism, little Dahomey would have been swallowed up by her neighbors. When King Gueso undertook his disastrous expedition against Abeokuta, they saved his life by holding the battlefield despite frightful casualties while the male army fled. On another occasion under Gueso's successor, they preferred death on the battlefield to flight with the remainder of the army. Their formula for disparaging cowards was, "You are a man." When maneuvers were held, the attackers raced through all obstacles and ran across cacti and thorns, after which they returned to camp smiling, their skins lacerated, their wounds bleeding. Their military ability was equaled by their skill as elephant huntresses.

Their appearance [reported Captain Duncan of the Life Guards] is more martial than that of the men; on a campaign, I should prefer the women of that country as soldiers to the men. After all I have seen in Africa, it appears to me that the King of Dahomey possesses an army superior to any other west of the Great Sahara.

Female warriors at times might be considered the "Swiss Guards" of Africa, but there also were large female armies, like those of the sultans of Zanzibar and of the old kingdom of Monomotapa in southeastern Africa. The Monomotapa army had a whole province assigned to it near the Zambezi River, and it held the deciding voice in the election of kings. Farther to the north, there was an Amazon kingdom with the ruler as well as all members of the army belonging to the female sex: the kingdom of Galla.[1]

The women of Africa tended to have their own organization. Missionaries often complained that, wherever marriage was not matrilocal to start with, the women would leave their husbands and go home to the mother clan at the slightest provocation. In some tribes, like the Useguha, the women

[1] The *New York Herald-Tribune*, Paris Edition, of Dec. 2, 1964, page 10, describes an Amazon army of 5000 forming an elite body in the army of Dr. Hastings Banda, the founder and first premier of Malawi (Nyasaland). This female corps was instrumental in helping to achieve Malawi's independence and at the time of the report was guarding the crucial boundary with Tanganyika. (Editor–translator)

returned to their homes every few years as a matter of principle. All eyewitness reports on African tribes were full of astonishment at the sensitivity of African women: with the Warega in the Congo, insulting a woman was a *casus belli*. The influence of the woman was strong all over Africa. The wife of the last sultan of Nyangara was asked for advice by the most important chiefs of the land in every crisis. If one tried to buy any trinkets at all from a Manbutto, he would, according to Schweinfurth, always send one to his wife, on the grounds that it belonged to her.

The Banyai, according to E. Hahn, asked their wives for permission to do anything demanded of them, and if her answer was negative, no persuasion or reward could convince the man to disobey her. The same author tells us that the Hottentot and Bushman wives were veritable despots. With the Ovoherero, the man owned no home but lived in his wife's house as an unpaid laborer—a common practice all over East Africa. Often the men had six or seven wives whom they visited alternately and with whose farm work they helped without ever owning any of the produce.

The Beni-Amer in Northeast Africa placed the man in a pitiable situation. Not only was he exploited, but there was something of a conspiracy to ruin him. At the slightest offense, he was shown the door, his wife would have her entire clan give him a rough time, and only after much pleading and the intercession of the neighbors would he be allowed to buy his way back in with a camel or a cow. He also had to make expensive gifts to his wife after the birth of every child. When the husband finally was totally without means, he was chased away to nurse his wounds and make room for the next victim. According to W. Munzinger's report, the women, in addition, considered it utterly shameful to show any affection or consideration for these pitiful wretches. Similar conditions prevailed among the Dongola.

The purchasing of the bride, a widespread custom in Africa, is not necessarily a sign of patriarchy. It could be construed as such only where the bride is severed from her clan by this payment. A price paid at the wedding may also mean that the husband is buying his way into the wife's house, thus making it a male dowry of the sort that played such an important part in ancient Egyptian marriage contracts.

With the Tuaregs of North Africa and the Sahara, this price used to be fixed at four white camels with which the wife would then go into business; after a divorce, they remained her property. Since the woman had a perfect right to dissolve marriages, she could, in the course of time, acquire quite a collection of camels. Even the Ashanti princesses demanded that they be bought at an enormous price by their slave husbands, who had no choice whatsoever about buying their way into the harems full of other slaves just like them. Rejecting such a "proposal" would have been very risky.

Of the two African areas of strong matriarchy, the western one extended to the Atlantic islands. According to *Revue d'Ethnographie* of 1924, a queen governed the island of Gomeira in the Canary Islands at the time of publication, and an elective princess ruled the island of Oranga Grande in the Bissago Archipelago, who had a court, with a prime minister, a fiscal officer, a master of the port, and an interpreter. From this farthest western boundary, matriarchal systems stretch across the African continent in a broad belt.

The second matriarchal area, inhabited mostly by Hamites, originated in the North and penetrated down to East Africa. There are distinct traces indicating that both areas were more extensive in former days, as indicated also by some matriarchal enclaves. In the western and central Sudan, the ruling families are still matriarchal, while the lower strata are patriarchal—a dualism often associated with the path of Hamitic conquests.

According to H. Baumann, African centers of matriarchy are located in areas of strikingly superior political organization. In the West African matriarchal belt, there is "a higher political form, a splendid art, a greater plenty of musical instruments, more of a myth-forming imagination," though the matriarchal peoples of South Africa are aborigines of a very low cultural level.[2] Frobenius collected a number of stories

[2] In January, 1965, the newspapers reported the discovery of the most primitive group of humans ever seen in the Kalahari Desert area, a part of the aboriginal Hottentot population. Whether this

dealing with city queens, for in Africa the polis played a part akin to that in ancient Greece. Timbuctoo, Bokani, Raba, Gbatatchi, and Omdourman turned out to be cities founded by women. Women still occupy important posts in African city government.

---

group was matriarchal in its organization or not would be worth recording, once oral contact is established with these pre-Stone Age people. (Editor–translator)

XXI

LYCIA, LYDIA, CARIA
SUMERIA, BABYLONIA

Bachofen loved the Lycian Mountains, which grow almost into the Mediterranean from the Taurus, stretching into the blue Aegean like a matriarchal Switzerland of antiquity, the area that the Romans called "Asia of the thousand fragrant peaks." Bachofen's famous work on the Lycian people starts with the words: "Any investigation of matriarchy must start out with the Lycian people. For this fact, we have the most definite and most voluminous evidence."

The Lycians originally came from Crete and thus were a Mediterranean race. Their period of greatest prosperity was associated with the name of Sarpedon, the youngest brother of Minos, and Bellerophon, the Peloponnesian, who was deified like Minos, who after his death became a god and judge of the underworld.

Herodotus, who traveled in Lycia shortly after Cyrus' conquest of the country, reports:

> Their customs are partly Cretan, partly Carian, but they have the peculiar habit of taking their mothers', not their fathers', names. If one asks a Lycian who he is, he will name his ancestors on his mother's side. If a free woman marries a slave, the children are considered free, but if a freeman marries a foreign woman or a slave, the children are illegitimate.

Nicolaus Damascenus agrees: "The Lycians show more honor to the women than to the men; they call themselves after the mother and bequeath her property to their daughters, not their sons." Heraclides Ponticus goes into greater detail: "They have no written laws, only unwritten customs." Where women rule, tradition takes the place of formal legislation. There is nothing as characteristic of gynocracy as an

absence of "the law" and a presence of good manners that
are the consequence of an enchanting confidence in motherly
justice. Bachofen says:

> It is certain that one believed in a closer relationship of
> women to the divine being and attributed to them a better
> understanding of divine will. They bore within themselves
> the law pervading all matter. Justice speaks out of their
> mouths without self-consciousness and with certainty in
> the manner of conscience. They are wise by nature, proph-
> etesses proclaiming Fate, Sybil, or Themis. Therefore,
> women were considered inviolable bearers of jurisprudence
> and sources of prophecy. The battle lines drew apart at
> their command, and they arbitrated the disputes of the
> nations as sacerdotal umpires: a religious foundation on
> which gynocracy immovably rested.

Then Bachofen summarizes the countless bits of evidence of
matriarchy in Lycia:

> First of all, there is the status of the children: they follow
> the mother, not the father. Secondly, there is the inherit-
> ance of property: the parental inheritance is passed on to
> the daughters, not to the sons. Thirdly, there is family
> power: the mother rules and not the father, and by a logical
> extension, this custom also applies to the state.

In other ways, too, Bachofen found the Lycian example
especially important:

> It would be easy to jump to the conclusion of cowardice,
> effeminacy, and lack of dignity resulting for the men from
> female domination. The Lycian people effectively demon-
> strated how false that would be. Its bravery was especially
> famous. . . . Gynocracy and courage of the men in war,
> united in the case of the Lycians, appear as correlatives
> also in other places such as Crete and Caria, whose peoples
> were closely related to the Lycians. Aristotle postulates
> that most warlike and courageous people were governed
> by gynocracy . . .

The Tel-el-Amarna finds were made long after Bachofen's
death, and so he did not have the satisfaction of knowing
what a place his beloved Lycians occupied in the diplomatic
correspondence of the eighteenth dynasty of Egypt, which

called them *Lukki.* Thus they appeared around 1500 B.C. as civilized, urban, and commercial people whose territories reached far into Anatolia.

Lycian gynocracy was responsible also for that unwritten, subtle law that made the men wear female clothing when they were in mourning. The mother alone owned everything born and therefore had exclusive rights to grieve for those who had died. If the father was irrelevant to the living child, he had no right either to mourn for a dead one. Only through a feminine mimicry, a kind of death couvade, could he participate in the fate of human mortality. The splendid Lycian funebrial culture, as extensive as the Egyptian, was also entirely feminine, featuring rows of female names along rows of tablets, flanked by the monuments of harpies, great egg mothers in the shape of birds.

Bellerophon, the national hero, never exceeded the power field of his mother earth. As the horseman riding Pegasus, fighting down from cool heights, he victoriously fought against the Amazons and then, allied with the Amazons, against Chimera, the nightmare animal of impure blend, but he never reached solar space, crashing instead on the bogs of the earth and limping away. "His victories I will sing, but his death I would not contemplate," Pindar says of him. Bellerophon's daughter Laodamia, according to the legend, became a queen.

Bellerophon's victories included the overthrow of the Amazons, for young daughters' realms seem to have drifted away from their tribes or penetrated Europe from the Caucasian area at the time. From the Sinai Peninsula to the Sarmatian plains there was great confusion wrought by the appearance of the young female warriors on horseback. Rameses II mentions in his correspondence that the Mysian women fought on horseback under the leadership of their queen. (The Mysians were a branch of the Lydians, neighbors of the Lycians, and relatives of the Carians.) Such was the custom of the country for nearly a thousand years.

The Carian queen Artemisia led a part of Xerxes' army and, as the historians report, exceeded all the male generals of the Persian army in bravery and strategic insight during the Greco-Persian War (480 B.C.). A later Artemisia was the originator of the famous mausoleum, the crypt built for her brother-husband Mausolos, after the construction of which she abdicated in favor of her younger sister Ada, who was married to her younger brother Hidrieus. Less unconsolable than Artemisia, she continued to rule after Hidrieus' death and was confirmed on her throne by Alexander the Great. As in Egypt, so in Caria the brother held his right to the throne only as the husband of his sister-queen, although, if she chose a stranger, he also was considered her brother.

In Lydia, the royal house traced itself back to the Amazon Omphale, whose husband of the day always was her slave, like those slave husbands of a later time in Africa. According to the Hercules legend, Hercules was her husband for a time, as a punishment for his outburst of unrestrained fury that caused him to kill an innocent person. As a sun-hero and future ruler, Hercules had to learn his manners, and so, he had to learn self-discipline under the most humiliating circumstances. Hercules, unlike Omphale's other husbands, of course, managed to avoid getting killed and after this experience is reputed to have gone about the earth in search of Amazon kingdoms, all of which he pledged to destroy. The Lydian throne, on the other hand, was handed down from queen to queen. Not until the times of the Medes do we hear about a Lydian king: Croesus, who seems to have prospered in his job.

The capital of Lydia was the Paris of Asia Minor, greater Greece, and the Mediterranean island world for almost a millennium. From there, one imported the most elegant cloth, perfumes, and the fine, high-heeled shoes so much in demand in Sappho's circles—Lesbos was a mere cat's jump away from the Lydian coast. Whoever thought that the Chaldeans were too expensive had his horoscope prepared by the Lydian ladies. Everything in circulation among our astrologists and other "prophetesses" under the name of *The Egyptian Dream Book* was copied from the work of Artemidoros of Daldis, who worked out his interpretation of some three thousand dreams in five volumes during the second century B.C.

Not only was the Lydian capital a cosmopolitan city creating fashions and giving every care to the human body, but it also was a male beauty center, featuring such attractions as permanents, gold jewelry, manicuring, and dental cures for the gentlemen. Strabo reports that gigolo types were selected and supported by the ladies. Women were allowed to marry whom they pleased and obtained divorces at their discretion and attended to public affairs, while the men took care of the house. This "inverted" order of things was mentioned by Herodotus in the fifth century and described in great detail. This impeccable historian assures us that, though he had seen much of the world, only Egyptian pyramids and Babylonian architecture could compare in splendor with a Lydian mausoleum. According to the inscriptions, it was not only designed and financed but also built—stone for stone—by women.

Babylonian civilization was a successor to the Sumerians. The realms of Sumer and Akkad were separated only after the eruption of the Semites in the third millennium B.C. Akkad was Babylon. Men with narrow skulls, like the Afghans, venerated the goddess Ishtar in old Ur and Uruk, and she picked a fight with the king of the youths, Gilgamesh, when he came from the cedar forest. Gilgamesh in the Sumerian national epic enunciated some of the most touching things that men had ever said:

My young friend, the panther of the field, has turned to earth,
Egidu, the friend whom I love, has turned to earth.
Shall I not also have to lie down, never again to rise?
How could then my cheeks not be hollow, or my countenance bent,
How could my heart not be sad, nor emaciated my body,
How could I not resemble a wanderer of distant paths?
Therefore I hasten across the fields, far away.
How could I be silent? How can I shout it out:
My friend, whom I love, has turned to earth!
Since he is gone, I find my life no more.

Excavations have unearthed golden animal heads with blue beards, just like those described in the epic. They are products of a civilization in maturity and decline. In those days, many thousands of years ago, the sexes balanced one another miraculously. Both spouses were completely equal in matters of divorce and adultery. The marriage contract contained provisions for divorce, inheritance, and adoption. If a freeman took a slave girl for a concubine, she and her children thereby gained their freedom. If a free woman married a slave, the mother's freedom was transmitted to the children. Dowry and engagement presents of the bridegroom remained the wife's property in all circumstances. She was protected against her husband's creditors, could conclude contracts, give evidence before a court of law, sue her own husband, and even repudiate or disinherit her own sons for disobedience, or have them expelled from the city altogether.

Boys and girls went to the temple schools together and learned geometry, grammar, and even square roots. Anyone engaged in business had to keep exact books. There was a literary language spoken only by women to women, the Emesal. All of this obviously was not the beginning but the culmination of a great cultural cycle. What might it have been that preceded the workings of the balance between the sexes, before it inclined toward the men under the influence of the Semites? Was it even then a shallow matriarchy? It seems a pity that we shall probably not learn much about the answer to that question, although Sumerian tradition claimed a conscious past of four hundred thousand years before the Great Deluge. But most likely the waters destroyed all the evidence of earlier civilization. What a pity!

XXII

ROME

At no time did the Romans pretend that the rule of men and patriarchy were a god-given or nature-ordained form of life. They were never so blinded by pride, for their genius was one of sobriety. On the contrary, the Romans always emphasized the abnormal element in their way of life, and, since they did not know China and since Greece and Judaea had become political ciphers, they considered themselves the only important people practicing patriarchy. They believed that they were a great exception to a general rule. To some extent they were right in thinking so, for their greatest enemies were matriarchal peoples: at first the small Italic tribes, the Etruscans and the Volsci with their Amazon queen and their Diana priestess Camilla, then their greater and more distant enemies, the Carthaginians, Egyptians, Scythians, Celts, and Teutons. However, not only were they surrounded by matriarchal peoples; an obedience to their Sabine mothers lay in their blood. Horace still reminds his readers of the times when the sons had to chop wood at the strict orders of their mothers.

Why that handful of rather dubious elements gathered from all directions became the creators of the Occidental empire and how they ever managed to become the proud Romans are perhaps parts of the greatest riddle of human history. Nor is it easy to understand how, in the midst of an ancient mother-dominated civilization, there arose an enclave of male predominance, whether one assumes the Asiatic origin, the Spartan from the Sabinian side, an autochthonous one, or any other.[1] The original Roman way of life, which

[1] The author, otherwise partial to the acceptance of national legends and folklore, seems unwilling to go along with the tradi-

in some ways was a new form of human existence, was of such force that, long after the disappearance of the Roman state and after the disappearance of anything like a Roman nation, this singular institutional complex remained suspended for many centuries without a material base and so forcefully brought the invaders whirling through Europe under its spell that they all genuflected before it and tried to re-create an empire they had never seen with their own eyes.

Even Spengler's formula that, in contrast to the race, which is a product of Nature, a nation is created in body and spirit by a common fate cannot satisfy one on this point, nor can one possibly accept an "economic interpretation." From what sources did those Romans take their characteristic strength of will, that incomparable, distinguishing Roman characteristic which was the fountain of their being from their beginnings and which comprised that common fate of theirs rather than being molded by it? We cannot place the entire responsibility on a "tradition" doctored after the event.

The Romans never seem to have thought about interpreting away their matriarchal influence through substitution of a masculine-oriented mythos, which might have been an obvious thing to do. In matriarchal Etruria, the matriarchal influence was later eradicated with diligent fury and even purged from the language, but the three great Roman kings of Etruscan descent, Tarquinius Priscus, Servius Tullius, and Tarquinius Superbus, were never explained away from the Roman throne.

Roman practice also did not really stamp out matriarchal tendencies but solidified them at the popular level where they survived. For this reason, the Roman state was actively concerned with keeping that basis in its current form and wanted to preclude any sudden developments which might have caused those latent roots to sprout unwelcome plants. Cato's ceaseless warning was: "Remember the laws through

---

tional Roman legend that the ancestors of the Roman people were survivors of the Trojan War, fugitives from Troy who found their way to Italy under the leadership of Aeneas. Though seemingly somewhat fantastic, the story of a very foreign origin seems to be borne out by the existence of Rome as a patriarchy in the midst of matriarchal Italic tribes. (Editor–translator)

which our ancestors limited the liberties of the women, through which they bent them to the will of the men." Any changes along these lines meant danger to the state.

Cato here exhibited a well-founded fear. Bachofen demonstrated with the example of Tanaquil that, in the beginning of Rome, this power-giving, hetaeristic queen of the Asiatic mold raised three men on the throne, though pious legend later reinterpreted her into the essence of Roman matronhood. Never did this mainstay of male domination forget the foundation on which it was based. *Roma,* the *urbs,* was a female earth navel that Romulus found in the moist underbrush. Around this navel stone surrounded by weeds, the *Forum Romanum* was built; it was the center of Rome, and Rome was the center of the world. One important lot for the new city was donated to it by a noble prostitute, the *nobilissima meretrix* Acca Laurentia; another piece of ground was given to the people by the vestal virgin Gaia Terratia, for the land was the property of the women.

The Latins named themselves after Latia, the wife of Saturn, and the Romans called themselves Quirites after their Sabinian mothers. The names of *Roma* and Romulus come from the Etruscan clans of the Rumate and Rumulna. The name of the Quirinal hill goes back to a Sabinian legend. The royal power was of feminine origin: the kings, some of whom were foreigners, received title and rank only by marriage with a woman of the ruling family. Porsenna led away female captives from Rome, because they were more important than the men, just as the Romans did later with the Celts and the Teutons. Romulus and Servius Tullius knew only their mothers. Finally, the Roman people originally consisted of thirty female clans called *curiae.* These clans had been assigned the names of thirty Sabinian women by Romulus as an expression of thanks for the long, happy era of peace, which was their work, after the Roman-Sabinian war that they had stopped by separating the hostile armies.

Later on, men founded families within these thirty clans. They called themselves patricians: *qui patres scire possunt* —"those who know their fathers." These families separated as an elite from the rest of the female clans. The word "plebeian" originally referred to all Romans; *pleo* means "to fill," and this term is related to the Greek *plethos,* meaning "substance." Thus the lowly *plebs* were mere creatures of indefinite substance, "filling" the ranks of the population—or perhaps of an indeterminate "filling" of the female receptacle, which would indicate why "those who know their fathers" were something so special as to become aristocrats.

Patricians became the bearers of the idea of the paternal state, which was diametrically opposed to the uninhibited female realm. The question here was not one of rich or poor—for one and the same person may be rich and poor within his single lifetime—but one of whether the male or the female element should govern. The sudden separation of the male family from the female clan was one of the climaxes in the age-old battle about the shape of the relations between the sexes, even though other nations had experienced similar events at an earlier time.

Matriarchal society had been the natural condition of things, for motherhood was biologically the only certitude. In addition, the mother exerted all of her prenatal influence on the foetus. The father remained a legal fiction that was never transformable into a certainty. It had been a just balance, for the woman alone bears the burden of her sex and bears long and heavily the thing which is so easy for the man. (This theory was first formulated by Rosa Mayreder.) Brevity in the participation in reproduction corresponded to uncertainty about the results. The constant and the transitory factor made up a disharmonious pair. The social form closest to Nature, therefore, was neither the male-dominated nor the female-dominated family but the female clan as a preserver and administrator of new life and of all material property.

The male impregnators, true to their natural function, migrated to and from this ruling feminine institution in a quick and always changing progression. This biologic-substantial order, based entirely on the natural fact of motherhood, seems to have achieved greater well-being and to have worked better than any other. The mother-dominated family, too, was still clear and true and, moreover, distinguished itself from the female clan by a deeper human relationship between the sexes. An order contrary to Nature was established only with the emphasis on fatherhood, no matter what proud heights may have been ascended by the partiarchal state.

First of all, biological calculation was badly confused by going back to procreation as the decisive event. Instead of birth, the only certain moment, one now considered as important only the eternally insecure moment of conception. How could one be sure of it, and, with it, of paternity? One tried to make sure of it by locking up the women and girls. The female half of mankind in this manner was prevented from earning its living and contributing to the production of goods, so that it became a burden on the men. Therefore, the women and girls were locked up even more securely so that the man should be sure that he was carrying this burden for his own children at least. In China, the extreme case, the male became so disenchanted by this stunted and uneducated product of his own making that he had to create a second female type, the "daughter of the flowers," for his physical and spiritual recreation, though he reproduced by means of his domesticated female. This is a well-known, often discussed chain of events.

The Romans tried another appoach. They appealed to the women's "own" sense of honor. Unfortunately, this appeal was not really the women's "own" feeling, and it was significantly called *virtus,* which comes from *vir,* the Latin word for man, as pointed out by Briffault. In order to make sure of things, there were the laws. Cato frequently reminded his listeners of them: "If thou findest thy wife in adultery, thou art free to kill her without a trial and without fear of punishment. If thou committest adultery, she has no right even to lift her little finger against thee."

But seldom in history has a law been honored so largely in the breech. Despite the encouraging impunity of killing adulterous wives, a Venus temple was erected in 285 B.C., paid for by fines collected from women for adultery at a time when republican virtues supposedly were at their peak. Thus it went with many laws. The law allowed no women to bequeath any property or conclude any business deals, and the laws did not recognize her children as belonging to her. In fact, however, the Roman woman lived in dignity and freedom, much freer than the Athenian. The coeducation of boys and girls promoted this status. The Roman matron was addressed by all persons, including her husband, as *domina*, which means "mistress." She received his guests as well as her own and visited whom she pleased. Domestic work, except for spinning, could not be demanded of her, while male slaves did the cooking.

The older the Roman matron became the more her standing rose in the community. Everyone had to make way for her on the street. Anyone insulting her with insolent words was brought to trial. One might be tempted to interpret this trait as a reminder of filial respect and masculine obedience. The opposite seems to be the case. The Romans could afford these niceties because they were such sober adults devoid of all infantilism; their masculine rule was not at all imperiled by their women. Roman manhood was far more vulnerable to the allures of hetaerae. Wherever Caesar was expected, his soldiers shouted: "Guard your wives, the bald lecher approaches." Nothing made Caesar prouder than the descent of his family, the Julians, from Aphrodite, and he diligently employed himself in showing himself worthy of this descent in an erotic manner. In contact with Egypt and Asia Minor, Roman generals easily succumbed to vice. It was rumored of Caesar that, if he had not been stabbed, he would have had Cleopatra come to Rome, made her his wife, and appointed Caesarion his successor in power.

A certain laxness on the part of inexorable patriarchs toward female adultery within their homes seems inexplicable until one notices that the paternity on which the Romans insisted was of a physical rather than an emotional variety. Paternal authority was far more important than paternity. "No other people has as great an authority over its sons as we." It was a matter of authority and pride rather than love. The power of the patriarchy was a sober means of achieving the state and keeping it immune to the dangers of an incalculably vacillating and emotional youth. This principle, realized at an early stage and without exception, had no other purpose than serving the male empire, a creation of a mature, realistic spirit.

The family forms exist for the state, not for the fatherly feeling. Unlike the patriarchal authority among the Jews, the *patria potestas* had its roots in civil, not in religious, areas and therefore was without the divine complement of a Father-God. The Roman state, occupying the place of a "great father" itself, was a rational structure, not a structure of the soul, and so, it was less encumbered by tatters of libido, fear, love, and hatred. A God-Father revered by a patriarchal people caused an ambivalence of love and hatred; the Romans had founded their father state in a different mode of consciousness called *patroos* or "founder of states," a purposeful clarity.

The women under Roman civil law not only had no legal right to their own children but also lacked the right to adopt children. Men could adopt them, even after they died, if their last wills and testaments specified it. The adopted son had no relationship to the wife of his adopted father; he remained motherless. The adoption resulted only from a pure mental act, without a pretended commonality of blood such as the gesture of giving birth to adopted children in primitive matriarchal nations. This state was changed only by Emperor Justinian.

Roman husbands occasionally lent out their wives: that is how little they cared about their sole possession of them. At the orders of the men, polyandry belonged to the accepted norm and republican virtue. Quintus Hortensius, for instance, asked Cato to arrange for the loan of his daughter, who was already married, so that he might "create children on such noble soil" for the greater good of the state. Cato felt honored but somewhat unsure of his son-in-law and asked his friend and admirer rather to accept his own wife in compensation. Thus the virtuous gallant had to extend profuse thanks for old Marcia. Some years later, after Quintus died, Cato took her back.

It is difficult to determine at this point whether this sexual communion comprised a remnant of Sabinian matriarchy, reinterpreted for Roman republicanism. Such an influence is clearly discernible in the Roman estimate that a father's brother (*patruus*) is less important than a mother's brother (*avunculus*). It appears also in the word *matrimonium*, meaning marriage, and in *consobrini*, meaning siblings, but originally standing only for sisters. Above all, however, it is apparent in *parricidium*, signifying the murder of either mother or father, and used even to refer to murders in general, for the *quaestores parricidii* were the duumvirs entrusted with the investigation of murders.

It is related to *pario, pareo,* and *appareo,* "to appear." The act of birth is the appearance of that which is hidden. *Pario* and *Pales* are obviously related. Pales is the original mother giving birth to all things, which is recognized as Pales, a male impregnator of the earth in the shape of a donkey. *Parricidium* was the word for an injury inflicted on the original mother in the shape of one of her creatures. Such an injury is implicit in any murder, no matter whether it victimizes a man or a woman. The degree of personal relationship is unimportant. The sin committed against procreative, birth-giving Nature determines the penalty earned. Atonement must follow any offense. A parricide cannot be buried, for his return to the earth's folds must be denied him. He was sewn into a sack and cast into the water in order to prevent him from touching Mother Earth. (That is Bachofen's theory.)

Underneath a well-defined line, the female element remained alive and free even in Rome. It had exclusive possession of emotional life and the religious sphere, though both varieties of experience atrophied somewhat in the Roman Empire. The royal female clan continued its existence in the vestal virgins. The Roman priesthood lived on in the high priest, the *flamen dialis,* and his wife, the *flaminica.* They were both incomparably sacred and incomparably unimportant. The *flaminica* was always elected from one of the oldest noble families and always sacrificed a ram at every new moon according to ancient, prerepublican customs. At her death, the *flamen dialis* lost his job and reverted to simple citizenship: an echo of the female law of succession in royal times.

The other surviving Italic tribes never were completely converted to patriarchal laws. Maecenas the Etruscan had no paternal line; when Horace wanted to flatter him, he recounted only his mothers in his epistles. The prerepublican, purely material existence and undifferentiated liberty was concretely practiced in the Saturnalia. The freeing of slaves also was practiced in the name of a great nature goddess,

Feronia. Female predominance, which here, as everywhere else, also signified the right to sexual freedom, came into its own with the feasts of Ceres and of Mater Matuta.

The priesthood, wearing donkey masks, then took the place of Pales, the phallic god. No patrician lady or matron of the highest nobility was allowed to be remiss in her sacred duty. Lesbian practices and holy obscenities, in honor of Bona Dea especially, exceeded the cultic rites of African rain priestesses, for primitive peoples have always considered rain the consequence of erotic stimulation of a divinity. As late as the reign of Tiberius there was a great scandal because a young roué, who had fallen in love unhappily with the wife of a high official, had bribed a priest to lend him one of the donkey masks, although no profane citizens were allowed to enter Ceres' temple. The ladies also were not allowed to pray for husbands or sons but only for members of their uterine line.

More honest than nineteenth-century society, republican Rome never spoke of a "physiological weakness of women" or made believe that they "belonged in the house." The Romans did not pretend that independence meant only an "illusory happiness" for women. Through Cato, the reason for their political and legal subordination was frankly admitted. He warned, as quoted above, "Remember the laws through which our ancestors limited the liberties of women, through which they bent them to the will of the men." And he added, "As soon as they become equal to us, they will be our superiors."

XXIII

CELTS

Female predominance among the Celts began in the astral sphere. Crowned bird fairies sway back and forth between the spheres, chirping wisdom and locking up saucy sorcerers in shiny graves. Ladies of lunar substance, tall, transparent, and beautiful, give their tellurian lover a few kingdoms after a night of love or dismiss him with droopy eyes and a long, white beard, depending on their whim and fancy. Shiny energies float before them and toy with cosmic laws. Their grace is responsible for the rotation of the stars. Since their freewheeling nature easily conforms to the aristocratic class differences of civilization, the enchanted man easily confuses elflike beings, queens, priestesses, goddesses, and free women.

Just as in patriarchal society the male lords usually saw that "the daughters of the earth were beautiful" and drew the customary inferences from that observation, a supernatural femininity in Celtic lands made a similar observation regarding the sons of the earth and came down to join them. Superiority is determined by the question of who condescends to join whom. The cosmic hour was midnight. The male day was enclosed by two female nights, and time division was by the night. The moon was the lord of time and bestowed somnambulism, oracles in its phases, and the gift of prophecy in the intoxicating beverage made of the sticky mistletoe juice. In its silvery light, naked and woad-painted priestesses danced in Gaul and Britannia.

Ireland and Scotland were female settlements, named after the ladies Erin and Scota. Ireland's oldest document, the *Book of Leinster*, describes in detail how matriarchy was forced upon the conquered Picts by the victorious Gaelic tribes. Irish and Gaelic heroic clans took the names of the mothers—not the fathers. Livy reports that the Celts had the female rule of succession on their thrones and inherited property according to matriarchal provisions. Several different historians tell of independent Celtic queens as leaders in war; the most famous of them, of course, was Boadicea. Celtic warriors were so accustomed to take female predominance for granted that a group of British prisoners, when brought before the Roman Emperor Claudius, ignored him and the imperial insignia and headed straight for the throne of the Empress Agrippina, making their obeisances to her, much to the shock and chagrin of Roman society in general and of Tacitus in particular.

The Celts of Britain and Ireland retained their matrilocal marriages up to, and including, the age of chivalry. The lady of the castle chose whomever she pleased, much like the lady of Arabia, who was "the property of no man, accustomed to give herself generously and freely." Emer, for instance, said:

> Rise, wonderful Ailill! Thou shalt have rest, bravest of the brave. Put thy hand around my neck—the beginning of the joy of love. Blissful is the gift of love, when man and woman kiss one another. But if that should not suffice for thee, excellent knight, I'll give thee of myself from the knee to the navel, to heal the pangs of love.

This quick, rather naïve intimacy without any cynicism may be traceable to the custom of having the young girls and ladies of the house immediately prepare a hot bath with herbs for any strange knight who was their guest, keeping him company all the while and then artistically massaging him—"le tastonner doucement."

In the Irish original of the story of Tristan and Isolde, there does not occur any difficulty about the problem that so much troubled Gottfried von Strassburg, the author of the thirteenth-century German version: deceiving King Marke regarding the virginity of the bride. In Cornwall the substitution of the virgin Brangane would have been unnecessary on this occasion, for Marke would never have expected to find Isolde a virgin. On the other hand, the position of the nephew as heir to the throne was genuinely Celtic. In old myths, legends, stories, and literature, the sister's son tends to play the part of the hero, as matriarchal law would dictate.

In the Celtic nobility, both sexes were trained in sports and had well-built bodies, but Strabo said of the common people that their "domestic" men tended toward obesity and were ordered by law not to exceed a certain measurement, while their women were taller, better-looking, and more supple. The woman also did the wooing. A Greek, the guest at a wedding of a Celtic chief's daughter, describes how all the young men of the neighborhood had been invited to the banquet, although there was no fiancé. The girl then appeared, a golden cup filled with wine in her hand, gave all those assembled a professional once-over and chose her bridegroom by handing him the cup.

On the British Isles, matriarchy lasted well into Christian times, although it died out much earlier on the continent because of the Romanization of that region. When Hannibal marched through Gaul, however, an agreement drawn up between him and the inhabitants stated that any difference of opinion regarding the damage done by his troops in passage and compensations to be paid for it were to be decided exclusively by the supreme council of Gallic women, with no right of appeal from this college of matrons for either party.

XXIV

THE TEUTONS

The ethereally cheerful Celtic moon world was opposed to the heavy, Germanic realm, which rose from the earth navels, cloudy-prophetic or warlike and shiny. Its three Nornes were called "rulers of gods and men." Profundity, dignity, wisdom, and power grew near the mother rocks on the Rhine.

In war, every Germanic army had a prophetess, without whose advice nothing was attempted. At home, priestesses were more respected than priests, seeresses more than seers. Entire tribes were fascinated by the divine oracles of such maidens or waited at a respectful distance from the towering castles in which they lived to receive the divine verdicts that they reached in cases of disputes between two peoples or prior to great enterprises. Saxons and Franconians summoned the popular assembly only for nights of full moon or new moon. According to Tacitus, "one could gain the greatest ascendancy over the Germanic tribes by securing girls of noble families as hostages." The chiefs preferred going away as hostages or sending their sons rather than part with their daughters.

The uterine line was preferred long after Romanization set in. In the times of Frederick I (1152–1190), the children of a free woman and a serf father or the children of a serf woman with a free father always took on the status of their mother. As late as the eighteenth century, Germans observed the principle that legitimate and illegitimate children had the same status in relation to their mothers. The Lay of the Nibelungs as recorded in the thirteenth century names three Burgundian kings as sons of Queen Ute without mentioning their father.

The Lombards, or Langobards, were named after their

tribal ancestress Gambara. Visigoths and Ostrogoths always moved into the home of their wives and their property and titles were inherited only through their wives, so that Hermingisil in Saxony, lying on his deathbed, instructs his son Radger to marry his widow after his death, "according to the laws of our forebears." Heirs apparent do not feel legitimate until they possess the queen. Edbald, the Kentish king, therefore marries his stepmother. Ethelbald, king of Wessex, marries the widow of his father Ethelwulf. Another queen of Wessex prefers to continue the rule by herself. Holland, too, had a queen without a consort in the days of Tacitus.

In Scandinavia, until the eighth century the succession went from mother to daughter and only through her could be inherited by a husband. Hamlet's mother bestows the throne along with her hand in marriage. Old German poems from the third and fourth centuries have the women wooing the men. The Salic Law, which took over in Germany in the Middle Ages, is clearly traceable to Roman influence; there were ten versions of this law, and some of them allowed co-determination for females in important decisions.

Female predominance survived longest in the old German criminal code, which meted out twice as much punishment for offenses against the life, the person, or the property of women as of men. An original matriarchy is especially confirmed by Tacitus' report that the Teutons considered themselves more closely related to their mother's brothers than to their father's, which always was a characteristic sign of the transition. Lamprecht proved in detail that matriarchal law existed in Teutonic society, although he did not prove anything like the rule of women. Specialists in Indo-Germanic history, for reasons of comparative philology, doubt that their group started out with matriarchal institutions.

There is a modern thesis that the Old Stone Age, matriarchal Cro-Magnon race already resided in Europe when the Indo-Germanic invader race arrived on the scene, both races tending to be blond, though the Cro-Magnon man was taller and much heavier than the Nordic race coming from the area of southern Russia. The two races then mingled and formed the Teutonic tribes. If this theory should be confirmed, one might presume that the Germanic peoples took their matriarchal institutions from their Cro-Magnon inheritance.[1]

The Germanic tribes also had another very matriarchal type of institution: the Amazon element, the armored maidens, the Valkyrie. At the first terrible collision of the Romans with the Cimbri and Teutons, the battle with the armed women was more difficult for the Romans than the fight with the men. The later linguistic distinction between the "distaff side" and the "sword side" would have been very much mistaken at a time when the tall Teutonic maidens' dowries included no spindles ("distaff") at all, but rather a complete suit of armor with spear, sword, and shield, not for the bridegroom but for the bride's own usage. The Romans always found many female corpses on German battlefields, and the archeologists have unearthed many skeletons of Germanic women with the insignia of war and in full armor.

---

[1] The thesis of the prior existence of the Cro-Magnon race has generally been accepted, and most German authorities, including the racist professors of the Third Reich, acknowledged that there was a strong admixture of the heavy, broad-built Cro-Magnon race in the stock inherited from the more delicately constructed, supple Nordics, who may or may not have come from southern Russia. (Some authorities believe that they originated close to the fringes of the melting icecap at the close of the ice age.) Whether matriarchal institutions crept into the conquering society of northern and central Europe from the Cro-Magnon origins or were a natural result of the beginnings of agricultural pursuits—carried on entirely by women in Germanic tribes of the early stage—is an open question. (Editor–translator)

XXV

THEORIES ON MATRIARCHY

In recent years, a great deal of research has been done on human nature, which is why once more so little is known about it. Anyone trying to understand it is first almost drowned in facts before he might even approach a law from which they derived, in fact, before he has any idea whether he is proceeding in the right direction. Above all, one must decide which phenomena belong to the same level of consciousness and which are primary phenomena. Is one to conclude that the essential criteria in matriarchy are perpetuation of the name and the right to inherit, or who moves in with whom, who makes pottery, who dances, and who cleanses the wells? There also is this fundamental question: Who is the dominant partner, the one that works or the one that is supported? From the "little man's" point of view, from the point of view of "wage slavery," that would be no problem. In reality, however, the answer has generally been the opposite from that of Marx, for work—hard, exhausting work —at some cultural levels comprises a jealously guarded privilege of the dominant woman, while the hen-pecked husband is condemned to loiter and putter about.

That is why results that long ago seemed certain are again being questioned. Formerly, one considered agriculture, or at least the cultivation of root crops, a feminine invention. One obsolete prejudice on the "natural division of labor" had it that the woman, while gathering plants and roots of the vicinity for vegetable foods during the absence of the male hunters, happened to find some grain growing in an uncultivated state and planted it along with the other vegetables.

For psychoanalysis, on the other hand, agriculture, like any sort of work in the soil, is a classic example of a substitute for forbidden mother incest, which would make it a typically male invention and occupation. Jung, observing this probability, said that, in agricultural pursuits, the libido regresses from the sexual to the food-procuring level, because it was deprived of its immediate object. Hahn says the same thing in terms of mythology, when he calls the plow and plowmanship religious ceremonies, with the plow representing the phallus of the bull used as a draft animal, the sacred bull inseminating Mother Earth.

Frobenius, discarding psychoanalysis as well as the older materialism, saw the rise of agriculture as a ceremony of thanks, which it was considered among a mountain tribe of the northern Cameroons. It is immaterial in this connection whether this interpretation also might be subjected to psychoanalysis; the important thing here is the fact that there was another theory possible, different from utilitarianism or incest substitution. He observed the tribe when it climbed down to the deserted plains in the fall and gathered up the grain growing naturally. In the spring, these people returned, made some holes in the fields, and placed some of the grain inside which they had gathered up. But—and this is the surprising thing—the grains they had sowed were the very ones they were *not* allowed to harvest.

The first step apparently was the gathering up of grain growing naturally. There then arose the ideal custom of returning some grain in gratitude to the Mother Earth who had been wounded by the cutting of her produce. The fruits of these sacrifices, however, were sacred and therefore ineligible for secular consumption. Only at a later time did agriculture take on a more secular and rational character. The custom described above goes back to the pre-agrarian period and proves that agriculture arose as an ideal from demoniacal phantasmagoria. A practical, purposeful utilization of agriculture did not occur until rational planning and provision for the future caused the atrophy of ideals. . . . [And] We can trace many more secular institutions of our civilization to the same depths of cultural fermentation. . . . Everywhere, there is expression in the beginning and secular purposefulness, that is, expediency, at the end.

The swastika, too—the tree of life that has grown small feet and rushes forth into time—also began as a contemplated image of an imagining (image-forming) humanity. Much later, it became a spoked wheel which had the advantage of saving weight and material in its quality as a wheel. The proverbial and childish error that "necessity is the mother of invention" is refuted by ethnology, psychology, linguistics, and anthropology, which show up other sources of invention, the primacy of magic and gods. First comes the temple, then the house; first the altar, then the hearth; fire was a god revered with prayers and sacrifices a long time before people fried chicken over it. In mystical and religious eras, people lived meaningfully and free of purpose, because their entire existence transpired on the level of feelings, whereas expedient action transpires on a rational plane of the sort produced by civilization. The dogma of necessity projects current problems arising from an overpopulated and exploited earth into an age lying far behind us, when it was not necessary to fight a "struggle for existence" against a skimping environment but the need of the hour was to fend off an aggressive Nature menacing a sparse mankind with its plenty. There was too much, not too little, of everything. The problem was to keep it all away. It was an immense, though differently structured battle, a battle against superabundance, especially since it was largely fought in the sub-tropical regions.

The most powerful human invention, the production of fire by friction, certainly was the product of erupting inner resources, not acquired from Nature by trickery or theft. Adalbert Kuhn, with his ingenious psychological and linguistic empathy, recognized the cognation of Prometheus, the fire giver, and *pramantha*, the male fire log. In India, making fire is an action interpreted entirely from a sexual point of view, seeing the phallus in the staff-shaped *pramantha* and the vulva in the drilled piece of wood lying underneath. The fire thus obtained is the divine son Agni, "the glistening tongue of the gods." Making fire is always designated by the verb *manthami*, which means "to shake" or "to rub violently." *Pramantha*, then, is someone or something that produces fire by violent rubbing, but it also has the meaning of "precaution" or "previsioner." Kuhn connects the verb *manthami* with the

Greek *manthanein*, "to learn," which is to allude to the stirring of the spirit in learning. The root *manth* is connected with *manthano prometheomai* and, thus, with Prometheus. According to Jung, the word *pramathyus*, related to *pramantha*, means "robber" or "one who rubs." Every criminologist, by the way, knows the close connection between an untamed autoeroticism and compulsive pyromania.

Fire, then, was not invented where it is cold but rather in the tropics, where it is hot, because the temperament of the people there is also hot. Fire is a relocated burning of the libido. A restrained, accumulated desire simply chooses another means of expression.

By way of comparison, let us look at the explanation for fire drilling offered by Alfred Russell Wallace, once a natural scientist of some renown. Frobenius quotes him as asserting that natives of Indonesia had seen the wind twirling a branch around in a hole created when another branch was torn out of its trunk; there, they saw their first sparks of fire. Presumably, they then thought, "Bravo, now let's stop having raw meat."

C. G. Jung, the great Swiss psychiatrist, on the other hand, sees the beginnings of technology as sexual activity moved outside the body in the shape of scraping, rubbing, and drilling, somewhat analogous to making fire.

If there is any resistance (external or internal) to original sexuality, the libidinal accumulation will most readily overstimulate those collaterals likely to compensate the resistance. Those, however, are the most proximate functions serving as introduction to the sex act: the function of the hand, on one level, and the function of the mouth on the next. The sex act against which the resistance was directed is then replaced by a presexual step, ideal cases of which are the sucking of the thumb or the picking of the nose. The presexual step is characterized by numerous possibilities, because the libido has not yet centered on a definite locale. A libido remainder regressively re-entering this step sees many possible utilizations: the libido is taken from its proper place and translated to another substratum. Since, however, a relocated coitus is not, and never can be, capable of yielding the natural satisfaction of the one in the proper place, this first step in its relocation also was the first step toward that characteristic dissatisfaction which has later driven man from discovery to discovery without ever letting him achieve satiation.

For the Hindus, the entire world is an emanation of the libido and arises from desire.

Jung then also occupies himself with the Hindu expression "light of speech." When the "autoerotic cycle (mouth-hand) breaks up," the mouth will continue the interrupted sexual rhythm as a lust call, as love call, music, speech, poetry, and spirit, while the hand continues it with fire drilling, invention, and technology. "Thus Indian metapsychology interprets speech and fire as emanations of the inner light, which we know to be the libido. Speech and fire were their forms of manifestation, the first human arts arising from the relocation."

As varied as the theories on the origin of human inventions are also those on the origin of human social forms, where the matriarchy emerges as the central question of all cultural origins, for it involves nothing less than the quest for the origin of human society as such. Whereas for many ethnologists, the family is the typically feminine institution, Frobenius considers both family and clan typically masculine. Frobenius is opposed by all other anthropologists in his theory that the horde is a feminine institution. Briffault traces all social groups to the female group, not the family, while the patriarchal family seems to him a derivative alien to the male instinct. Some are of the opinion that patriarchy and matriarchy must be considered together with totemism and exogamy, since all four interact upon one another, although they never explain very clearly whether totemism and exogamy belong together or whether they are of separate origins.

BACHOFEN'S THREE-STEP THEORY

In the chapter about symbols, the changing image of human nature, as seen by the great Bachofen, has already been outlined: his three-step theory, of which two were female material and one was male spiritual. From the morass cult of a Pan-Aphrodite, an era of unregulated sexual intercourse, when female substance as such was dominant, there rose the Demetrian stage, the genuine, matrimonial matriarchy with determination of name and inheritance, which achieved great power and dignity because mankind voluntarily subordinated itself to the mysterious primacy of the matron. As a third step, there followed patriarchy which meant the complete vanquishment of substance by idea, sun, and spirit. At this stage, the evolution seems to stop, for the Dear Lord knows of nothing better.

These steps do not rise from one another without sanguinary upheavals resulting from an excess of domination by man or woman. We have here the Klearch theory of misuse in another variation. Klearch, too, had asserted that every break in system must have been preceded by an unbearable pressure, as a consequence of which society was turned upside down. According to Bachofen the woman, exhausted by her constant sexual misuse in hetaerism, fought long battles and achieved the Demetrian form of existence with its matrimonial rules. This form, passing its peak, degenerated in turn into Amazonhood, with the enslavement of the man, which at that particular stage was not a singular, but a worldwide, phenomenon. Finally, with the heroic age, the male counter movement began, establishing the predominance of patriarchy, even though its Apollonian purity was clouded later by material irruptions of a Dionysian nature.

It is, however, a strange assumption about the transition from the first to the second step that this female being, this insatiable, sensual substance herself insisted upon sexual limitation. Presumably this substance is always desirous of fertilization, as demonstrated by Bachofen with countless symbols, with the barrel of the Danaïds, the sieve, and numerous other examples. He also calls upon the testimony of the hermaphrodite Tiresias, who stated that the female enjoyment in the act of coitus was ten times as great as that of the man.

It is far more significant, however, that in searching for proof for such an important assumption as the abolition of hetaerism by the action of the female, that natural hetaera, Bachofen can never think of anything but the word of

Strabo, valid for Arabia alone; whereas, in connection with other statements, he always seems to be turning a book shelf upside down when he cites his proof. Strabo's story, repeated at least half a dozen times by Bachofen, deals with an Arab princess and her sixteen brother-lovers. As customary among many nomad tribes, each one of them used to ram his walking stick into the ground before her tent as a symbol for the fact that he was inside. The princess, tired of these incessant visits, thought of the trick of always ramming such a stick into the ground at the entrance to her tent when she was alone in order not to be disturbed.

As the sole support of Bachofen's three-step theory, this stick is too weak. The immense reality of Demetrian power itself, on the other hand, has been represented unforgettably in the most beautiful portions of his life work, whereas the thing which is called into question is only the cause of the transition into this stage from the previous one. Concerning the strict matrimonial customs or the monogamy of matriarchy, progressive anthropology has proved extensive toleration for all areas dominated by matriarchal customs as well as an easy change of partners. Only patriarchates enforce connubial fidelity for reasons of sure paternity, and then only for the woman.

Concerning the Amazons, agricultural—that is, Demetrian —races have never produced Amazon conditions in natural evolution. It is rather a process typical for pasturing and steppe peoples with rituals demanding the sacrifice of the horse.

Bachofen sees the proof for a pre-Demetrian, original matriarchal stage with promiscuous commingling of the sexes, as demanded by the original Aphrodite, in premarital temple prostitution. The dowry thus acquired, he says, was the compensation paid to an antimatrimonial nature goddess. But since Bachofen's death a great deal of new knowledge has been gathered about temple prostitution, artificial premarital defloration, and related issues. Temple prostitution and premarital artificial defloration occur in some patriarchal societies as well as matriarchies. They relate not only to the Aphrodite cult but also to the moonblood taboo of the ripped hymen on one hand and, on the other, to the popular idea that no woman can fulfill her wonderful functions without direct, supernatural intervention, so that a god must deflower her because no mere mortal could give her the power of reproduction. The "great unknown," in this case, can take the place of the god, when it comes to temple prostitution.

In other cases, the priesthood of the temple performs the service. The Brahmans derive the greater part of their incomes from deflowering girls. If, therefore, the ladies of the Russian court threw themselves at the monk Rasputin, who had intercourse with them in his capacity as a holy man, this was no blasphemy but an ancient religious practice. Divine elements can be absorbed into the body only through the mouth, like the eucharist, or by way of the sexual channel.

Scholarship has not borne out any conclusions hastily drawn from the kind of dowries given in matriarchies or patriarchies. Service marriage, too, may have several different meanings: in case of a shortage of money or animals, it may amount to an earning of the bride and may end with the abduction of the woman into the male clan, in which case it is patriarchal; it may also mean that the man earns his way into the house of his wife or her parents, in which case it conforms to matriarchy. A dowry may be paid by the man to the woman as the price of her consent to marriage, as it was in Egypt, while a dowry in cases of patriarchy and polygamy is nothing given to the man but guarantees the material security of the woman in case of divorce and thus remains her inalienable property.

Bachofen's greatness is not diminished by such objections to his assumptions. His distinction did not lie in the particular mode of transition he postulated, but in his manner of tracing matriarchy through all of its many faces in the diverse realms scattered all over the earth.

THE VAERTING PENDULUM THEORY

The Vaertings postulated a hypothesis akin to the old Klearch thesis of abuse, spruced up with a bit of Marxism. Their cardinal point is that "power corrupts," regardless of who might exercise that power or how he might have acquired it. For this reason, rulers and subjects presumably exchange those characteristics which were previously considered their hereditary nature. In case of female predominance, the men become domestic, coy, fond of children, faithful, fat, weak, dependent, and stupid, as do women in case of male predominance. The ruling sex always shows a proclivity for increasing the pressure, which at first has the effect of strengthened enslavement but finally reaches a point where the worm turns so much as to induce the boot to desist, after which the worm grows into a menace to the boot.

According to the Vaertings, power probably has preformed several swings of the pendulum in the course of cultural history, during which a stage of equal rights for both sexes is only viable for a brief interlude. The ascending sex always misuses its power for the enslavement of the other and thus provokes a counter-movement. Although, however, the Vaerting law would seem to indicate a necessary predominance of the rising female in the future, the Vaertings state that the pendulum must be arrested, making for a permanent stabilization of human bliss at a stage of equal rights.

Some remarks have already been made above regarding this appealing theory, which is at least clever. Those remarks were necessitated by the discussion of the female characteristics in the male-dominated society and male characteristics in the female-dominated society.

One objection often raised against the sum total of the Vaertings' work—including the writings of H. Schulte-Vaerting and Dr. M. Vaerting—is that "Whomever God gives an office, He also gives ability." The Vaertings make no allowance for a divine Providence granting office and ability or for a Nature giving birth to leaders and followers, the competent and the incompetent, lords and slaves as such. If, however, the two sexes have an equal endowment and their differences in strength and ability are the products of artificially imposed restrictions, where did the first swing of the pendulum come from?

The first hypothesis, because of this question, is then reinforced in the Vaertings' works by a second: that primitive nations tended to give birth to a very much larger number of males than females. Their superior numbers then supposedly gave the men the controlling voice. But there is no shred of evidence in favor of this hypothesis. One ought not to draw direct analyses regarding humans from numerical proportions among animals, even if we had an exact and reliable manner of knowing the proportion of males to females in the animal kingdom.

The second major objection against the pendulum theory is the fact that we know of no single example of a nation that returned from patriarchy to matriarchy. There is, to be sure, an equal-rights period here and there, but it has always been observed to be a transitional phase from matriarchy to patriarchy. Sir James George Frazer, perhaps the greatest expert on prehistorical, historical, mythological, folkloristic, and purely ethnological material regarding such questions, says:

> Any theory claiming that a people previously practicing patriarchy had changed over to matriarchy would have to cite very convincing proofs to become credible, since inner probability as well as analogy speak against it. For it seems very improbable that men, once they have become accustomed to passing on their rights and privileges to their children, would later disinherit them and bequeath their rights, property, and privileges instead to their sisters' children. Whereas a large number of symptoms in other parts of the world would testify for a transition from matriarchy to patriarchy, there is not a single example to my knowledge of any transition in the other direction, from patriarchy to matriarchy.

The only possible beginning of such a tendency might be seen in the fact that the Kwatiutl Indians, tracing their descent in the male line, have somewhat altered their practice under the influence of matriarchal neighboring tribes and now also accept the maternal grandfather's totem into their table of ancestors. But that is all the evidence we have.

The advantageous position of the American woman is not a reaction against a previous male abuse of power but a phenomenon of an entirely different, new, and singular nature. The initial scarcity of white women, combined with Anglo-Saxon chivalry, necessarily had to give women the advantage if given an equal opportunity. This factor must be added to the freedom and responsibility of the farmer's or cattle breeder's wife. The most important element, however, was the alteration in the cultural mood of the race through the influence of the American soil, with its ancient, matriarchal soul, which the Indians did not have the opportunity to live out to its ultimate destiny. What does the Vaertings' theory of abuse have to do with that? In contrast to the Europe of the past centuries, there is no trace of an abuse of power in American history on the part of the male. One seeks too easy a solution if one attempts to ignore any racial differences as a matter of principle, no matter how unpopular they may be at this time.[1]

---

[1] A solid note of skepticism may be in order regarding the mystical explanation of cultural changes undertaken by the author on the basis of blood and soil and a natural spirit arising out of the soil into its inhabitants regardless of their previous ethnic background. This skepticism seems so much the more in order with regard to observations she makes about the United States, because she manifests a thorough dislike of the United States at various spots of her work. Moreover, her theoretical commentary on the position of American womanhood does not quite jibe with her previous remarks on the subject made in her chapter on North America.

The major mistake in perspective, which she shares with most American writers on the subject of American sociology, is to view the American people as a completely new nation. American nationhood, of course, began with the Revolutionary War, but the members of that nation all went to North America carrying an ancient culture with them, a culture that was largely Christian, Western European, and materialistic and that they merely transplanted into their new environment and continued. American culture has, in many ways, carried on the European tradition, and quite consciously so. The age of American civilization should, therefore, be taken to be the age of Christian European civilization, with only the comparatively slight variant that there occurred a direct infusion of contributions from most of the European national cultures at various times.

The Vaertings' theory of the female reaction triumphing over male domination is not to be dismissed so lightly, when it comes to the United States, for although it is true that there was a shortage of women *at the western frontier*, the cultural climate of the United States was largely shaped in the eastern states, which did not experience the same shortage, and which were dominated largely by the extremely patriarchal English Calvinists and Dutch planters. The emancipation of the American woman was largely carried out in opposition to the Puritan-descended culture and

The Vaertings, ransacking other cultures for evidence to substantiate their thesis, cite a notation by Nymphodorus that Pharaoh Sesostris had introduced matriarchal laws in Egypt. This would lead one to believe that Egypt must have had a patriarchal society before that. But this superficial remark of Nymphodorus finds no confirmation in any other writings regarding ancient Egypt, and Egypt never had a patriarchal society. The Egyptians were conservative ancestor worshipers and wrote down their chronicles with great care, but never mentioned patriarchy at all.

Regardless of the infeasibility of the pendulum theory itself, the Vaertings' works contain many important subsidiary points. Above all, they demonstrated how a masculine-oriented historiography perverted the evidence of matriarchy or just omitted the accomplishments of women in translations. Male historians always tended to comment with glowing enthusiasm on male achievements and to derogate the success of female rulers.

THE REMNANTS THEORY

Heinrich Schurtz, despite his books on ethnology and cultural history, was above all a specialist for male associations. That is the field of his achievements, crowned by the work *Altersklassen und Männerbünde* ("Age Groups and Male Associations"), an almost global study of this typically male group,

---

through the abolition of standards set by the misogynist Puritan clergy in combination with the domineering Dutch *patroons*. The feminist movement and the suffragette movement certainly carried enough drama and even violence with them to qualify for a counter-revolution. And the results have far exceeded the bounds that could be attributed to "Anglo-Saxon chivalry," with so large a share of the property in the United States controlled by women.

Finally, the American phenomenon of the dominant woman seemed a singular phenomenon to the author and is attributed by her to the unusual conditions prevalent in the United States, but it has generally held true that America was not so much *different* from Europe as it was some twenty or thirty years *ahead* of Europe in almost all respects. Women's rights have taken just as strong an upturn in Europe as they have in America since the author completed this work. The position of the European woman is rapidly catching up with that of her American sister. (Editor–translator)

with its long house of the primitives, skull cults, rituals, aspirations, and ideas. Blüher, in his interpretation of the state as a social structure produced by homophiliac eroticism, reverently refers to Schurtz's material. Schurtz shares with Frobenius the opinion that male associations and age group systems are related. He was, however, absolutely opposed to female beings and their world. Whatever he cites on this topic on the basis of secondary material, such as Ploss' *Das Weib in der Naturund Völkerkunde* ("Woman in Science and Ethnology"), is accepted reluctantly. Matriarchal rule, which he was unable to eliminate from human annals, was something he swept aside as bothersome refuse and a coagulation of everything that was uninteresting to a real man, women's and children's buncombe that had no more than an apparent vitality. Female associations, he thought, merely aped their male examples.

The following passage from *Altersklassen* concerning the trend toward associations is typical of him:

> Even the most superficial female soul at least knows curiosity, though it usually is no more than a stale, infertile impulse without any deeper consequences. The better representatives of the male sex, conforming to their inclination toward contemplation, here also show a very different characteristic, which is the desire to solve the riddle of existence, or at least to have it explained by other, more advanced men.

But all of antiquity, or at least its "better representatives," also "conforming to their inclination toward contemplation" and to the desire "to solve the riddle of existence, or at least to have it explained by other, more advanced men," strove humbly to become communicants of the sacraments of the female Eleusinian mysteries.

The matriarchy is far too powerful an influence throughout history to be a mere unwanted phenomenon that is to be stricken out in Schurtz's sense. In order to circumvent matriarchal laws, the Choctaw Indian became an American citizen; for otherwise his property could not be inherited by his own son, since he had no right to dispose of his property, which belonged to his maternal clan. The Beni Amer man had to buy his way back into his own house with humiliations, presents, fines, and the mediation of his compassionate neighbors, because "his own" house belonged to his wife. Gray-haired Africans did not dare join an expedition, a purely masculine affair, without asking their wives, even though it was a matter of only a few days. The Aleutians could not stand living apart from their mothers for two months' time. Among the bushmen and the Seri Indians, only the old women can decide which males may join the tribe and first conduct a rigorous examination of the candidate. The same old women also act as leaders in moving from place to place. Similar examples could be cited in great quantity.

Finally, if female-dominated social forms are no more than remnants of antiquated ills and subsidiary phenomena, female associations ought to be found at the periphery of pronouncedly male groups. But that is not the case. It is precisely in typically matriarchal areas like Assam that the great female mother-clans with continuously changing husbands comprise the sole social structure, and there is no determined male association or firm inner nucleus from which the female group could have been expelled. How could female rule be a remnant of anything, when it is the only social form to be seen far and wide?

FROBENIUS' CULTURAL SPHERE THEORY

For Leo Frobenius, as for Spengler, cultures are "organisms of the highest order," each one a living entity with its own growth processes, with birth, childhood, maturity, senility, and death. It is not the will of man that brings forth cultures, but rather the culture that lives upon the people. Like plants that grow only in certain vegetational zones, cultures also are tied to a certain area to which they are endemic and germane. Modern biology has discovered that environment, inner life, and sphere of influence comprise a unit for each living being. When a culture migrates, it is altered by its new soil like windblown seeds, "though the regeneration of the cultural soul, which may be intensified by certain conditions changing the environment, cannot be explained chemically, physically, or meteorologically." Frobenius sees the rise of the

Occidental cultural soul as an outgrowth of early Aegean civilization. "Culture is earth which has become organic through man," he says, and—

> Vegetation and culture are in touch with the soil in two different directions, one growing into, and the other growing out of, the earth. In both cases, the movement in the proper direction means life itself. I call the root-forming culture chthonial, outgrowing culture tellurian. The plant in its dual nature includes the chthonial and the tellurian element.

To Frobenius, culture, or *paideuma* (soil soul), is primarily either chthonial or tellurian. The polarity of root origin and sprout origin comprises the unity of plant life and corresponds to a duality of original cultural life. The two original polar forms of culture are the chthonial-matriarchal and the tellurian-patriarchal, of which the chthonial is centripetal, inclusive, creative, and cavernous, while the tellurian is centrifugal and possessed by a strong feeling for space. The two opposite cultural spheres from which everything arises may sometimes overlap but never merge, though each is the complement of the other. Higher forms are due to this fact.

> Each cultural form has a pre-polar, a polar, and a post-polar stage. Each one in its pre-polar stage first forms hordes without any arrangement other than the animal classification of men and women. There is not yet any matriarchy or patriarchy, because there has not yet occurred any cleavage revealing polarity for the purpose of differentiating human types.

At the polar stage, however, which itself has four steps, there is a clear order in both spheres, for even in their first step the spheres become virulent: "Each one appears as a perfect organism in the orderly spaces that properly belong to it."

This new doctrine of the cultural sphere would naturally eliminate the sociological, linear sequence. In order to comprehend it, "one must first abolish that ancient, naive belief in the sequence hunters-shepherds-farmers." Many ethnologists, indeed, have turned away from that belief. Frobenius, however, does not believe in a sequence of matriarchy-patriarchy. The two polar spheres, he says, have existed since the beginning of time as coeval opposites in every field of the spiritual, cultural, and physical, in the economy, in the division of labor, in housing, and in handicrafts, in everything that concerns a profound approach to Life. Matriarchal people are magical, while patriarchal ones "experience everything as a symbol and therefore are mystics." Frobenius continues: "Predominance of fathers or mothers is therefore only a single manifestation of culture, which shows identical differences in all directions."

Tellurian-patriarchal is architectural growth from the soil. Man lives on a pole-bed in a house on piles and cooks his food on a spit. This way of life corresponds to the mental image of the newly-born child's soul rising out of the soil like a plant, undergoing the various ages until senility, and returning to earth only to be reborn as human.

It is a vertical cycle. Therefore the elders rule society.

This culture is dedicated to vegetation, characterized by intensive agriculture and Dionysian joy. The body of the deceased is surrounded by holy jubilation, because he will soon return. . . . The earth seems limitless like the vast fields surrounding the clan buildings. All people of tellurian culture are characterized by an intense feeling for wide spaces.

Chthonial (feminine) culture emanates from a dwelling in the ground and digs its dwelling, its bed, and its storage chambers into the earth, with spacious rooms in the interior, ramified like the fibrils of a root. Food is baked inside a mound, in an earth oven. Only slowly does chthonial existence liberate itself for continuance as an aerial root. Despite all art and delicacy, it always returns to the idea of life in the motherland at the beginning of things, . . .

While the tellurian way of life strives up vertically and then spreads out into the far distance. "The dying chthonian can look forward only to Hades, shadows, and the realm of specters." Therefore chthonians celebrate earthy matter, the flesh of the body. "Chthonial culture commences with domesticated animals, with flesh, blood, discipline, and bonds with geographical spaces, for animal husbandry, needing more room, brings about an earlier fixing of boundaries."

According to Frobenius, it was a grave error to think that nomads could roam aimlessly; on the contrary, each horde had its closely delimited pasture grounds. For the male, tellurian culture, on the other hand, limitless space begins after the last cultivated acre, and every field no longer cultivated rejoins boundless space. Property extended as far as one's arm and one's energies could reach. "Tellurian means rest in boundless space. Chthonial means unrest in limited space." Agriculture is matriarchal in its very essence. Woman determines soil, property, selection of spouse, and especially chooses the husband deliberately and exactly for his bravery, good looks, strength, and ability.

She has taken on all duties and obligations, milks the cows, tans the leather, weaves the cloth, puts up and breaks the tents, loads up the beasts of burden, and decides whither the next move shall go. She bests the woman of the patriarchal-tellurian culture, because in addition to all these other duties she is also a mother and home-maker. The men lie around lazily or come home from the hunt or wars.

When the tents are broken, the men provide warlike protection in the location of new pasturing grounds, soldiers working for the women. Chthonial culture only knows the matriarchal horde, tellurian culture only the patriarchal clan. In the real steppe, this matriarchal horde lives in a circle of huts, protected by an abatis of thorny underbrush. All ideas are materialistic. "The child splits away from the mother. In the steady unfolding of progeny on the road from grandmother to granddaughter, the female body becomes immortal, just as some lower forms of life strip away any part of their matter which has become useless" and in this way remain immortal.

While the soul is eternal in the male-tellurian, eternity in the female-chthonial rests in the body. From this fact one can explain the female selection of the fittest and glorification of the physical. Original polarity had it that "males appear as the wooers, the mobile, the expansionist, and the resplendent," all of which are centrifugal qualities. The female element, on the other hand, always appeared in the form of hesitation, selection, absorption, retention, conservation, and object that is to be wooed.

In the spread of culture, the cleavage of polarity occurred in a large division whose spatial dimensions can now be understood. The great steppe regions of Central Asia, Eastern Europe, and Central Africa became the home of centrifugal cultures, while the coasts of the Mediterranean and southern Asia were regions of centripetal cultures, which means matriarchy. The movement and the incursion of the mobile, centrifugal, patriarchal elements into the territory of the centripetal resulted in the rise of great civilizations in India, Western Asia, the Aegean, Rome, France, and England. Naturally the cultures of the mobile elements were more capable of development, while those of the resting elements were more creative. All the problems of so-called world history have their foundation in this phenomenon.

In the first stage, which is the primitive revelation of polarity, each cultural sphere is especially virulent. The young protagonist enters the stage, "claiming hegemony in all things as the central purposes of Life. Anything else is subsidiary." In the case of matriarchy, Frobenius thinks, the first impact was tremendous, because some of the most powerful characteristics of the centripetal were active in it, such as an appreciation of facts and the finality of the idea of justice. Conditions during this "episode of the greatest women's revolution must have led to astonishing phenomena of one-sidedness, such as Amazonhood, legal hetaerism, and the pawning of men. During this stage, the man is the servant, and his metaphysical requirements are completely ignored." During the second stage the polarity, so brusquely revealed in the first, becomes a part of an organized whole and is merely utilized as any other established fact.

It would hardly be worth one's while within the framework of this book to go into the details of all of Frobenius' stages. For the understanding of the theory it would, however, be of some importance to see where he divides polaric from post-polaric or prosperity from decay. During his fourth stage, he sees the new polarity of individual man and the mass confronting one another. In the beginning of culture, power and essence reside in the nature and character of the tribe, whereas our contemporary world makes it possible for individual, strong personalities to work upon their own nations and thus to reach mankind. On the polar stage, the effective agent is the nation. In the postpolar stage, the effectiveness of the nation withers away.

In his doctrine of cultural spheres, Frobenius at times diagnoses rather bold symptoms for the female or the male sphere. For instance, the stage of female predominance in his writings knows of no "mothers," but makes them all promiscuous women, while the veneration of "mothers" is restricted to male-dominated societies, because they are the ones who consider matrimony sacred. He also asserts that patriarchal societies place no emphasis on virginity prior to marriage, only on absolute loyalty to the patriarchal clan after it. On the other hand, he claims that female rule jealously guards virginity as an inducement to the man to prove himself over and over again, while the female examines carefully whether he really is the most capable and the handsomest one, and she would really like to keep something back for a still handsomer male.

> Once the women in a matriarchy have married, however, the selection does not end. At a later time, someone emerges who is more courageous, more renowned, and more successful than the husband, and the female then strives to arouse a strong passion in him, too. Thus it comes about that indifference to virginity and insistence on loyalty after the wedding ceremony characterize male-dominated societies, while a carefully guarded virginity and infidelity after marriage characterize female-dominated ones.

Frobenius especially emphasized this thesis, "because we here have a symptom by which we may categorize societies in the proper groups." But the symptom probably applies only to Africa, with which Frobenius was very familiar. All of his observations may apply to matriarchal Hamites, who are close to a chivalrous, Arablike stage, or to the patriarchal Zega.

In most other parts of the world, however, we have too many examples to the contrary that matriarchy is dominated by *old* women and not by young ladies of the evening with their admirers, and that these old women are clan elders, for matriarchies reaching back to prehistorical stages live in the clan, not in the horde. Young women in such societies are not ladies of the evening but are proud of the number of lovers they had before marriage. Veneration of mothers always depends upon the dependence of the sons. On the other hand, the contempt for old women and preference for young ones for erotic purposes in the case of patriarchies are so well known that it suffices merely to mention them. One may accept or reject the thesis that animal husbandry from the very beginnings was matriarchal or that patriarchy and agriculture have always gone hand in hand. Perhaps the opposite is just as "original." Matriarchy, intensified to the point of gynocracy, has actually occurred in every kind of life, even those kinds that precede animal husbandry, such as the Seri society. Making agriculture the result of the male feeling for wide spaces seems somewhat farfetched. No doubt there is more of a feeling for wide spaces in the adventurous and glorious exploits of warrior races, conquerors, and Vikings. On this point Frobenius probably became a prisoner of his concept of the plant as an image of culture.

On the whole, however, the doctrine of the cultural spheres is an important contribution, the product of some demoniacal-geniuslike intuition. The cultural spheres are "spheres" only from a superficial point of view. They rather act like maelstroms reaching very far toward the bottom in order to whirl up something unrecognized and unachieved.

THE SOCIOLOGICAL HYPOTHESIS

The thesis of Marx and Engels that economic production and the social form that it brings about make up the foundation for the political and intellectual history of every epoch forms the basis of the sociological approach to patriarchy and matriarchy. History, therefore, is no more than the story of class struggles between exploiters and exploited, dominant and dominated classes, at various levels of social development. The causes of all things are purely economical: religion, ethics, and art are only among the many facets of "ideological superstructure." Matriarchy, therefore, can only arise if, during an era, the woman determines the production process and thus becomes the "dominant class." Sociology places this era at the only possible stage, the primitive agricultural level. Matriarchy should therefore be a transitional phenomenon, that brief period when the male is still a roaming hunter, while the woman has arrived at primitive agriculture. According to Müller-Lyer,

> . . . the woman becomes predominant, because the results of the hunt are much less certain than those of agriculture. She acquires an economic ascendancy and becomes the center of the economy around which the man rotates like a planet around the sun.

According to Dr. P. Krische,

> . . . there thus transpired that revolution so singular in the cultural history to date by which the woman became the governing class of human society. It led to a classical period of matriarchy, which, although it only lasted a short time, left some distinct traces behind, remnants of which are still distinguishable today.

The sociologists claim that, before the matriarchy, there was neither matriarchy nor patriarchy, but only the horde. This horde tended to be dominated by the male, because he held the hunt, which was the means of production, under his control. He comprehended the advantages of agriculture much later than the female, but as soon as he understood it, he removed it from her authority, so that a more advanced agriculture is characterized by male predominance with a very consciously patriarchal jurisprudence leading to the enslavement of the women. Male predominance at this level is reinforced by the man's mental superiority, which he acquired because he kept the woman as a work animal bound to the soil while he employed himself in the sale of excess products and thus won experience in business and human relations. Although the soil remained community property during matriarchal days, the man created the concept of private property in real estate. He found that he liked property and tried to expand it through handicrafts, trade, and warlike conquests. The Müller-Lyer work outlines this economic process as follows:

1. Wealth arises.
2. Wealth is acquired by the male.
3. The habit of buying the bride results.
4. The woman becomes the subordinate of the man.
5. Patriarchy replaces matriarchy.
6. The man removes his family from the clan.
7. Clan inheritance is replaced by male inheritance.
8. The clan disintegrates.

This rational-sociological hypothesis has been widely circulated in popular writings in England and Germany, such as those of Cunow, Müller-Lyer, Krische, and Eildermann. Instead of starting with objections against the assumption of a sequence hunt-pasture-agriculture and the presumption that the woman invented the planting of crops, it may be more practical to investigate the premises of this hypothesis: Is there an essential correspondence of matriarchy and primitive agriculture? Could the woman acquire economic superiority by using the changeover in control of production at this stage?

According to Müller-Lyer, the fishermen also still belong to the matriarchal stage, for he thought that fisheries were the purview of the woman at the coasts, as agriculture was in the hinterland. When agriculture advanced and there was trade and prosperity, the man appropriated these avenues to success. According to Dr. P. Krische, the sociological assumption is that "it is certain that normal human development proceeds as dictated by the production process and matriarchy always disappears when agriculture enters a more advanced stage." But just how certain is this sociological thesis?

Matriarchy prevailed in the most advanced and the most ancient city cultures—pre-Aryan India, Egypt, Lycia, and Lydia, to name just a few. Some, such as Egypt and Lycia, never had anything else. This objection is sometimes answered with the argument of the "luxuriating life of marshy deltas," that the means of production simply exceeded the capacity of the clans to control them. According to Dr. P. Krische,

> . . . the technical evolution that otherwise required long periods of time here took place so hastily that, just as in the rapid industrialization of Western Europe in the nineteenth century, the ideological superstructure of this radical economic change was unable to keep pace in the same measure as it would have in an unhurried progress. Therefore, age-old customs and concepts of the matriarchal period persistently remained within the rapid development of these first city cultures.

They must have been persistent, indeed, to last thousands of years. But where did this persistence come from if the means of production determine mental processes? Moreover, Lycia, the classical motherland of trade and architecture, consists of mountains with a very sparse vegetation, without any "luxuriating life of marshy deltas," corresponding somewhat to the city-states of the Tibetan matriarchies with nine-story buildings, trade, animal husbandry, and industry. Since the icy climate of Tibet at an altitude of fifteen thousand feet permits very little agriculture, Krische thought that Tibet must have had a much warmer climate in former days. As for Sparta, the reluctance of her warriors to abolish the matriarchy is something he attributes to "agrarian conservatism." But in Sparta, the ruling caste was a pure warrior race and practiced no agriculture at all. The means of production of the Spartan state remained in the hands of the politically disenfranchised helots, because the Spartans thought as little of helots as they did of agriculture. Sparta practiced the first opposite thesis to that of Marx, namely, that power depends upon the means of production; it proved that power depends upon the will and ability to exercise it.

Contrary to the "certainties" of the sociologists, the nomads and animal breeders of Africa are overwhelmingly matriarchal; whereas the agrarian tribes have been patriarchal as long as their history can be traced back, even though it is not necessary to go as far as Frobenius did and assume that the female sphere of culture is to be identified *as a matter of principle* with animal husbandry and the patriarchal male sphere with agriculture. The eastern Hamite animal herders are all patriarchal, but the western ones are matriarchal, and nobody knows why. According to Fisch, there are several animal-herding, matriarchal, horseback-riding peoples in northern Togoland.

W. Junker says: "Among the Bega, the women rule in a manner which is hard to reconcile to the temperamental nature of these proud and untamed nomads." The bushmen and Hottentots living near the Kalahari desert, who are some of the most primitive hunters in the world and have no agriculture at all, also live under a perfectly matriarchal social pattern. The great matriarchal and chivalrous culture of old Arabia was based on animal husbandry. The ancient mother clans of Assam have well-developed commercial relations and have the men perform the work and fight in the wars, although they have remained completely dependent upon their women. The Tuaregs of the Sahara live under a gynocratic organization as their ancestors, the old Libyans, did, with the women breeding camels, carrying on trade, and building cities, without having ever known a primitive agricultural stage or a change in the ownership of the means of production. The gypsies, too, are well known for their nomadic ways and their matriarchal society. Dr. Krische thought the gypsies must have been sedentary agriculturists at one time and thus have acquired their matriarchy.

The Australian aborigines, who belong to the most primitive and least developed peoples in the whole world, show a very distinct set of traces of a matriarchal society which they must at one time have destroyed without any change in the ownership of the means of production, since they have no production at all. The same is true of the Patagonians, who have remained stationary on the level of fishermen. The Seri Indians, on the Gulf of California, who have no clothes, stone implements or other tools, and who hover around a cadaver for days until all the raw meat has been devoured by them, have a strongly developed matriarchal society. They are a perfect example of the fact that the matriarchy is possible at all cultural levels, disregarding the question of who owns or controls the means of production. And we need to concern ourselves no further with the "ideological superstructure" discussed by the Marxists, since we have thus effectively dismantled the ethnological substructure which they postulate for the support of their historical theses.

Despite these facts, the sociological hypothesis will probably be accepted by an ever growing public, especially by people who have never heard of Seris, Bega, or Tuaregs. As Plato says, "If the audience has no experience with, or knowledge of, the subject, it is a great relief for the speaker." There also is the Marxist party line to be considered, taken as gospel truth by people who live on the introduction of politics into everything from original morass to modern furniture. That party line labels all things with the label of its superficiality and shortsightedness. Marxists lack the depth of creative contemplation. They do not notice that it is just as comical for a rationalist to explain the events among a magic-based mankind with a theory about the ownership of the means of production as it would be for a savage to explain the ticking of a watch with the theory that his grandfather's spirit is sitting inside. Historical materialism views world history with the mentality of a petty union official. It projects the only world it can understand, the world of asphalt, printed paper, collective bargaining, and accident insurance policies into all levels of existence, since it does not know any better. Insights, views, and perspectives of other horizons, with their many, equally valid solutions to problems, are no longer open to it. Sociological dogma will therefore completely satisfy an increasing part of the literate world and will even be transfigured into truth, once all human urges other than acquisitiveness have atrophied, for at that stage, world history and economics will really coincide.

INDEX